Another Fork in the Trail

*vegetarian
and vegan recipes
for the backcountry*

Laurie Ann March

TouchWood
Editions

First published in the United States of America by Wilderness Press.

First published in Canada by TouchWood Editions with ISBN 978-1-894898-97-3. www.touchwoodeditions.com

LIBRARY AND ARCHIVES CANADA CATALOGUING IN PUBLICATION
Cataloging in Publication data available from the National Library

Front cover photos copyright © 2011 by Laurie Ann March
Cover design by Scott McGrew
Book design by Lisa Pletka
Book layout by Annie Long

We gratefully acknowledge the financial support for our publishing activities from the Government of Canada through the Canada Book Fund, Canada Council for the Arts, and the province of British Columbia through the British Columbia Arts Council and the Book Publishing Tax Credit.

1 2 3 4 5 14 13 12 11

PRINTED IN CANADA

To my children, Tobias and Kaia: you are my miracles.
The way you both look at the world reminds me
that the wonder of childhood still lives within all of us.

To my husband, Bryan: you always give me the courage
to follow my dreams and attain my goals. Your unconditional love
and unfailing support mean the world to me

Acknowledgments

My gratitude goes to everyone at my publishers, Keen Communications and Touchwood Editions, for believing in my work and for their support throughout the creation of *Another Fork in the Trail.* Also thanks to Roslyn Bullas for having faith in my abilities as both an author and a cook and her encouragement throughout this journey.

Thanks to my mom, Janet Langman, who has encouraged my creativity since I was little and has always inspired me, both in the kitchen and in life. Victoria and Nigel March, my parents-in-law, have been like a second family to me and I thank them for their unfailing support.

I have the utmost appreciation, as always, for my husband, Bryan. Not only is he a wonderful husband, but he also cleaned up my messes, did the laundry, and took care of our two wonderful children when I was consumed with cooking and writing. And thank you, my darling son, Tobias. You've become such a big boy and you are so brave when it comes to trying new foods. Your honesty—coupled with your enthusiasm to help in the kitchen, with your baby sister, and at camp— is amazing. Kaia, thank you for being the darling baby girl that you are and for always making me feel young at heart.

Samantha Rogers, you are the best friend that a girl could ask for and you deserve a pat on the back for listening to my constant chatter about food, dehydrators, and everything else under the sun. Michael Rogers, you are a great friend and your support has not gone unnoticed—thanks for mowing the lawn and making me smile with the little pranks you played on Bryan. To Erika Klimecky; although we've yet to meet in person, your enthusiasm about my books and my future writing projects has not passed without appreciation. Our mutual love of writing and photography connects us across the miles. Shelley and Claude Lauzon, thanks as always for being there and for all you do for the kids.

To my readers and workshop participants, your passion for mixing outdoor adventures with culinary ones and your desire for ideas are always an inspiration. As a wilderness cooking teacher I've discovered that it is as much a joy to teach as it is to learn from you.

There are so many other people who have my gratitude. It is a long list that includes family, friends, the connections I've made online, and people I've met through a mutual love of backcountry camping. There just isn't enough space to thank you all individually, but please know that your support and encouragement have not gone without notice.

Contents

List of Recipes

Desserts and Baked Goods (continued)

Beverages

More Elaborate Dishes

Preface

During my time as a young student at a local university, I had a bit of a rough time when it came to food. Back then, most of the mainstream campus fare was greasy, unhealthy, and pretty much unpalatable. I ended up having my lunches with a group of students who had embraced a vegetarian and vegan lifestyle. Some of my friends were eating this way because it was merely a better choice and others because of religion or ethics. I had simply chosen this diet because it was the only thing that appealed to me at the time and it was a better alternative to what was being served in the student center eateries. This shift in diet provided me with a chance to experience foods and flavors that I normally wouldn't have been exposed to, especially having grown up with parents who were meat-and-potatoes folks serving a very British menu. Foods unique to me, such as quinoa and silken tofu, became the familiar. Throughout the writing of my last book, *A Fork in the Trail,* I would often find myself looking back to those days for inspiration, which led me to include a variety of meat-free options in the book. That also spurred some changes on the home front, and over the past few years our family started embracing eating vegetarian and vegan foods several times a week. This has been a change that I've welcomed whole-heartedly.

When my first book was released in early 2008, I felt a little lost. I missed being in the test kitchen and out in the backcountry creating recipes. My passion for creating new recipes was not vanquished as I had expected and quite the opposite had occurred. Inspiration was still flowing long after the book hit store shelves. I found myself wishing that I had included more vegan fare. During my workshops and at book signings, I had the opportunity to talk to a variety of people, many of whom required a special diet on the trail due to being vegetarian or vegan or having celiac disease. They added to that inspiration, and the idea for *Another Fork in the Trail* was born.

While other wonderful vegetarian cookbooks have been written for those frequenting the backcountry, no one had tackled the subject in the way that I wanted to or had addressed the issue of gluten-free eating on wilderness trips. I approached my publisher immediately with the idea and then again later in the year. It was somewhat fitting that I was standing in Ontario's beautiful Algonquin Provincial Park, admiring the fall colors that graced the sugar maple canopy, when the message came across on my new BlackBerry. My publisher thought it was a great idea too! I was excited and up to the challenge, although, at that time, I didn't realize what a challenge it would be. As soon as I arrived home, I set to work on compiling the recipes I had already created and started brainstorming ideas for new ones.

I was already adept at creating recipes for the backcountry, so my first order of business was to take some time to refresh my knowledge of the philosophies surrounding vegetarianism and veganism. It was imperative that I research the hidden sources of meat and meat by-products that often lurk in foods and that a nonvegan might not think to consider—products such as instant pudding, Worcestershire sauce, and marshmallows. I also wanted to ensure that I was well versed on what foods contain gluten. That was certainly eye-opening, to say the least. I was simply shocked at the number of commercially prepared foods that contain some trace of gluten and how ill it could make someone with gluten intolerance. I spent time chatting with people who have celiac disease and with those who lead a vegan lifestyle on the trail so that I could thoroughly educate myself. As an avid backpacker and canoeist with vegetarian tendencies, I set out to create a series of recipes that would be suitable for backcountry trips, recipes that even people who aren't vegetarian could enjoy. The irony is that, during the writing of this book, I had to address the subject of dietary restrictions on a personal level. Even though my situation is different, in many ways I now have a greater personal perspective of the difficulties related to meal planning with a special diet and the importance of it.

Once again, lightweight yet delicious recipes are the main focus of this book. The recipes vary from quick and easy to more involved fare, such as backcountry gluten-free baking. Many of the recipes require home preparation and the use of a food dehydrator; after all, this is a cookbook. Cooking and dehydrating foods at home will reduce the work you have to do at camp as well as the weight in your pack. Not to mention, the wonderful thing about animal-free recipes is that they rehydrate much more easily than meals containing meat. I've also created these recipes to be enjoyed by others who aren't vegetarians or vegans or those who aren't on gluten-free diets under the premise of never sharing a recipe that I wouldn't make for my family and friends or enjoy myself.

I hope that you take pleasure in the recipes and anecdotes contained within this book and that your delicious backcountry meals will enhance the enjoyment of your journey, making any of the hardships encountered fade into memory. As I always say, good food really brings people together at the end of a tough day.

Laurie Ann March
March 2011

Chapter 1

An Introduction to Wilderness Cooking for Vegetarians

On Being Vegetarian and Vegan

Many reading this will already be well-versed on what being a vegetarian or vegan is because it is part of their day-to-day lifestyle, but let's talk about it for those who may be new to the lifestyle or for those omnivores who have been designated camp cooks and are reading this book as such.

Who is a vegetarian? A vegetarian is a person who eats a plant-based diet that does not contain meat products. One type of vegetarian is what we call ovo-lacto or lacto vegetarian. Ovo-lacto vegetarians will consume dairy and eggs as part of their diet, while lacto-vegetarians will not use eggs but will use dairy in some of their meals. Some vegetarians may still eat foods that are made by living creatures, such as honey. Strict vegetarians will not consume items such as dairy, eggs, or honey but may still wear leather, down, or wool products. Some vegetarians don't eat land animals or fowl but will eat fish; they're called pescatarians. In some circles, this is not considered vegetarian at all. The strictest of all vegetarian lifestyles is veganism.

Who is a vegan? A vegan is a person who eats a plant-based diet that does not contain any product or by-product of an animal, bird, fish, or insect. True vegans will not use leather, wool, or down-filled products or anything else that comes from an animal, bird, fish, or insect.

Nonvegetarians often wonder why people would give up a diet that includes animal products. People choose to be vegetarian or vegan for many reasons. Spiritual beliefs can play a significant role in dietary choices. For example, people who are of the Hindu belief system make up a good portion of the world's vegetarian community. Ethics are a reason for many vegetarians too. Some feel that killing a living creature is just wrong. Others are concerned with how animals are treated, sometimes quite cruelly, and slaughtered only to become someone's supper. Recently the number of vegetarians has increased due to concerns about the environment.

Some people are merely disgusted by the thought of eating meat. This happened to me when I held a position as an office administrator for a veterinarian who specialized in treating animals that were being raised for food. In typing reports I learned about some of the illnesses that farm animals can contract. This brings up another reason that people choose to be vegetarian—animal-borne diseases. The thought of *E. coli,* avian flu, or BSE (mad cow) is enough to turn some away from meat altogether.

Health can be a factor in making the decision to adopt a vegetarian lifestyle. Often vegetarians, who plan their food choices well, eat healthier because they consume more fiber and less saturated fat than the typical North American. Plant-based fats such as olive oil and flax oil have health benefits that aren't found in butter and many other animal-based fats. Often nonvegetarians think that cutting out the protein that comes from meat is unhealthy, but there are many ways to ensure that one has complete proteins, B12, and iron with a plant-based diet.

Some people who aren't vegetarians don't realize that merely removing the meat from a dish—for example, peeling the pepperoni off a pizza—or cooking the food where it will contact meat—such as portobello mushrooms being cooked on the same grill as a steak—still exposes the vegetarian to a product he or she has made a concerted effort to avoid consuming. This can be frustrating for the vegetarian.

On Having Celiac Disease

What is celiac disease? Contrary to what some may assume, it is not a mere allergy. Celiac disease is an auto-immune response caused by ingesting gluten. This genetic disease can permanently damage the small intestine. Intolerance to gluten affects the person's ability to absorb essential nutrients and, for some people, causes great gastrointestinal distress. Those of you who have celiac disease or are close to a loved one with the disease already realize how difficult it can be. Many people think that it is only the gluten in wheat that causes issues, but barley, rye, certain brands of oats, and many other commercial products contain gluten. It is sometimes found in products one wouldn't think of, such as some spice blends, canned soups, powdered mixes, vitamins, and medications.

Being a vegetarian with celiac disease can be difficult, as it does narrow one's food choices considerably and can be expensive. Most commercially available backcountry foods are not gluten free, making it especially hard for outdoors people with such restrictions. That is why creating your own foods at home and drying them for use in the backcountry is the ideal choice for anyone with special dietary concerns.

Food for Wilderness Trips

I remember our first backcountry trips and the prepackaged fare that made us almost dread mealtimes. Not only were the freeze-dried meals expensive, but there was also little control over the flavor, level of spice, or ingredients. It wasn't until I started speaking with my readers and workshop participants that a lightbulb went on and I realized just how difficult those meals from the outdoors store would be for someone with special dietary needs, such as celiac disease or food allergies. It used to be that the alternative was to take fresh food from home. Many of us started this way, me included. While the control and taste are there, the style of cooking fresh foods on the trail is too cumbersome for more than a night or two; it can also be heavy and can lead to food storage issues resulting in food-borne illnesses.

That brings me to the style of the trip. Whether you backpack or paddle, weight should always be a consideration. With backpacking and kayaking, you want to pay close attention to bulk as well. With canoeing trips the bulk isn't as crucial, but one should still consider it carefully, especially for longer trips. And who wants to have to double or triple a portage?

When planning your menu, think about things such as can and bottle bans as well as fire bans. In certain areas laws state that you must utilize reusable containers. While common sense indicates that glass bottles are dangerous, I am amazed by the number of people who take them into the backcountry and leave them there, whether by accident or design. Many backpackers use canned goods, but the trend is moving away from that because the goods can be cumbersome and weighty. Fire bans can be a concern for those who enjoy having a cooking fire. If you are a campfire cook, you should always check to see if the area in which you will be traveling is prone to fire bans and double-check the status before you hit the trail.

Other important considerations are the season and area in which you will be hiking. If the weather is cold or wet, you should expect to have increased needs as far as food and camp fuel are concerned. Spoilage can occur quickly in hot weather, so it is best to choose nonperishable or dehydrated foods during those times. In the cooler weather you can expand your menu because the risk is reduced.

I also recommend taking at least a full day's worth of extra rations and some extra snacks in the event that an emergency or severe weather delays your progress. Unpredictable things can happen in the outdoors and it's best to be prepared.

Outdoor Cooking Equipment

Camp kitchen setups are as varied as the people carrying them. There are no hard-set rules and you'll have to find what works best for you. Some people, especially those who solo, prefer an ultralight approach and others prefer a more elaborate setup. A more complete kitchen is easier in situations where gear weight can be split between two or more people. The following list will give you an idea of some of the items that one can consider for a camp kitchen; however, you will have to pick and choose items according to your style of wilderness travel and the menu that you create.

- Single-burner stove with windscreen (I recommend one with a refillable fuel bottle that can accommodate various fuel types if you are planning to travel internationally) or an ultra-light stove that uses alcohol or Esbit

- Fuel (The amount depends on the type of stove and cooking times of your chosen menu—I always take an extra half bottle or canister depending on the stove type.)

- Heat exchanger (recommended for cold-weather trips to reduce fuel consumption)

- Matches in a waterproof container

- Cooking grid (if weight isn't a concern and you are in an area where you can have a cooking fire)

- Backpacker's oven (Outback Oven, reflector oven, or BakePacker)

- Lightweight pot set designed for backpacking (I recommend avoiding titanium if you plan to do anything other than boil water.)

- Pot lifter

- Pot cozy or Nalgene insulator

- Insulated work gloves (for handling hot pots, cooking grid, and so on)

- Folding spoon that can double as a ladle (one with measurements is quite useful)

- Folding spatula

- Salt/pepper shaker (I prefer an all-in-one unit.)

- Backpacker's pepper grinder (an "essential" luxury item)

- Rehydration container (A pot, plastic container, or large wide-mouth Nalgene insulator would work.)

- Cup, plate, bowl, and cutlery for each person

- Water treatment solution (filtration pump, UV pen, tablets, or liquid)

- Personal drinking water bottle for each person

- Water containers (Nalgene bottles, Platypus bladder, or other container)

- A few extra ziplock bags in case of leftovers

- Parchment paper

- A sharp knife (I like a Swiss Army or locking blade knife.)

- Collapsible sink, camp soap, dishcloth, and scrubber or pot scraper

- Pack towel to dry dishes or a mesh bag to air-dry them

- Tarp, tent wing, or other shelter to cook under during inclement weather (It is important that this is not a tent or shelter where you will also be sleeping.)

Equipment at home is equally important and you may already have most things you need for pretrip preparations in your home kitchen. This book relies heavily on dehydrating your own foods, giving you a balance between food weight and great taste. While you can use your oven to dehydrate many of the foods for your trips, I strongly suggest that you purchase a food dehydrator for the task, as it will be more efficient and the results will be better. I have had the opportunity to test units by Nesco and Excalibur. Both companies have excellent units and have stood up to a great deal of dehydrating with my creation of two wilderness cookbooks. A good, sharp paring knife and chef's knife are very important. A coffee grinder used specifically for spices and other foods is very useful, as is a food processor. While not a complete necessity, I like to use a mandolin slicer because of its ability to create uniform fruit and vegetable slices for dehydrating.

Cooking Methods

How you will cook in the backcountry will depend on a number of factors, including the type of activity, location, altitude, duration, season, and individual needs. Most methods such as boiling, frying, heating, foil packet cooking, and grilling are familiar and straightforward. Backcountry baking, on the other hand, will need some explanation and a little practice. While what I am about to write may seem daunting at first, it is a worthwhile skill to learn as it will enhance your menus, especially on longer trips, and it's much easier than it first appears.

You will need some additional equipment for baking. My preference is a product known as the Outback Oven by Backpacker's Pantry. You can bake almost anything that you can bake at home in this type of oven and achieve the same results—imagine enjoying fresh-from-the-oven goodness on a wilderness adventure. There are two sizes of this product. I prefer the Ultralight, which uses a pot and lid that you are already bringing and consists of a heat shield, riser, thermometer, and convection tent. The other model, the Plus 10, comes with everything the Ultralight model has plus a 10-inch lidded frying pan. The convection tent is also larger on the Plus 10. While it isn't as light, the Plus 10 is preferable when baking for three or more people, and it's brilliant for making pizzas. When using this type of oven, you need a stove that has the ability to simmer. Outback Ovens are not for use with stoves where the canister is directly below the flame or with alcohol-burning stoves.

The BakePacker is another type of backcountry oven. It is basically a grid that sits in the bottom of your pot with a bit of water. This system allows you to steam-bake items in a bag. The downside is that you don't get the golden brown color or crusty exterior on baked goods like you would with a normal oven.

Reflector ovens use a hot campfire for baking. They are made of metal and reflect the heat back to bake the item within. Most reflector ovens fold flat for storage. While a few places sell reflector ovens, you can also make one quite easily. Other ovens are available from cottage or hobby gear makers, and you will find links to these, as well as oven plans, on **www.aforkinthetrail.com.**

Of course, there are many other ways to bake in the backcountry. Some of these methods are baking in a frypan, foil packet, or orange skin, or on a stick over a campfire.

Spices, Condiments, and Fats

Spices and condiments can really enhance a meal, but for the vegetarian, vegan, or person with celiac disease, it is extremely important to be aware of the ingredients. Some spices contain traces of gluten with ingredients such as wheat starch, and some condiments, such as regular Worcestershire sauce, contain meat products such as anchovies. Even some less expensive brands of tamari sauce have meat ingredients, so be sure to look for true tamari sauce and read the labels carefully. If you are traveling with a group, it is advisable to allow each person to adjust the spices according to his or her preferences. I take salt and pepper but will also include other spices and condiments as my menu dictates.

Oils, butter and substitutes, shortening, jams, maple syrup, brown rice syrup, agave syrup, and other items can be stored in small leak-proof Nalgene containers. If you are an ovo-lacto vegetarian and are taking butter, it is best to take regular salted butter as the salt acts like a preservative and the butter will keep longer. In very hot weather, ghee or clarified butter is a great alternative. Soy- and olive oil–based spreads work very well but aren't good for baking.

Using This Book

Dehydration times listed in the recipes are approximate; you should check food periodically as it's drying. The cooking and rehydration times are also an approximation. Outside factors such as weather, humidity, altitude, and heat source can affect the cooking or baking time. You should read a recipe, including the instructions, twice before you make it. Familiarizing yourself with the recipe in this manner will give you better results.

Serving sizes are what I would describe as average to hearty. All recipes, except for the baking ones, can easily be cut in half. Those of you who are solo hiking or solo paddling might consider making the recipe and eating it for dinner at home and then drying the leftovers or drying the entire recipe and dividing it into single servings. Because dehydrated food will keep for an extended period, doing the latter will give you food for additional trips. If a recipe involves dehydration, then the approximate time is listed at the beginning. Where applicable each recipe includes icons to help you choose an appropriate dish.

 indicates that a recipe is suitable only for ovo-lacto vegetarians.

 indicates that a recipe is vegan

 indicates that the recipe is gluten free.

 indicates that a recipe is especially lightweight and therefore more appropriate for an activity such as backpacking or thru-hiking.

Special Ingredients

A few ingredients in the book need some further explanation and instruction. Also see the section called "Ingredient Substitutions" beginning on page 32.

Mushroom Powder

Mushroom powder can add great flavor to soups, pasta and quinoa dishes, mashed potatoes, and other meals. To make mushroom powder, simply grind dried mushrooms into a powder using a spice or coffee grinder.

Roasted Garlic Powder

To make roasted garlic powder, gather 1 bulb of garlic, some olive oil, and a pinch of kosher salt. Cut the top off a bulb of garlic. Drizzle the cut with olive oil and sprinkle with a little salt if desired. Wrap in aluminum foil. Bake the garlic at 350° 30–45 minutes. Remove from the oven and let cool. Squish the garlic out of the skin and spread it on a lined dehydrator tray to dry 5–7 hours. When the garlic is dry, process it in a spice grinder or blender until you have a powder.

Roasted Red Peppers

To roast peppers place the whole pepper on a baking sheet in a 350° oven 45–60 minutes. Remove from oven when the skin starts to blacken. The skin will separate easily from the flesh. Allow to cool before peeling off the skin. A little trick is to put the hot pepper in a bowl and tightly cover the bowl with plastic wrap until the pepper cools. The skin will come off more easily. You can also grill the peppers until the skin starts to blacken and peel. If you prefer, you can buy roasted peppers at the supermarket; just look for those packed in water.

Celery Leaves

Many people do not realize that the leaves found on celery stalks are good in salads and other dishes. They impart a mild celery flavor. Most often, the leaves are at the top of the celery; however, if you look closely, you can sometimes find them hidden between the stalks.

Lemon, Lime, or Orange Zest

Citrus zest adds another layer of flavor to a dish because of the aromatic oils in the fruit rind. The easiest way to zest citrus fruit is by using a fine grater or a tool specifically designed for the task, but in a pinch you can use a knife. Remove the outer layer of skin, being careful not to get any of the white pith. If you use a knife, you will need to cut the pieces into tiny slivers. Citrus zest dehydrates well.

Candied Lemon, Lime, or Orange

Making candied citrus fruit gives you an interesting ingredient to use with breakfast in oatmeal, couscous, quinoa flakes, or granola. It is also delicious added to chocolate or carob bark, GORP (good ol' raisins and peanuts), and baked goods. Sometimes you can buy these candied items in the baking section of larger grocery chains, but if you turn up empty handed, you can easily make your own. I find that the taste and texture of homemade is much more desirable.

Use a vegetable peeler to remove the very outer rind from an orange, a lemon, or a lime. Try to avoid getting any of the white pith. Cut the rind into strips about ¼-inch wide. Place them in a heavy-bottomed pot with 1 cup of water and bring it to a boil. Drain and repeat the process two more times. Then set the rinds aside. Put 1 cup of water into the pot with 2 cups of fine granulated sugar over medium heat. Heat until the sugar dissolves completely. Then bring the mixture to a boil. Turn the heat down to medium-low and add the citrus rinds. Simmer 10–20 minutes or until the rinds become translucent. Drain and let cool. Once cool, toss the pieces in fine granulated sugar. Tap off any excess sugar and store in an airtight container for up to one month.

Candied Lemon, Lime, or Orange Powder

Take candied citrus fruit as made in the recipe above and dehydrate it 7–10 hours at 105° or until completely dry. It will be hard, brittle, and sugary. Place the dried peels in a spice grinder and grind until you have a fine powder. This powder can be used in a variety of way, such as a flavoring to breakfast grains or baked goods or sprinkled on pancakes.

Ginger

When buying ginger, look for pieces with a firm and smooth texture. Older ginger will be more fibrous, and young ginger will have a sweeter flavor. Freezing ginger-root is a great way to store it and helps it grate more finely. An easy way to peel ginger is by scraping it with the edge of a metal spoon.

Candied or Crystallized Ginger

Just like the candied citrus fruit, this is often available in the baking section of larger grocery chains. It is a great addition to sweet breakfasts, trail snacks, and desserts. Even dipping half of each slice in chocolate makes a delicious treat. If you can't find candied or crystallized ginger, then you can make your own. However, it is best to use very young ginger for this recipe, as older ginger can be fibrous.

Peel the ginger and slice it very thinly. Use the tines of a fork to poke numerous holes in each slice and set aside. In a heavy-bottomed pot combine 1 cup of water with 2 cups of fine granulated sugar over medium heat. Heat until the sugar dissolves completely. Then bring the mixture to a boil. Turn the heat down to medium-low and add the ginger slices. Simmer for 30 minutes until the ginger is translucent. Drain and let cool. Once cool, toss the pieces in fine granulated sugar. Tap off any excess sugar and store in an airtight container for up to three months.

Vanilla Sugar

To make vanilla sugar, place a vanilla bean in a ziplock freezer bag of fine sugar and let it sit for a few days.

Physical Needs and Nutrition

When you travel in the backcountry, whether you are backpacking or paddling, you burn more calories than you would in your day-to-day activities at home.

Terrain, distance, climate, and pack weight come into play. You will use more calories when you are trying to keep warm. For paddlers this caloric burn depends on the difficulty of the trip, length of the paddling day, roughness of the water, and the number of portages. It is important that your body gets the fuel it needs.

You will require a good balance of nutrients to ensure proper nutrition in the wilderness, and that should include carbohydrates, proteins, and fiber. The carbohydrates help satisfy the need for immediate energy and the protein will help with the rebuilding of muscle and long-term energy.

Sometimes people lack understanding of the vegetarian lifestyle and think that lack of protein is an issue; that is not the case. There are great ways to get protein in the diet, including foods such as quinoa or combinations of grains and legumes. Having enough fiber in the diet isn't generally an issue for vegetarians and vegans either. Pickier eaters may consider supplementing with a multivitamin.

How you eat depends on the trip and your needs. There are days on the trail where munching frequently throughout the day is necessary to keep your body properly fueled. This is very important for breakfast skippers. Foods such as nuts, seeds, homemade energy bars, dried fruit, and the like will provide energy as you snack along the trail and will keep you from hitting the wall because you ran out of fuel.

Safe drinking water is another important component that is often overlooked, and if you are hiking at a higher altitude, you need to consume more than you would at sea level. I can't tell you the number of times that I've traveled with people or met people on the trail who were starting to show the signs of dehydration. Symptoms include weakness, lack of coordination, excessive thirst, nausea, and headache. Dehydration can become a serious issue—one that could be potentially deadly. Be sure to drink frequently.

Food Storage: Safe Practices at Home and Camp

One topic that comes up during my workshops is food storage. Air and moisture can be the enemy when it comes to storing dehydrated foods. With that in mind, it's very important that you compress as much air out of the storage bags as possible. If you aren't using the meals you've dehydrated within the first month or two, then place the meals in the freezer. Here they will keep for six to eight months without taste or quality being compromised. Sweet potatoes are the exception to the rule and should only be stored for two to three months because they will lose flavor.

After the food has thawed completely, open the bag a little to let out any condensation that might occur. You might even have to put the food in a new bag. Then squeeze out the air and close again. If you aren't freezing the meals, keep them in a cool, dark place or in your refrigerator. Check meals carefully a few weeks before you leave on your trip—if there is even the slightest sign of mold, throw the meal out. It means that the meal didn't dry properly or became contaminated. This has only happened to me once, and it was because the bag wasn't sealed or stored properly.

Storing Fresh Ingredients

While I usually try to avoid taking a lot of fresh foods because of weight considerations, you have a few options. Some require the use of a small cooler and ice and others require some creative packing. On weekend hiking and paddling trips, fresh food can be a nice alternative if you don't mind the extra bulk and weight.

Vegetables

I've discovered that organic produce stays fresher for longer. Fresh potatoes, especially baby new potatoes, will travel well and are nice wrapped in aluminum foil and baked in hot coals. Fresh yellow onions last a week or more in a pack. If the skins show signs of wrinkling, use them right away. On a short trip where weight is not so much of a consideration, you can bring eggplants or zucchini and grill them over a fire or panfry them with herbs, balsamic vinegar, and olive oil. I have had fresh, organic green peppers last a week in my pack. They are generally smaller than nonorganic peppers and fit nicely into a plastic container, which prevents them from being crushed. I also have been known to carry avocado in the same manner, but I generally buy one that is underripe and let it ripen in my pack. When I put veggies in a plastic container, I open the container every day for a few minutes to let the humidity escape and allow the contents to breathe. Vegetables such as fresh carrots, celery, and green peppers are delicious dipped in hummus. You can even grow sprouts on the trail to add a fresh crunch to wraps and trail salads. A fresh cucumber can be a nice addition to lunch or dinner especially if kicked up with a dressing.

Always store fresh mushrooms in a paper bag, or they will spoil quickly. If I take fresh fruits or vegetables in my pack, I wrap them in a paper towel to reduce bruising and then in a plastic bag that isn't airtight. Every day at camp I unwrap and check them and allow the air to dry any condensation. If something is ripening faster than I expected, I will juggle the menu to use the item before it spoils.

Fruits

Fruits such as oranges are sturdy, so they carry well and will last a week or more. If you wrap an apple in some paper towels and place it in the center of your pack, it will last more than a week. More delicate stone fruits such as peaches, nectarines, and cherries bruise easily; they travel better in a hard-sided container. Avocados, tomatoes, and other very fragile produce can be carried in a Froot Guard, and bananas can by placed in a Banana Guard. Both products are available from **www.bananaguard.com.**

Cheeses

If you are an ovo-lacto vegetarian, you might want to include cheese in your menu. Hard cheeses such as Parmesan, Grand Padano, dry Monterey Jack, and old Cheddar will keep longer. If you want to store cheese for longer than a few days, wrap it in vinegar-soaked cheesecloth and put it in a ziplock freezer bag. If you want to use it for more than a week, go one step further and dip the cheesecloth-wrapped cheese several times in paraffin wax. Cheese also keeps well wrapped in plain brown paper or butcher paper and placed in a ziplock bag. Grated cheese does not keep long and should be used on the first night or two; the same is true for creamed cheeses such as mascarpone, herbed cheese, and the like.

Vegetarian Cheeses

Many types of dairy- and casein-free cheeses for vegetarians are on the market. Often these products are made from rice or soy. These products will only keep a day or two without using a cooler bag and are best used in cooler weather.

Fresh Tofu and Tempeh

In cooler weather fresh tofu or tempeh can be carried but is weighty. You can press the tofu at home with a tofu press or a heavy pan to remove a great deal of the liquid and then package it in a ziplock freezer bag to reduce the weight a little. Shelf stable, firm, silken tofu is available in some supermarkets and is your best option if you'd like tofu on longer trips.

Storage Ideas

There are many ways to deal with storage when it comes to food for wilderness trips. I prefer reusable containers because I like to reduce my environmental footprint, so I lean toward items such as BPA-free Nalgene containers when feasible. I also use freezer bags and LOKSAK products. Freezer bags can be washed at home and reused if they aren't damaged as long as you air-dry them well. LOKSAK makes two products, OPSAK and aLOKSAK, both of which are element proof. Both are food safe and the OPSAKs are an odor-proof bag rated for higher temperatures.

I use a selection of the following containers and bags:

* Nalgene bottles in sizes 30–500 milliliters
* ziplock freezer bags, ranging in size from small to large
* reusable OPSAK and aLOKSAK bags, in a variety of sizes
* a hard-sided container for items such as crackers or tortilla chips
* mini ziplock bags or contact lens containers for salt and spices
* extra ziplock bags for leftovers or emergencies

It is advisable to store foods by meal in larger ziplock bags rather than store many meals in one ziplock bag. The bags often fail if they are opened and closed repeatedly, and being stuffed into a pack each day can be hard on them. Remember to check the ziplock seals daily and to carry a few spare bags just in case. The exception is with energy bars. I like to wrap them individually in waxed paper or baker's parchment and then place several in a ziplock bag together. The waxed paper makes an excellent fire starter.

Protect GORP or trail mix from being crushed by storing it in a wide-mouth Nalgene bottle. Sometimes I store my GORP items separately from one another and mix it each morning. That way I will not have to dig through the mixture if I want to use an ingredient such as raisins in another recipe.

It is important that you also store your food safely. I double bag much of my food to prevent moisture from getting inside because it causes food to spoil quickly. At camp I try to keep the food pack out of the sun to reduce its temperature.

It is also important that you hang your food or use an approved bear canister in areas where there are bears; some parks and trails have hanging cables, poles, or bear-proof boxes. But bears aren't the only problem—raccoons, mice, and other critters can be bothersome as well. If you are in bear country or above the tree line, be sure to use an approved bear canister. It is best to find out ahead of time what type of container is approved for the area in which you plan to hike.

Because I don't like to hang all of my gear or my entire pack, I carry a nylon bag designed specifically for hanging food. The bag packs up small but will hold a considerable amount of food. You could also use a coated nylon dry bag. Bear-proof canisters are also available, but unless I am hiking where one is required, I find that hanging the food is just as effective. If you are on a paddling trip, you may have the luxury of a separate food pack or barrel, which should be hoisted up between two trees. You should hang your food before dark if possible—not only does this reduce the risk of attracting little nocturnal pests, but it's easier to find a suitable tree when you can see what you are doing. Be sure to use a good-quality rope for food hanging. The inexpensive, yellow rope that you can buy at the hardware store breaks much more easily than you would think. Use a marine-grade or climbing rope that won't stretch if saturated with water. If your clothes smell of food or you spilled food on them, you should hang them as well. Toothpaste, camp soap, and other scented items need to be hung with the food pack for safety.

As much as you try to avoid having leftovers, sometimes it happens. Depending on the item, you can store it for use the next day. Intentionally creating leftovers, such as bannock or muffins, makes the next day a little easier. Before storing baked goods, let them cook completely; then place them in a clean ziplock freezer bag or other suitable container. Unless the weather is very cool, be careful when storing food such as rice, as it can develop bacteria that will make you ill. If you have any doubts about the safety of leftover food, it is best to err on the side of caution. Depending on where you travel, you might be able to burn your leftovers. I prefer to pack garbage out as it has less impact on the environment. At night hang the garbage bag in a tree just as you do your food pack.

Packing food for backpacking and paddling trips can have a steep learning curve. Here are some tips that I've found helpful:

- Plan your menu.
- Take a copy of your menu with you so you can refer to it. I keep mine in my waterproof map case.
- Pack each meal separately in a larger ziplock bag.
- Bring extra ziplock bags in case one of them tears or you have usable leftovers.

- Repackage grocery store finds into ziplock freezer bags.
- Pack the name of the meal, water needed, and other trailside instructions with each meal. (Don't write it on the outside of the bag in case it wears off.)
- When baking, line your pots with parchment paper to make cleanup easier.
- Store liquids in leak-proof containers, and put these in a ziplock bag just in case.

Hygiene

Good practices surrounding hygiene are essential both at home and in the backcountry. More often than not, when a person gets ill in the wilderness, it is due to poor hygiene practices, food-borne illness, or contaminated water. Proper hand washing is imperative both on and off the trail. You should always wash your hands before handling food. If water is limited and you are using an alcohol-based hand sanitizer to disinfect your hands, be extremely careful and wait a few minutes for the alcohol to evaporate before lighting a stove or cooking fire. Keep your body clean as well, as bacteria can travel. Water should be treated and you should be careful not to contaminate water containers or other utensils with untreated water. This can put you at risk of contact illnesses from bacteria such as *giardia* and *cryptosporidium*.

Keep It Personal

I like to have my own personal water bottle for drinking, and I expect my campmates to do the same. This can prevent me from getting ill if someone else's hygiene is lacking or if they contract a cold. I also feel that it is a good idea for each person to have his or her own eating utensils, plate, cup, and bowl. Don't share foods such as GORP. Give each person his or her own personal snack bag or have each bring a container for the mix. I also like to divide the GORP into daily portions as opposed to a larger bag, even if it is my own personal bag. Why? This can prevent issues with bacteria because you are taking a handful of GORP, putting your hand to your mouth, and then putting your hand back in the bag each time.

Cleanup

When dishwashing be sure to use a soap product that is specifically geared for wilderness camping. These camp soaps are generally concentrated so you don't need a lot. Use camp soap with care and keep it out of lakes and streams. Be aware of any environmental impacts it could have. Steer clear of sponges—they harbor bacteria. When disposing of dishwater, ensure you follow LEAVE NO TRACE guidelines. Take any pieces of food out of the water and then scatter the water well away from camp and water sources so it is spread over a larger area.

If you drop food on the ground, pick up as much as possible. Put the food in your garbage bag to be packed out and rinse the area well. Always keep a very clean camp kitchen so that you don't attract rodents or, even worse, a bear.

Meal Disasters

While I am an experienced cook both at home and in the wilds, I am not infallible. I have had my share of meal disasters and I've witnessed a few that others have had. I try to learn from my mistakes and hopefully so can you.

Watch the Water

One of my first experiences with dehydration and rehydration was spaghetti sauce. I wrote "2 cups" on a sticky note for a total measurement that was to include the dried ingredients. When I got to camp, I added 2 cups of water to the ingredients rather than putting the ingredients in first and adding enough water to bring it up to my required measurement. Oops.

When rehydrating your meals, it is always best to err on the side of caution until you get the hang of it. Less is more when it comes to water. If you use too much water, you'll not only have a runny dish but you'll also lose flavor if you try to drain some of the water off. Don't rely on the measurements preprinted on water bottles, as I've found they aren't always accurate. Use a folding spoon with measuring increments marked on it, or mark a cup or bottle with measuring increments before your trip. As good as my memory is, I still write measurements on a sticky note. While you think you won't forget, it can happen, especially if you are drying a lot of meals.

Don't panic if you end up with tomato water instead of spaghetti sauce. You can use potato starch or cornstarch to thicken it or you can cook your pasta in the sauce. The pasta will soak up the extra water. You can do the same with sauces for rice dishes. Another alternative is to reduce the water by simmering your sauce, but this can increase fuel consumption.

Prevent the Burnt Offering

If you are baking with an Outback Oven, it is important to remember to put the riser in place. It only takes a few moments for the baked item to scorch and burn if the riser has been forgotten. I remember making a cinnamon-swirl coffee cake from a mix, and it smelled delicious for about 30 seconds before the smoke started billowing out of the oven. I forgot the riser and there is no way to recover from that mistake.

If you burn something like chili to the bottom of your pot, you might be able to rescue it. Don't stir it! Transfer the unstuck portion to another pot or your bowl and then clean out the burnt pot. However, if you stir it, you will also stir the burnt flavor through the entire dish.

Keep It Level

A level spot for your stove is of great importance. If the stove and your meal aren't somewhat level, they can teeter and the next thing you know, you are faced with a dinner disaster. If your food happens to land on a rock, it's easy enough to recover most of it; however, ground covered in pine needles is quite problematic. This happened to my husband on one of our trips. Thankfully it wasn't too big of an issue because it was a dessert that was lost. That brings me to another lesson learned.

Keeping a stove level is also an important safety issue when it comes to using an alcohol stove. Because these stoves use fuel in an uncontained manner, unlike their white gas and compressed gas counterparts, the fuel can spill and continue to burn. This could cause a fire, damage to gear, and personal injury. The flame on an alcohol stove is sometimes very difficult to see. I'd like to say that we've never had an issue but we have. Thankfully it had just rained and we were in a car campground. The stove was on a picnic table that was saturated with water and contained about 2 ounces of denatured alcohol. The pot wasn't centered on the stove properly and the works toppled. The entire table was aflame. As luck would have it, the water stopped any damage from occurring, but had we been on a wilderness trip, this could have had serious consequences. This is also why I tend to lean toward using white gas stoves. It isn't advisable to use an alcohol stove on trips where you will be with small children.

Eat Clean

A male friend dropped a noodle on the ground when serving his pasta. Partway through his meal he was playing a gentle tug-of-war with a deer mouse who had wandered over to munch on the spillage. My friend thought this was adorable until the mouse climbed the rock beside him and proceeded to leap toward the plate. The mouse missed and landed on the fellow's shoulder. He screamed and the plate of noodles was airborne. Cleanup, of course, was crucial and not just because we were in bear country; little critters such as mice can be destructive—though the last thing you want to do is something that will bring a bear into camp.

Be Careful with Spices

It is important to use spices sparingly and never pour them over the pot. The inner lid, the one with the small shaker holes in it, once came off my spice bottle when I was shaking it over the pot. What was to be a sprinkle of cayenne ended up being a significant addition—one that I couldn't correct. It was so hot that we couldn't eat it. The other issue with pouring spices over the pot, and this is important at home too, is that it allows small amounts of steam to get into the spices, which can ruin them.

Check Your Gear Twice

Double-checking your gear is important. If you are going on a group trip, you should ensure that everyone is clear on who is bringing what. A friend and colleague of mine embarked on a trip last year where three sets of couples were traveling together. Each couple thought that the other was bringing a pot set. Everyone realized their mistake when they set up camp the first night. Thankfully one of the couples had decided to bring a Plus 10 model Outback Oven, which has a lidded frying pan. They had to cook for the entire week from the pan, and they even made coffee in it. If they hadn't had the pan, it could have very well ruined their trip.

Bring an Extra Meal or Two

It's always a good idea to bring some extra food. Emergencies can happen. You could need the extra food because of one of the meal disasters we've talked about, or it may be something more serious, such as being camp-bound because of severe weather or an injury.

   Sadly, there are times where you might have to bail out a campmate like I did a few years ago. This could be from poor planning on the other person's part or because of someone forgetting to use his noodle, which was the case with my campmate. There were two couples and we were cooking dinner. The other man decided he was going to drain his pasta water in the wooden privy—a practice with which I have huge issues. One issue is how unsanitary the practice is and the other is critter related. The pasta started to slip from the pot, and as he tried to stop it from happening, he dropped the towel and burned both his hand and his leg. The pasta went down the privy hole and their dinner was lost. Luckily it was a mild scald and I had something in my emergency kit to help. They would have gone hungry had I not packed extra rations for the trip.

Bring Extra Fuel

It's always a good idea to bring a little extra fuel. I generally try to bring at least enough for one extra day. Why? Well, if you were to have a meal disaster like some of those I just mentioned, you may need the extra fuel. There may also be a situation where you use more fuel then you plan due to weather. Weather conditions can cause the stove to use more fuel or may affect your decision to have extra-hot drinks to take the chill off. It is also a good idea in case your water filter fails or you run out of chemical treatment, as you may need to boil water to make it safe to drink.

Chapter 2
Dehydration Basics, Commercially Dried Foods, and Grocery Store Finds

About Dehydrating Foods

Drying has been a reliable and simple method of food preservation for centuries, and it is ideal for those of us who love to travel in the backcountry. While you can use fresh foods, there is the issue of pack weight and spoilage over the long term.

There are several ways to dehydrate your own foods; however, some are more accurate and cost effective than others. Because you are using air circulation with very low heat to dry the foods, it requires a bit of time, and the length of time will depend on how you decide to dry your foods, the humidity of the air, and the foods and the size of the food pieces. Drying times, with these variables in mind, can range 5–20 hours.

Types of Dehydrators

Homemade dehydrators vary in style and construction. One method is to make a wooden box with trays and use a light-bulb as a heat source. These homemade versions tend to be bulky and lack the ability to control the temperature, which can cause problems with some foods. Another version of the homemade dehydrator uses solar energy. While a novel idea, these don't work particularly well for some foods, and you are at the mercy of the weather. Because these are used outside, bugs may also get on the food. You can find instructions for creating homemade dehydrators on the Internet.

Using your oven is another method. Some modern convection ovens have a dehydration setting, and because convection ovens use a fan, you'll achieve better results in these compared to standard ovens. You'll want to set your oven between 140° and 165°. The food goes on a lined cookie sheet and the oven door is left ajar. With some ovens, you may have to use something like a wooden spoon to keep the door open. While an oven can be an effective tool for food dehydration, there are drawbacks. First of all, many modern ovens only have a lowest temperature setting of 170°, and that is too high for proper drying. That high of a temperature will cause your food to continue cooking and can also cause casing on certain fruits and vegetables. Casing is where the outside dries too quickly, creating a seal that prevents the inside from drying properly. You are also limited to drying two trays of food at a time, and you must rotate them frequently to make the drying even. If using the oven, you'll have to check your foods quite often to ensure proper drying. It is also not the most energy-efficient method of food dehydration.

I prefer to use a retail dehydrator that fits nicely on my countertop. The one I have used the most is a relatively inexpensive unit that can accommodate numerous trays and has a thermostat. Recently, because of my work and high level of usage, I upgraded to a more expensive and feature-laden model with a timer. Because these types of appliances have a fan, the drying is more uniform and that, coupled with the size, makes them more energy efficient. You generally don't need to rotate the trays because of the airflow and can often turn on the dehydrator in the evening and turn it off when you get up in the morning. Models with a timer are very helpful but not entirely necessary.

Advanced Dehydration

While you may be apprehensive at first when it comes to using a food dehydrator, once you have dried your first few meals, you will greet the task with less trepidation and may even start to experiment with your own recipes using some of the ones in this book as a guide. The following tips will help you succeed.

It is a good idea to line your dehydrator trays with baker's parchment paper or to buy fruit leather trays that are made for your unit. Some models use a nonstick liner and others a plastic tray. You'll need to line the trays when you are drying foods that contain more liquid, such as sauces, soups, stews, fruit leathers, and whole meals such as chili. Small pieces of fruits and vegetables will fall through the tray's grid if you don't use a liner. Larger pieces of fruits and vegetables can be dried on trays that are lined with a plastic mesh screen purchased from the dehydrator manufacturer. Plastic wrap that is rated for use in microwave ovens also works well. I prefer the liners made for my dehydrator primarily because they are reusable. Using a liner makes cleanup much easier as well.

When drying soups that have more liquid, you can use the vegetables as a dam to keep the liquid from running off the lined tray. Then, as the liquidity of the food has been reduced, just spread the vegetables out a little more for even drying.

Most fruits for use in fruit leather can be used without cooking first. Sauces such as traditional spaghetti sauce should be cooked before drying. When you are ready to dry your sauce, soup, stew, fruit leather, or whole meal, measure it and then write that measurement on a sticky note. Place a liner on the food dehydrator tray and then pour the food on the liner. If your dehydrator has trays with a hole in the center, leave about an inch of space without food at the inner and outer edges of the tray. For square or rectangular models without a center hole, just leave the inch of space around the outer edge. Spread the food out so that it is about ¼-inch thick. On some dehydrators ingredients pool toward the center of the unit, and spreading the food a little thinner in the center of the tray will make drying more even. Set the temperature on your dehydrator according to the manufacturer's instructions.

Fresh vegetables such as potatoes, corn, asparagus, broccoli, and cauliflower need a quick blanch before dehydrating. To blanch them, merely put them in a metal or silicone strainer and put the entire strainer in a pot of boiling water for a few moments. Then put the strainer with the vegetables still in it into a bowl of cold water to stop the cooking. You can also use your microwave to blanch vegetables. Simply add the vegetables and a little water in a microwavable bowl or steamer bag. Cook them on high for about 2 minutes in a 750-watt microwave. Reduce the time for higher wattage units. Frozen and canned vegetables can be put directly on the dehydrator because they are blanched before freezing. Use either a solid liner or a mesh one depending on the size of the pieces.

Be sure to measure the food before you dry it and write this measurement down so you will know how much liquid to add back when you rehydrate the food. To this note you may want to add the name of the meal or food, the number of servings, and the date you dried it. Pack this with the food in a freezer-grade ziplock bag.

If dried properly and packaged well, these items will last for up to eight months in your freezer before flavor loss occurs. Unfrozen, the shelf life is several months, as long as the package remains tightly sealed and is stored in a cool, dry place.

Rehydration Basics

One of the benefits of vegetarian and vegan foods on the trail is the ease of rehydration when compared to meals that contain meat. Tofu is the only exception to this. It does not rehydrate well at all. You can rehydrate foods in one of several vessels—such as a large, wide-mouth Nalgene; a ziplock freezer bag; or a pot. My preferred container is the wide-mouth Nalgene, but I do use the others from time to time. Many of the foods, especially lunches, can be reconstituted with cool water, thus saving time and fuel weight. Rehydrating with cool water will lengthen the time with some foods, so pay careful attention to the "At Camp" instructions, as I will mention water temperature there if it will make a difference. Also, take a copy of your menu with you. I suggest listing the foods by meal, so you can refer to it in the morning to see what you have planned for the day. This lets you know if you will need to keep your stove handy because you've decided on a hot lunch, and also allows you to position your lunch in a convenient place when you pack your backpack. It also lets you see if you need to add water to your lunch meal at breakfast, if you aren't planning to use your stove at lunch. For example, if you are having the Mediterranean Garbanzo Bean Salad (see page 107) for lunch, you will need to rehydrate it in the morning. Let's say you started with 2 ½ cups and now have 1½ cups of dried mix. Because it is morning and you do not need this until lunchtime, you can use cold water and let the mixture rehydrate as you travel. Put the dried mix into a Nalgene or other leak-proof rehydration container and add a little less than 1 cup of water to end up with close to a full 2½ cups. It is always best to err on the side of caution when it comes to adding water. You can always add more water later if needed. Place the container in the top of you backpack or clip it to the outside of your pack.

At lunch you will have a Mediterranean Garbanzo Bean Salad that tastes just like it did before you dehydrated it at home—and you didn't even have to pull out your stove. If the dish is thicker than you like, just add a little more water. You can also plan to add water to your dinner at lunchtime, and the meal will be rehydrated by the time you are ready to eat. If you reach camp and the meal hasn't come back, which is rare with vegetarian foods, put the contents in your pot and bring the meal to the boiling point. Remove the pot from the heat, replace the lid, put it in a cozy if you have one, and place the pot in a safe spot to allow the final bit of rehydration. The heat will speed up the rehydration. You can put a rock on the lid if you like so it doesn't get knocked off. If you decide not to initiate rehydration of your dinner earlier in the day, you can add boiling water at camp, and then place the food container in a cozy to speed up rehydration. If you use boiling water in a Nalgene bottle, it is advisable to open the bottle on occasion to release the pressure from the steam. It is this pressure that makes the Nalgene my favorite container for rehydrating foods. The pressure seems to help the food take in the water better.

I have one Nalgene bottle just for rehydrating our meals. When I do the dishes, I wash it well and rinse it thoroughly with boiling water. I do bring a few ziplock freezer bags too, as they are handy when rehydrating meals with multiple ingredients. When using very hot water with a ziplock bag, you will need to be careful so that you do not burn yourself from the water or the steam.

Multi-ingredient Rehydration

Some items will produce flavored water that may overpower the dish you are rehydrating. Dried mushrooms, green peppers, and olives are examples of foods that can overtake a meal pretty quickly. I have indicated in the recipe if ingredients need to be rehydrated separately. The best way to do this is to use freezer bags for the smaller ingredients and a wide-mouth Nalgene for the portion of the dish that requires the largest volume. Be sure to let the steam out of the Nalgene as the food expands. I can't stress enough the care you need to take when pouring very hot water in a ziplock bag. If weight and bulk aren't an issue, you could take a few small plastic containers for multi-ingredient rehydration.

Commercially Dried Foods

There are times where spontaneity means that there isn't time to prepare foods for a trip. Generally I try to keep some home-dried meals on hand, but there have been times where I've had to pick up a commercially dried meal. They can be pricey, but some brands will do well for a last-minute addition to the pack. The following companies have vegetarian and vegan options.

* **Alpine Aire**—has a variety of meatless meals

* **Backpacker's Pantry**—offers fare for the vegan and vegetarian as well as organic meals; also clearly marks allergens on the packaging

* **Mary Jane's Farm**—the Outpost line of foods has a great selection of vegetarian options that are also organic

* **Harvest Foodworks**—most of its line is vegetarian but requires a bit of cooking time as the ingredients are dehydrated rather than freeze-dried; this Canadian company ships throughout North America

Sometimes purchasing specially dried ingredients will help you with your backcountry cooking. Availability may vary by region but many companies offer online ordering.

* Powdered vegan egg replacer
* Powdered soy, almond, or rice milk
* Freeze-dried fruits and vegetables
* Tomato powder
* Peanut butter powder
* Dried soup base
* Powdered vegetable shortening

* Dried mushrooms (Asian grocery stores are a great resource for these)
* Honey powder
* Instant wild rice
* Dried sliced potatoes
* Dehydrated legumes
* Maple sugar and maple flakes

Grocery Store Finds

* Shelf-stable tofu
* Textured vegetable protein
* Muffin mixes
* Cake mixes (look for single-layer varieties)
* Gluten-free baking mixes
* Pizza dough mix
* Pancake mix
* Instant mashed potatoes
* Instant couscous
* Precooked rice in pouches
* Curry sauces
* Premade pasta sauces in plastic pouches

* Sliced potatoes
* Flavored rice
* Minute Rice or other 5-minute rice
* Instant soups
* Instant sauce mixes
* Coconut powder
* Creamed coconut
* Wraps
* Flatbreads
* Bagel chips
* Rye crispbread
* Shelf-stable soy, almond, and rice milk boxes

- Shelf-stable juice boxes
- Dried mushrooms
- Bulk soup mixes
- Dried hummus mix
- Granola bars
- Cereal bars
- Instant hot cereals
- Kava
- Instant coffee
- Instant hot cocoa/hot chocolate mixes
- Vegetable chips
- Wasabi peas
- Spiced nuts
- Sugared nuts
- Dried tortellini
- Ravioli
- Gnocchi (some varieties don't require refrigeration)
- Corn bread mix
- Pringles
- Cheeses (look for shelf-stable varieties or harder cheeses)

Online Resources

The Internet has made it much easier to find ingredients and prepared meals. I've listed some resources here, and an up-to-date list can be found at **aforkinthe trail.com**.

- **Gourmet House Wild Rice (www.gourmethouse.com)**—instant wild rice (not available in Canada)

- **Gibbs Wild Rice (www.gibbswildrice.com)**—instant wild rice and wild rice cereal

- **Walton Feed (www.waltonfeed.com)**—dehydrated ingredients, egg mix, powdered soy milk, peanut butter powder, and shortening powder

- **Mumm's Organic Sprouting Seeds (www.sprouting.com)**—organic seeds for growing sprouts on the trail

- **Minimus.biz (www.minimus.biz)**—single-serving condiments, dressings, and other travel-size items

- **The Spice House (www.thespicehouse.com)**—specialty extracts and spices

- **King Arthur Flour (www.kingarthurflour.com)**—dried egg products, organic ghee, specialty flours, mixes, and spices

- **Bob's Red Mill (www.bobsredmill.com)**—quinoa, millet, teff, spelt, amaranth, gluten-free flours, grains, flax, and a variety of mixes

- **Bauly Specialty Foods (www.bauly.com)**—freeze-dried and dehydrated fruits and vegetables

- **Emergency Essentials (www.beprepared.com)**—freeze-dried and dehydrated meals and ingredients (not available in Canada)

- **Harmony House Foods (www.harmonyhousefoods.com)**—textured vegetable protein (TVP), vegan soup mixes, freeze-dried and dehydrated fruits and vegetables, and dehydrated beans

- **Miles Outside (www.milesoutsideorganic.com)**—gluten-free, organic baby food for the littlest hikers

- **Indian Harvest (www.indianharvest.com)**—supplies of specialty rice and grain products (not available in Canada)

- **Nesco/American Harvest (www.nesco.com)**—food dehydrators

- **Excalibur (www.excaliburdehydrator.com)**—food dehydrators

- **MEC (www.mec.ca)**—gear and a small selection of freeze-dried fruits and other ingredients (not available in the United States)

- **Briden Solutions (www.bridensolutions.ca)**—freeze-dried and dehydrated foods, as well as scrambled egg mix (not available in the United States)

- **Shalit Foods (www.shalitfoods.com)**—Canadian supplier for hard-to-find products, such as red quinoa and specialty rice, from companies such as Indian Harvest

- **Feel Good Natural Health Stores (www.feelgoodnatural.com)**—Canadian supplier for items such as quinoa flakes and amaranth

Trader Joe's (**www.traderjoes.com**), with stores throughout the U.S., has a great selection of spices, nuts, dried fruits, dried vegetables, and dried beans and legumes, as well as foods such as couscous and soup mixes. Some of the items are in bulk bins, so you only have to purchase what you need. Unfortunately, online ordering is not available at the time of this writing.

Chapter 3

MENU PLANNING

When teaching workshops and talking to other outdoors people, I am often asked about how I handle planning food for a trip. It's a bit of a learning curve and a challenge to find the balance between nutrition and food weight. I remember some of the first trips I took and how much extra food we brought. We'd create a perfect menu and then at the last minute we worry that it wasn't going to be enough food for the trip, so we'd add more to the pack only to bring it back home. A few trips later we decided that it was time to get realistic and evaluate what we were doing. We made a menu, with a plan for some emergency rations, and stuck to it.

Our simple meal plan is comprised of three main meals and a few snacks for each day coupled with the occasional dessert. I add in a few extra snacks for cold-weather trips. While I suggest using dehydrated foods, adding in fresh food can really complement the backcountry menu, as long as you don't mind a little extra weight. Paddlers will have more flexibility in this respect unless they have long or difficult portages.

You'll also want to consider that you may eat more in the backcountry than at home because of the amount of energy you are expending; however, you might find that your appetite is decreased in the first few days, increasing as the trek progresses. When looking at peoples' menus, I often see plans that include items such as candy bars—not always a good choice. While a candy bar might give you a burst of energy, it is nutritionally lacking and will be short-lived. You may experience a sugar crash, which makes you feel lethargic and zapped of energy. This isn't a good thing when you still have a half day of hiking or paddling ahead of you. When you don't consume enough calories, you tend to live off your body's food stores instead of giving your body the fuel it needs. Nutrient-dense foods will serve you better both on and off the trail.

Planning for Solo Trips

Solo hikers and paddlers may want to prepare a simpler menu than people on a group trip. Avoid heavier items such as baked goods and backpacking ovens if weight is an issue. If you cook multiple serving meals, package them in single servings and take along a copy of the menu. The benefit of going solo is that you can plan what you like and you don't have to consider the likes and dislikes of a campmate.

Planning for Larger Groups

With larger groups, planning can be a little difficult because you must consider the needs and wants of each person in the group. Some larger groups like to plan food so that the menu is shared; each person is responsible for a meal to feed the entire group. Other groups plan it so that certain people bring specific ingredients that get contributed to group meals. Both methods can cause difficulty in the planning, organizing, and execution. Add fussy eaters, special diets, and varying appetite sizes into the mix and it can be a recipe for disaster. If someone forgets to bring part of his or her share, it can result in the whole group going hungry, and that can create some stressful situations. I suggest handling things a bit differently.

If your group will have more than five people, create subgroups, limited to three or four people. Sometimes groups will form naturally by couple or family, and other times it will form by dietary choices. An example would be a trip where you have vegetarians and nonvegetarians traveling together. The logical division there would be by diet. The subgroups make it easy because each subgroup is responsible for its own food and the related gear. The subgroups then cook and eat around the same time of day in the designated kitchen area at camp. Before the trip it is best to have someone create a proposed menu plan and then share it with everyone. Then each subgroup can plan its menu with the cooking style of the proposed menu as a guide. Adjustments can then be made to suit the needs and tastes of the subgroup's members. With everyone eating in a similar style, in the same area, at the same time, it makes for a relaxed and communal atmosphere. We've found that this really adds to a trip and it is a great time to reflect on the travel of that day. This method is better because when you cook in a larger group, there is less flexibility in the menu and it can be difficult for those with special dietary needs. Organizing by subgroup does reduce the amount of gear needed, as each group can share a pot set, water filter, and stove.

Assigning chores is of great benefit and will make life in the camp kitchen much more organized. Morning is a good example. While one person starts to take down the shelter and fills the packs, the other can prepare breakfast. This approach to cooking while preparing to break camp is time efficient and will help you to get on the move early while still enjoying a hearty start to the day.

Mailing Foods

When you are going on extended hiking or paddling trips or embarking on a thru-hike, you may need to mail parcels ahead or shop along the way. On some trails shopping in tiny grocery stores can be difficult for vegetarians, especially vegans, as well as people with celiac disease, because selection may be very limited. Mailing food is a great alternative even if it does mean small delays associated with the need to be in an area when the post office is open. It is crucial that all of your ingredients are dried properly and thoroughly, sealed well, and packed carefully. A sturdy cardboard carton is the best choice and you may want to include food-safe oxygen absorbers in the food packages or in the carton itself. These will help preserve the freshness of the food. Oxygen absorbers can be purchased from Walton Feed at **www.waltonfeed.com** or Sorbent Systems at **www.sorbentsystems.com.** Speak to someone at the post office that you are sending the parcel to give them a heads-up and ensure that you mail the package in time, so it will be waiting for you when you arrive.

Special Diets and Picky Eaters

Individuals with special dietary needs, other than what is covered in this book, or severe food allergies and those who are extremely picky should be responsible for their own food. It is simpler for one person to prepare their special diet rather than expect the whole group to conform. If you have a picky eater, especially a child, you should test the food choices at home to ensure that he or she will like the food on the trail.

Most recipes in this book can easily be made with low-sodium diets in mind. I've included a selection of gluten-free recipes and regular recipes for menu items such as pizza crust so that you may select the one that suits your dietary needs.

Those who are diabetic should consult their physician, nutritionist, and diabetic education center before going on backpacking or paddling trips. Increased physical activity can cause a diabetic to have increased insulin sensitivity, so adjustment to the carbohydrate intake and medication dosages may be needed to prevent severe hypoglycemia. Diabetic outdoors people should always pack extra carbohydrate-rich foods in case of such emergencies and should test their blood glucose levels more frequently than at home.

Food allergies are of particular concern and it is best that someone with a severe food allergy plan his or her own menu. Severe and life-threatening allergies should be discussed with your campmates before the trip, as should emergency measures. If someone has a deadly allergy to an ingredient, then it is best for the entire group to avoid including that ingredient in any of the foods in order to prevent cross-contamination. I'll address some other food substitutions in the next chapter, "Recipe Creation."

Resizing Recipes

Sometimes you will need to resize a recipe to suit your needs. It's not as difficult as you might think; however, you should test the recipe at home first to ensure that the size adjustments are successful. Most of the recipes here can easily be resized, either doubled or reduced by half, as long as you follow a few simple guidelines.

* When doubling a recipe containing onions, leeks, or shallots, only increase the amount of these strong aromatics by half.

* Be careful with hot spices such as cayenne, hot paprika, and other hot peppers when you double a recipe—you can always add more when you serve it.

* Mark the number of portions and predehydrated volume on a piece of paper and place it in your storage bag or container.

* Never measure ingredients directly over the pot or bowl. If too much of something falls into the dish, you could have a dinner disaster.

* When doubling baked recipes for a larger group, it is often better to prepare two of the recipe as opposed to trying to do one dish. You can cook one, and while everyone enjoys a small serving, cook the second. If you want to serve both at the same time, use two stoves or cozy one while you wait for the other.

Menu Plans

Print a small copy of your menu plan and take it with you so that you can refer to it each morning and plan accordingly for the day. Make notes about what ingredients you may have to rehydrate at breakfast time for consumption at lunch. This preparation saves you from digging through the packs, which is especially helpful in inclement weather. The following sample three- and six-day menus were taken from actual wilderness hiking trips.

Three-day Menu Plan

Day 1—Lengthy Travel Day

Breakfast	Creamy Brown Rice Farina
Snack	Cashews
Lunch	Olive Tapenade with crackers
Snack	Alegria Trail Candy
Dinner	Red Quinoa and Curried Lentil Stew
Dessert	Double Ginger, Almond, Blueberry Fry Cookies

Day 2—Moderate Travel Day

Breakfast	Green Tea and Ginger Quinoa Pancakes
Snack	Maple Balsamic Walnuts with Apples and Dates
Lunch	Pumpkin Hummus with pitas
Snack	Garam Masala Roasted Chickpeas
Dinner	Greek Lentils
Dessert	Mayan Black Bean Brownies

Day 3—Hike Out

Breakfast	Carrot Cake Quinoa Flakes
Snack	Cashews
Lunch	Jicama, Savoy Cabbage, and Mango Slaw
Snack	Date, Pecan, Blueberry, and Ginger Bars
Dinner	Stop at a restaurant on the way home.

Six-day Menu Plan

Day 1—Moderate Travel Day

Breakfast	Cinnamon Griddle Toast
Snack	Fresh orange
Lunch	Greek Red Pepper Dip with crackers
Snack	Roasted Nut and Mango Energy Bars
Dinner	Chana Masala

Day 2—Lengthy Travel Day

Breakfast	Pumpkin Breakfast Bars
Snack	Black Cherry Apple Leather
Lunch	Caribbean Hummus with pitas
Snack	Sun-dried Tomato Flax Crackers
Dinner	Pasta alla Puttanesca
Dessert	Double Ginger, Almond, Blueberry Fry Cookies

Day 3—Lengthy Travel Day

Breakfast	Harvest Apple Granola with soy milk (Start rehydrating lunch ingredients with cold water.)
Snack	Grilled Cinnamon Pineapple
Lunch	Mediterranean Garbanzo Bean Salad
Snack	Citrus Seed Balls with Figs and Agave
Dinner	Late Harvest Soup with Saffron
Dessert	Chai Hot Chocolate

Day 4—Moderate Travel Day

Breakfast	Spiced Date, Cherry, Almond, and Carob Bars (Start rehydrating lunch ingredients with cold water.)
Snack	Veggie Chips
Lunch	Roasted Corn and Ancho Salsa
Snack	Walnut and Anise Stuffed Figs
Dinner	Mushroom Burgundy
Dessert	Cranberry Ginger Green Tea

Day 5—Short Travel Day

Breakfast	Quinoa Berry Muffins
Snack	Wasabi Peas
Lunch	Pear and Fennel Slaw with flatbread
Snack	Maple Sugared Walnuts
Dinner	Pizza

Day 6—Hike Out

Breakfast	Goji Berry Agave Granola with soy milk
Snack	Lime and Black Pepper Roasted Chickpeas
Lunch	Smoky Lentil Pâté
Snack	Grilled Cinnamon Pineapple
Dinner	Stop at a restaurant on the way home.

Additional items

Bring beverages; raw organic sugar or other sweetener such as agave nectar, rice syrup, or stevia; seasonings; soy milk powder; oil; vegan butter; an extra meal; and a few snacks for emergencies (in case you become ill, stormbound, and so on).

RECIPE CREATION AND INGREDIENT SUBSTITUTIONS

Drying your own meals allows you to adapt recipes from home or create new recipes, which will only serve to make your wilderness meals more pleasurable. The ideas are limitless and you may find inspiration from a variety of sources, such as a lunch at your favorite restaurant or a family classic adapted to suit your vegetarian lifestyle.

Adapting recipes is pretty simple. It can be as easy as dehydrating leftovers from the soup or ratatouille you had for dinner. The key is making sure that pieces are small enough to dehydrate and rehydrate properly. Being vegetarian has its perks—almost all vegetables dry very well with the exception of lettuce and most salad greens. Swiss chard, kale, and spinach dry nicely for use in soups and pastas. You can thinly slice vegetables such as zucchini, jicama, sweet potatoes, carrots, and parsnips and dry them to make your own vegetable chips. Frozen vegetables are already blanched and you can dry them right from the freezer. Legume- and bean-based dishes dry fabulously and rehydrate fairly quickly. When it comes to baked goods, many vegetarians are already adept when it comes to making adaptations and substitutions for dairy and eggs. I've included some common substitutions a little later in this chapter if this is new territory for you. Dried fruit can be rehydrated and used in place of fresh fruit in foods such as cobblers.

Creating recipes is fun, but a word of warning: ensure that you create and test the recipe at home a few times before using it on the trail. It's rough when you have to force down a meal that is the texture of cardboard or that didn't have a palatable flavor profile after being dried and rehydrated. Keep in mind that it's not like at home, where you can head to the pantry if you've messed up. You might find that you are inspired by the flavor combinations in another meal that you enjoy. For example, the flavors in a dressing for an Asian salad could make a wonderful marinade for tofu jerky or could be used to enhance a rice and vegetable dish. The ideas are as limitless as your imagination.

Ingredient Substitutions for Vegetarians

Many products on the market make ingredient substitution very easy for back-country meals, and you can make some more creative ingredient substitutions.

Egg Powder or Replacer

You can purchase egg powder that is suitable for baking but not for use as scrambled eggs. If you have an allergy to eggs or you are vegan, you can purchase egg-free egg replacer at your local health food store.

If you prefer, you can make your own egg replacer. It is similar to egg whites and works well in white cakes, muffins, and cookies. The addition of oil mimics a whole egg in baking. To make the equivalent of one egg, mix 1½ teaspoons tapioca starch, 1½ teaspoons potato starch (sometimes found with the kosher foods), and ⅛ teaspoon baking powder together and store it in a ziplock freezer bag. Then when you're ready to use it at camp, add ¼ cup of water and 1 teaspoon of vegetable oil. Beat the mixture with a fork until it becomes a little foamy.

Ground flaxseed can be used in muffins, breads, or other baked goods, but it imparts a flavor that might be unpleasant in a cake or cookies. Keep the ground flaxseed cool and away from air and light to prevent it from becoming rancid; this recipe is not suitable for use in hot weather or more than two days into a trip. Store the seeds in the refrigerator until you leave for your trip. To make the equivalent of one egg, use 2 tablespoons ground flaxseed. If you cannot find ground flaxseed, then grind whole flaxseed. Pack the powder in a ziplock freezer bag, removing as much air as possible and storing it away from sources of heat and light. When you're ready to use it, add 3 tablespoons of water to the ground flaxseed and let it sit 3–5 minutes. Add to your recipe like you would regular eggs.

Chia seeds also make a great egg replacer that can be used in baked goods. Chia turns gooey when water is added to it and becomes very much like an egg white in consistency. Use 1 tablespoon of chia seeds with 3 tablespoons of water to make the equivalent of one whole egg. If you don't want the texture of the seeds in your baking, you can grind the chia into meal first. The darker chia will make some baked goods a little gray in color, but you can also buy white chia seeds if appearance is an issue.

Sweeteners

Both white and brown sugar can be replaced with Splenda white or brown sugar. Read the instructions on the package for equivalents. Stevia is a good sugar substitute that is available at most health food stores. It is very sweet so you only need a small amount. Organic raw sugar can be substituted for white sugar in recipes as well. Maple sugar makes a great replacement for white sugar and adds a wonderful hint of maple. Honey and maple syrup can also be substituted for one another in most recipes. Because honey is more acidic, you may have to add a pinch of baking soda if you are using it to replace maple syrup. You can also substitute sugar with real maple syrup using ¾ cup syrup for every cup of sugar you are replacing. Keep in mind that it is liquid and may change the texture of the recipes, so reduce the recipe liquid by 3 tablespoons for every cup of maple syrup used. Agave nectar or brown rice syrup can be used as replacement for honey or maple syrup.

Cheese and Other Dairy

Many vegetarians do not consume dairy products, but these days there are alternatives. One can buy "cheese" made from rice or soy. Read the label to ensure the product is casein free. Some of the cheeses aren't good for melting but the rice "mozzarella" melts fairly well compared to soy mozzarella. You can even purchase soy-based "feta." Rice and soy yogurts are available, and silken tofu blended with vanilla and fruit makes a wonderful replacement for pudding. Mayonnaise-type salad dressings made from soy can be found easily, as can vegan-friendly "butter." Powdered soy milk is readily available and, although a little difficult to find, you can order powdered almond milk on the Internet. Coconut powder can be added to water to make coconut milk. If you aren't worried about pack weight, you can find shelf-stable Tetra Paks of soy, rice, and almond milk in larger grocery stores.

Whole Wheat Flour

You can increase the fiber in a recipe by replacing up to one-third of the white flour called for with whole wheat flour. This substitution, however, will change the texture, giving you a coarser and denser product. Pastry flour contains less gluten than all-purpose flour and is great for baked goods that require a finer texture.

Chocolate

Carob and carob powder are great substitutes for chocolate and will work well in most recipes; however, there will be a difference in flavor.

Gluten-free Substitutions

Oats

Sometimes oats are not gluten free; however, you can purchase gluten-free oatmeal. That said, quinoa flakes are a great substitute for oatmeal whether you are having it as a hot cereal, making muffins, or creating a crumble topping for your favorite baked fruit.

Couscous

Both Israeli (pearl) and Moroccan styles of couscous are made from wheat. Quinoa, millet, and amaranth make good substitutes. To make them instant, cook the grain and then dehydrate on lined dehydrator trays at 135° 5–8 hours.

Gluten-free Pasta

There are alternatives to wheat pasta. Rice noodles cook very quickly but don't have the same texture as traditional Italian pasta. Quinoa and amaranth pastas are more similar in texture to regular pasta and are a good source of protein. Sometimes you can find gluten-free soba noodles, but be careful to read the package, as some brands contain wheat flour. Small pastas such as orzo can be replaced with rice, amaranth, or quinoa. Some people with celiac disease are able to tolerate kamut pasta.

Gluten-free Mixes

A variety of great gluten-free mixes, for everything from cakes and biscuits to pizza dough, are on the market. Gluten-free pizza dough can also be used to make focaccia bread, cinnamon buns, and calzones.

Gluten-free Flour Substitutions

In gluten-free baking, it is often necessary to combine several types of flour to get a good consistency. Because of the lack of gluten, ingredients such as xanthan gum may be needed to aid with creating the proper texture. Sometimes you will need to increase the amount of fat and leavening ingredients to replicate the action of the gluten in wheat flour. Some gluten-free flours will cause your baked goods to be more crumbly.

All-purpose Mix

In some recipes you can substitute all-purpose flour with an all-purpose gluten-free mix such as one from Bob's Red Mill. Often these mixes contain a variety of flour types and ingredients such as xanthan gum.

Buckwheat Flour

Buckwheat flour can replace up to half of the white flour in your pancakes. It is flavorful flour and despite its name, it is wheat free. It is great in pancakes and breads.

Quinoa Flour

This flour adds more fat to your baking and can replace half of the white or all-purpose flour in a recipe. Quinoa flour also contains a good amount of protein. It works well in all sorts of applications from flatbreads to muffins.

Spelt Flour

Spelt flour can be used cup for cup, but you need to increase the baking powder in the recipe slightly as spelt is heavier. While spelt flour does contain gluten, it can be tolerated by some with celiac disease.

Teff Flour

Teff is an Ethiopian grain that can be ground into flour. The grain is tiny, so I suggest purchasing it already ground rather than trying to grind it yourself. You can substitute up to one-fourth of your flour with teff flour, creating a unique flavor profile for your baked goods. It can also be used as a thickener. Keep in mind that it has a slight sweetness.

Sorghum Flour

Sorghum flour, also known as jowar, has a fairly neutral taste and can replace white flour cup for cup, but add 1 tablespoon of cornstarch to each cup of sorghum. Sorghum works well when mixed with soybean flour, which will help reduce the crumbly texture it can create.

Millet Flour

This flour can be used to substitute up to one-fifth of wheat flour. It is similar to sorghum flour in that it can create crumbly results. It needs to be used with soybean flour, cornstarch, or xanthan gum to bind it.

Nut Flours

Nuts such as almonds and hazelnuts can be finely ground into meal and used to replace other flours in baked goods, but I recommend using them in conjunction with other gluten-free flour as they tend to make items very crumbly. These flours are very nutrient dense and flavorful, especially flour made from almonds, which are one of the most nutritious nuts. Nut flours can be used in place of breadcrumbs for breading.

Bean Flours

While you can buy flours such as chickpea or soybean flour, I often make my own. The texture isn't quite as fine as commercially available bean flour, but that is preferred for some recipes.

Take several cups of cooked and cooled chickpeas or garbanzo beans and purée them in a food processor. Spread on lined dehydrator trays and dry 5–7 hours at 135° or until the mixture resembles dried cracked earth. Grind the dried beans into a powder—a spice or coffee grinder works best for this. Chickpea or garbanzo bean flour is good for items such as flatbread and bannock. Black bean flour is wonderful for baked goods such as brownies or chocolate cake.

White bean flour is best for baked goods such as white cake, where the batter is a light color.

Pumpkin and Squash Flours

Flour made from pumpkins or squash can add great flavor and other nutrients to baked goods. Pumpkin flour or powder can be purchased through online specialty spice stores. You can also make your own. Different types of flour come from pumpkins and squash. The first is made from shelled raw or toasted pumpkin seeds, also known as pepitas, which are ground into a fine powder using a spice or coffee grinder. The second is made from the unshelled seeds of the squash or pumpkin. These are roasted and then ground. The third is made from the meat of the pumpkin or squash. You can take the raw pumpkin or squash meat, slice it into thin pieces, and dry 6–8 hours at 135° until thoroughly dried and then grind it into a fine powder. You can also use stewed or roasted pumpkin or squash that has been puréed. Dehydrate the purée 6–8 hours at 135° and grind into flour.

Wild Rice Powder

To make wild rice powder, take small amounts of wild rice and simply grind the grains into a powder with a spice or coffee grinder. The wild rice powder can be used to thicken soups and stews and it imparts an earthy richness, especially when paired with mushrooms. It can be used in baking by replacing 25% of the flour in a muffin, bread, or pancake recipe with the rice powder. The powder is also a great addition to hot cereals such as oatmeal.

White Rice and Brown Rice Flour

Results are best when you substitute up to one-quarter of wheat flour with white rice flour or brown rice flour. You will need to add more liquid and possibly more fat, as these flours are absorbent and the mixture may become crumbly because of the lack of gluten. White rice flour is fine and similar in texture to cake flour. Brown rice flour is more nutritious than its white rice counterpart; it adds more fiber and a mildly nutty flavor to your baked goods. It's best to buy a superfine version of rice flours or you may discover a bit of a grainy texture.

Barley Flour

This flour isn't completely gluten free, but it can replace up to half of wheat flour in baking. It works fairly well with cookies and pancakes.

Coconut Flour

This flour smells and tastes of coconut and can replace up to one-quarter of the wheat flour. It is especially wonderful in desserts or muffins, but you should limit the amount, or the baked good will be crumbly. It can also be used to thicken Thai-inspired sauces. It is delicious in chocolate- or carob-laden recipes and can also be used to thicken trail smoothies.

Tapioca Flour

Also known as cassava flour or tapioca starch, tapioca flour is best used in combination with other flours. Its high starch content adds a chewy texture to baked goods, and that also makes it an ideal thickener. It's ideally used with rice or millet flour as it adds a bit of sweetness to the other flours.

Masa Harina

Masa harina is used to make tortillas and tamales. It is made with dried corn that has been soaked in a special water containing lime. Then it is ground into very fine flour.

Cornmeal

Cornmeal is ground corn that can be yellow, white, or blue. It comes in different grinds from fine to coarse, which are used for different purposes. Fine cornmeal is often used to make polenta and baked goods.

White Chia Flour

White chia flour is made from ground chia seeds and can replace up to one-third of the flour you are using. Chia flour acts as a binder and can improve the texture of baked goods in combination with other flours. If you can't find chia flour, you can take white chia seeds and grind them in a coffee grinder or flour mill.

Potato Flour

Made from potatoes, this flour is naturally gluten free and is sometimes confused with potato starch. Because the finely ground potatoes hold moisture well, it is often used in baking.

Sweet Potato Flour

To make sweet potato flour, cook sweet potatoes in boiling water or a steamer until tender. Drain and purée the potatoes and spread on lined dehydrator trays. Dry 6–8 hours at 135° until thoroughly dried and then grind it into a fine powder. Sweet potato flour is good in baked goods and croquettes and is useful for thickening soups.

Xanthan Gum

Despite the artificial sounding name, xanthan gum is merely a natural bacterium from the fermentation process that will mimic gluten, to a point, in baked goods. It helps gluten-free recipes develop a similar texture to those baked goods created with wheat flour. It is sometimes used to thicken products because of its ability to gel when it is exposed to moisture.

Now on to the recipes!

Chapter 5

BREAKFASTS

Since the writing of *A Fork in the Trail*, I've discovered that breakfast is one of my favorite meals. Some mornings I like to crawl out of the tent early and enjoy a breakfast bar while watching the sun come up over the horizon. Other mornings it is the comfort of a freshly baked warm muffin that gets my day off to a great start. It is most definitely one of the most important meals, given that we have just fasted and need the energy to get on with the next leg of the journey.

There are many things to consider when planning the breakfast portion of your menu. Type of travel (backpacking, hiking, paddling, or portaging), weather conditions, season, amount of travel for the day, and energy needs are all important factors. If you are backpacking, you will need more energy/calories than you will if you are flat-water paddling with minimal portaging because your body simply burns more calories when you are hiking with a pack. You will also have higher caloric needs when it is really cold out. The seasons play a role as well. In the cooler times of year I prefer a warm breakfast after reluctantly crawling out of my nice warm sleeping bag into the crisp air.

You'll always find a few extra snacks such as energy cookies or bars in my pack. I carry these in case there is a situation when we have to break camp early, such as when we need to stay ahead of weather. Keep your length of travel for each day in mind and consider how long it will take you to rehydrate or cook your meal, clean up, and break camp. If you have a long, arduous day planned, it would be best to choose a breakfast that is quick to prepare and can be cleaned up quickly. Save the more elaborate and baked breakfasts for shorter days or rest days. Talk with your camping companions before the trip to get a feel for their style. If they prefer to break camp early every day, then you are best to leave the baked goods for a rest day. Discussing these things beforehand can prevent strife and unnecessary tension.

Ovo-lacto vegetarians may like eggs as a source of protein. Powdered, freeze-dried scrambled egg mix is great for omelets or French toast. Powdered, freeze-dried whole egg or powdered, freeze-dried egg whites are specifically for use in baking.

Oats are a good breakfast food but can sometimes contain gluten because of where they are milled. If you are cooking for someone with celiac disease, look for oatmeal and rolled oats that are specifically labeled as gluten-free. Bob's Red Mill is a good choice.

Soy milk can be purchased in powdered form, as can coconut milk and coconut cream. Adding a little of the powdered coconut milk to soy milk is delicious poured over granola, muesli, or hot cereal. To make vanilla soy milk you can either add a split vanilla bean to a bag of soy milk or add in a little pure vanilla extract. A recipe for almond milk powder can be found on page 228. To make a sweet almond cream, mix boiling water with marzipan in a freezer-grade ziplock and then carefully knead the bag until the almond and water are well combined. Ovo-lacto vegetarians may choose to use nonfat skim milk powder or a full-fat milk powder such as Nido.

Protein shakes and bars are very popular, but I feel that they are best left to the adventure racing crowd. I find that the taste can sometimes be unappealing, and some brands just don't mix well on the trail, so I tend to look for other sources of protein in my breakfasts, such as quinoa.

To save time I often will start the rehydration of some breakfast ingredients the night before. It's simple to put cold water in a Nalgene with your ingredients and hang it with your other food overnight. This might not be feasible if you are using a bear canister because of space limitations, so if you are hydrating the foods in the morning, use boiling water to speed up the process. Don't rehydrate bean- or legume-based foods overnight though—you'll end up with mush in the morning.

Baking for Breakfast

Having the comfort of freshly baked muffins or biscuits can really make a morning special. You can fry-bake or use an Outback Oven or BakePacker. The Outback Oven is my preferred method. This isn't the type of breakfast you are going to want on a hard day, so leave it for mornings when you aren't in a hurry to get moving or for layovers. You can use recipes from this book, modify your own, or experiment with commercial mixes. Look for commercial mixes that only require the addition of a few items such as oil, water, or eggs. You can use the vegan egg replacers mentioned earlier in the book in place of regular eggs. I've used vegan egg replacements for the baked recipes in this section, but if you are ovo-lacto vegetarian, you may prefer to use powdered whole egg instead. That said, some of the egg replacements I've used are of nutritional benefit. Chia, for example, is a source of calcium and potassium. You can use commercial pizza dough and biscuit mixes for both sweet and savory breakfasts. Sometimes, if I've arrived at camp early enough, I will bake the next morning's breakfast the day before to save time. I've even planned this into my menu to enjoy a baked breakfast on what would normally be too busy of a day to do so.

Use of Leftovers

Leftovers such as biscuits, flatbread, or even extra brownies from your dessert can be saved and used the next morning for breakfast. Just place them in a ziplock bag and enjoy them with your favorite hot breakfast drink.

Breakfast on the Go

On those days where it is necessary to break camp early, a more convenient breakfast may be in order. For these days I look to more portable breakfast options. Homemade energy bars, energy cookies, last night's leftover biscuits with nut butter, or a bagel can be easily eaten while you travel. Prepare things such as bagels or biscuits the night before and place them in a ziplock. In the morning all you have to do is grab and go. Look in the Snacks chapter for other things to eat on the go when time or conditions don't permit a sit-down meal.

Blueberry Hazelnut Quinoa

½ cup quinoa

⅛ teaspoon salt

1 tablespoon white sugar

¼ teaspoon cinnamon

¼ cup dried blueberries

⅛ cup hazelnuts

Brown sugar to taste

Enough soy milk powder to make ½ cup

¾ cup water, plus enough to reconstitute the milk

Makes 2 servings

Quinoa, pronounced "keen-wa," is a good source of amino acids. The addition of blueberries, cinnamon, and toasted hazelnuts makes this dish as comforting as a bowl of oatmeal but packed with protein.

At Home

Rinse the quinoa under cold water for at least 3 minutes. Drain well and then toast in a dry nonstick frying pan until the quinoa starts to pop. Allow it to cool and then place it in a ziplock freezer bag with the salt, sugar, cinnamon, and blueberries. Toast the hazelnuts in a dry nonstick frying pan until they start to become fragrant. Remove from the heat and let cool. Wrap the toasted hazelnuts and brown sugar separately in plastic wrap and place both in the bag with the quinoa. Pack the milk powder with the other milk powder you will take on your trip.

At Camp

Mix the contents of the quinoa bag with ¾ cup of water in a pot. Bring to a boil. Reduce the heat to a simmer and let the quinoa cook for 10 minutes, stirring occasionally. If it becomes too dry, add a little more water. Meanwhile use the milk powder and water to make ½ cup of milk. When the quinoa has finished cooking, divide it into 2 servings. Top each with milk and a little brown sugar, if desired, and sprinkle with hazelnuts.

Tips

If you are camping in cold weather and need to increase your fat intake, add a tablespoon of butter to the quinoa when it has finished cooking. For a warmer quinoa add the milk to the pot when the quinoa has finished cooking and heat through.

If you don't want to cook the quinoa in camp, you can cook it at home and dehydrate it for 6 to 10 hours. At camp you'd simply add ¾ part boiling water to 1 part quinoa and let it rehydrate for 15 to 30 minutes.

Carrot Cake Quinoa Flakes

Dehydration Time: 5–7 hours
Makes 2 servings

This hot cereal recipe has the comforting flavor of carrot cake and the gentle flavor of green tea combined with the protein-packed nutrition of quinoa flakes. If you like, you can sub-stitute oats for the quinoa; however, if you lead a gluten-free lifestyle, ensure that the oats are packaged in a gluten-free facility. I usually rehydrate the carrots and raisins while I have my first cup of tea.

At Home

Grate a carrot on the fine side of a box grater and dry on lined dehydrator trays for 5 to 7 hours or until dry and leathery. Grind the green tea to a fine powder in a spice grinder. Place the quinoa flakes in a medium ziplock freezer bag with the green tea and soy milk powder. Put the raisins and dried carrots in a ziplock freezer bag and place that bag in with the quinoa flakes. Mix the sugar and spices together and wrap in a small piece of plastic wrap. Then do the same with the nuts and coconut if you are using them. Put the bundles in the bag with the quinoa flakes.

At Camp

Remove the bundles from the bag of quinoa flakes and set aside. Add enough boiling water to the carrots and raisins to barely cover them and let rehydrate for 10 to 15 minutes. When the carrots have rehydrated, boil 1½ to 2 cups of water depending on the desired consistency. Add the quinoa flakes, sugar-and-spice mixture, carrots, and the raisins to the pot, cover, and let sit for about 2 minutes. Stir in the nuts and coconut if you are using them. Divide into 2 servings.

3 tablespoons carrots, dehydrated measurement

2 teaspoons gunpowder green tea, ground measurement

⅔ cup quinoa flakes

2–3 tablespoons powdered soy milk

2 tablespoons sultana raisins

2 teaspoons maple or brown sugar to taste

½ teaspoon ground cinnamon

¼ teaspoon ground nutmeg

2 tablespoons walnuts or pecans, coarsely chopped (optional)

1 tablespoon shredded sweetened coconut (optional)

1½–2 cups water

Tips

I like to grate several carrots when making this recipe. That way I have extra for this, soup, and trail salads.

If you don't have a spice grinder, just use an inexpensive coffee grinder and dedicate it to grinding spices.

To save time in the morning, start rehydrating the carrots and raisins the night before using cool water and a leakproof container.

Apple Berry Rooibos Quinoa Flakes

Makes 2 servings

I love the combination of apples, raspberries, and rooibos. Rooibos is a tea that comes from a bush grown in Africa. When the needles are dried, they turn a beautiful red color. The Afrikaans word for red is rooibos, *which is how the tea gets its name. It has a slightly sweet and nutty flavor. If you like, you can substitute oats for the quinoa; however, if you lead a gluten-free lifestyle, ensure that the oats are packaged in a gluten-free facility.*

At Home

Place the quinoa flakes in a medium ziplock freezer bag. Wrap the rooibos in a piece of cheesecloth and tie it with kitchen string. Wrap the sugar, raspberries, and apples separately in small pieces of plastic wrap. Put the bundles in the bag with the quinoa flakes.

At Camp

Remove the bundles from the bag of quinoa flakes and set aside. Boil 1½ to 2 cups of water depending on the desired consistency. Add the cheesecloth containing the rooibos and let steep for 5 to 10 minutes. Remove the cheesecloth bundle. Bring the liquid back to a boil and add the quinoa flakes, sugar, raspberries, and apples to the pot. Cover, and let sit for about 2 minutes. Divide into 2 servings.

Tip

After the cheesecloth bundle cools, squeeze out any excess liquid, wrap in the leftover plastic wrap, and place in an empty ziplock bag to be packed out. You may also wish to use a product such as t-sac—a tea filter made from unbleached paper.

⅔ cup quinoa flakes

1½ teaspoons plain rooibos tea

2 teaspoons maple or brown sugar to taste

2½ tablespoons freeze-dried raspberries, crumbled

1 tablespoon dried apples, finely chopped

1½–2 cups water

Chia Banana Nut Crunch Oatmeal

¼ cup freeze-dried banana slices

1 cup old-fashioned rolled oats

¼ teaspoon cinnamon

2 tablespoons chia seeds, toasted if desired

1 large fresh banana or ½ cup freeze-dried banana slices

Enough soy milk powder to make ½ cup, plus water as necessary

¼ cup pecans, coarsely chopped

Maple sugar or brown sugar to taste

Makes 2 servings

Chia seeds add nutrition to this hot breakfast, which is high in protein and omega-3 fatty acids. You can substitute a multi-grain hot cereal or instant oats for the oatmeal if you like.

At Home

Blend the freeze-dried bananas into a powder in a blender or coffee grinder. Combine with the oats and cinnamon in a medium ziplock freezer bag with a note containing the package directions for cooking the oatmeal or cereal that you are using. Toast the chia seeds by placing them on a baking sheet in an oven preheated to 350° F. Bake until lightly toasted. Let cool and wrap in a piece of plastic wrap. Wrap ½ cup of freeze-dried bananas—if you aren't using fresh—soy milk, pecans, and sugar separately in plastic wrap. Put the plastic-wrap bundles in the bag with the oatmeal. If you are using a fresh banana, pack it in a BananaGuard or wrap in a few paper towels. Place it carefully in the top of your pack to prevent bruising.

At Camp

Remove the bundles and the note from the oatmeal bag. Cook the oatmeal or multigrain cereal according to the package directions on your note. If you are using freeze-dried bananas, add a little cool water to them so that they will reconstitute. If you are using a fresh banana, cut it into slices and prepare the soy milk. When the oatmeal is to the consistency you prefer, stir in the toasted chia seeds, pecans, and banana slices. Sweeten to taste and serve with soy milk.

Tip

A dollop of peanut butter stirred into the hot oatmeal during the last few moments of cooking makes this taste like a gooey peanut butter and banana sandwich.

Creamy Brown Rice Farina

Makes 2 servings

This cereal has a striking similarity to cream of wheat. My husband loves to have this wheat-free alternative on cold winter mornings before heading out for a snowshoeing adventure. If you can find maple flakes, they make a great substitute for the maple sugar.

AT HOME

Place the brown rice farina, salt, and maple sugar in a medium ziplock freezer bag. Wrap the cardamom, raisins, and toasted cashews separately in plastic wrap and place the bundles in the bag with the farina. Pack the milk powder with the other milk powder you will take on your trip.

AT CAMP

Remove the bundles from the ziplock with the brown rice farina and set aside. Add the farina to 1 cup of water and bring the mixture to a boil. Reduce heat and let simmer for 4 minutes. Add the cardamom, raisins, and nuts. Cook an additional 1 to 3 minutes, being very careful not to overcook the farina. Serve with soy milk poured over top.

⅓ cup brown rice farina

¼ teaspoon salt

2 teaspoons maple sugar or to taste

¼ teaspoon cardamom

2 tablespoons raisins or other dried fruit

2 tablespoons toasted cashews, coarsely chopped or other nut of choice

Enough soy milk powder to make ½ cup, plus water as necessary

Lemon Ginger Scones with Cranberries

¼ cup rolled oats, ground measurement

½ cup plus 2 tablespoons unbleached all-purpose flour or whole wheat flour

1½ tablespoons sugar

1¼ teaspoons baking powder

2 teaspoons soy milk powder

⅛ teaspoon salt

Egg replacer equivalent of half an egg plus ⅛ cup water

1 teaspoon dried or fresh lemon zest

⅛ cup candied ginger, chopped

⅛ cup dried cranberries

A little extra flour

¼ cup butter, vegetable shortening, or vegan butter substitute suitable for baking

2–4 tablespoons water or half water and half lemon juice

Parchment paper

Makes 6 scones

This yummy breakfast scone recipe is my variation of more traditional Scottish fare. If you don't like the bite of candied ginger, you can easily switch this up by using extra dried cranberries or adding blueberries in their place. Sometimes I use orange zest, orange juice, and dried cherries for a bit of variety. Leftovers may be kept for the next day's breakfast or to have as an evening snack.

At Home

Grind the oats into smaller pieces in a food processor or spice grinder until the pieces are about one-fourth of their original size. Mix the oats, flour, sugar, baking powder, soy milk powder, and salt together and place in a large ziplock freezer bag. Place the egg replacer in a small ziplock bag and wrap the lemon zest, candied ginger, cranberries, and extra flour separately with plastic wrap; then put the bag and bundles in the ziplock with the dry ingredients. Pack the butter, vegetable shortening, or vegan butter substitute with what you will already be taking with you. If you decide to use lemon juice, be sure to pack a fresh lemon before you leave for your trip.

At Camp

Remove the bundles from the ziplock bag. Add ⅛ cup water to the egg replacer and stir with a fork until frothy. Add the lemon zest to the egg replacer and set aside. Add ¼ cup butter, vegetable shortening, or vegan butter substitute with the flour mixture using your fingertips until the mixture looks like small beans. Stir in the ginger and cranberries. Add the egg replacer mixture and 2 to 3 tablespoons of lemon juice or water. Just use enough liquid to moisten the dough. It shouldn't be loose or runny but more like the consistency of pizza dough. With the dough in the ziplock bag, lightly flour the ball and then gently knead about 12 times. Make sure the bag is open and lay it on a flat surface such as a rock or a camp plate. Add a little more flour and use your water bottle to roll the dough into a circle about ½-inch thick. Cut one side off the bag and cut the dough into pizza slice–shaped triangles.

Place in a pan lined with parchment paper, brush with a little reconstituted soy milk if desired, and bake for 10 to 15 minutes. Remove from the pan immediately and serve warm with butter or vegan butter substitute or your favorite jam.

Tips

If you plan to bake with a vegan butter substitute, choose a product that has more than 60% oil content. Ones with more water will cause your scones to be soggy.

If you don't want to pack a fresh lemon, use an extra pinch of dried lemon zest or half a packet of True Lemon with the water.

A little of your favorite syrup warmed up and drizzled over the scones is delicious on a cold morning.

Hazelnut Fig Granola with Popped Amaranth

1 tablespoon canola or vegetable oil

1 tablespoon amaranth seeds

2 cups rolled oats

1 cup hazelnuts, coarsely chopped

½ cup dried Turkish figs, chopped

¼ cup sunflower seeds

¼ cup canola or vegetable oil

¼ cup brown rice syrup or honey

½ teaspoon freshly grated orange zest

Makes 6–8 servings

Granola is a staple on many of our longer hiking and pad-dling trips because of the durability and high caloric rate.

AT HOME

Preheat the oven to 350°F. Heat 1 tablespoon of oil in a wok or deep skillet that has a lid over medium-high to high heat. Add the amaranth seeds and cook, moving constantly, until they start to pop and turn white. This happens very fast; about 15 to 20 seconds. Remove them from the pan immediately and set aside to cool. Mix the remaining dry ingredients in a medium-size bowl. Combine the liquid ingredients in a small bowl and then add to the dry ingredients. Stir well. Spread the mixture on a baking sheet lined with parchment paper. Bake for 25 to 30 minutes, stirring occasionally. Add the popped amaranth seeds in the last 5 minutes of cooking.

Remove from heat and let cool. Once the granola has cooled, package it into ziplock bags.

Tip

When popping the amaranth seeds, use a splatter screen or lidded pan and shake the pan as you would for old-fashioned popcorn, instead of using a deep skillet.

Goji Berry Agave Granola

Makes 6–8 servings

¼ cup quinoa flakes or wheat germ

2 cups rolled oats

1 cup pistachios, coarsely chopped

½ cup dried goji berries

¼ cup mixed seeds such as sunflower, flax, sesame, and chia

¼ cup canola or vegetable oil

¼ cup agave nectar

I first had goji berries, which are also known as wolfberries, when on a wilderness trip with my dear friend Roula Loukas, who is a raw foodie. My son is obsessed with wolves, and when he heard Roula was eating wolfberries, he excitedly asked her if he could try them. They are somewhat reminiscent of a cranberry with a little bit of tartness, so you can substitute cranberries if the goji berries are difficult to find.

AT HOME

Preheat the oven to 350°F. Place the quinoa flakes in a food processor and pulse once or twice until the flakes are reduced in size but not pulverized. Mix the dry ingredients, except for chia seeds if you are using them, in a medium-size bowl. Combine the liquid ingredients in a small bowl and then add to the dry ingredients. Stir well. Spread the mixture on a baking sheet lined with parchment paper. Bake for 25 to 30 minutes, stirring occasionally. Add the chia seeds in the last few minutes of cooking.

Remove from heat and let cool. Once the granola has cooled, package it into ziplock bags.

Blueberry Granola with Cocoa Nibs

¼ cup quinoa flakes or oat bran

2 cups rolled oats

1 cup slivered almonds

½ cup dried blueberries

⅛ cup cocoa nibs

⅛ cup pepitas

¼ cup canola or vegetable oil

¼ cup maple syrup

Makes 6–8 servings

My paddling companion, Shelley Lauzon, and I were at a Costco in Canada's capital city, Ottawa, and the taste-test ladies were giving out samples of chocolate-covered wild blueberries from Quebec. It was a flavor combination that I had never explored before, and the complex flavors of cacao with the fruity tartness of blueberries became the inspiration for this granola.

At Home

Preheat the oven to 350°F. Place the quinoa flakes in a food processor and pulse once or twice until the flakes are reduced in size but not pulverized. Mix the dry ingredients in a medium-size bowl. Combine the liquid ingredients in a small bowl and then add to the dry ingredients. Stir well. Spread the mixture on a baking sheet lined with parchment paper. Bake for 25 to 30 minutes, stirring occasionally.

Remove from heat and let cool. Once the granola has cooled, package it into ziplock bags.

Tip

If you can't find cocoa nibs, simply cut a few pieces of a good quality dark chocolate bar into tiny pieces and add it once the granola has cooled enough that it won't melt the chocolate.

Harvest Apple Granola

Makes 6–8 servings

The cinnamon and cloves add a warmth to this granola that makes it as comforting as Mom's apple pie. Using the apple syrup makes it a really apple-y breakfast. To make this granola even more of a comfort food on a cold day, pour a little warm soy milk into it at camp.

At Home

Preheat the oven to 350°F. Place ¼ cup rolled oats in a food processor and pulse once or twice until the oats are reduced in size but not pulverized. Mix the dry ingredients in a medium-size bowl. Combine the liquid ingredients in a small bowl and then add to the dry ingredients. Stir well. Spread the mixture on a baking sheet lined with parchment paper. Bake for 25 to 30 minutes, stirring occasionally.

Remove from heat and let cool. Once the granola has cooled, package it into ziplock bags.

¼ cup plus 2 cups rolled oats

1 cup pecans

½ cup dried apples, coarsely chopped

¼ cup jumbo dark raisins

¼ cup canola or vegetable oil

¼ cup Apple Cinnamon Syrup from page 79 or ¼ cup agave nectar

⅛ teaspoon cinnamon (use ½ teaspoon if you are using the agave instead of the apple syrup)

⅛ teaspoon ground cloves

Cherry Almond Couscous with Marzipan Crème

1 cup instant couscous

2 tablespoons dried cherries

2 tablespoons roasted almonds, chopped

1 tablespoon marzipan

Enough soy milk powder to make ½ cup of milk (optional)

1 cup plus 3 tablespoons water, plus enough to reconstitute the milk

Makes 2 servings

I have fond childhood memories of my mother making beautiful little fruit-shaped confections out of marzipan to adorn a festive white cake laced with cherries and raisins.

At Home

Place the couscous, cherries, and almonds in a medium-size ziplock freezer bag. Wrap the marzipan tightly in plastic wrap and place that in another ziplock bag and then into the bag with the couscous. Wrap the milk powder, if using, in a piece of plastic wrap and place in the couscous bag.

At Camp

Bring 1 cup plus 3 tablespoons water to a boil. Meanwhile make your soy milk if you are using it. Remove the plastic wrap from the marzipan and place 1 tablespoon of it back in the ziplock bag. Add 3 tablespoons of water to the marzipan bag, seal it back up, and carefully knead the bag until you have a mixture that resembles cream. Very carefully add the remaining water to the bag with the couscous. Let stand 5 minutes. Stir the marzipan mixture into the couscous and scoop it into bowls. Top with milk, if desired.

Tips

Marzipan comes in shelf-stable packages, so if you are planning this for after the third day of your trip, it is best to keep the paste in the original packaging, as it will keep for weeks. Once you open it, you will have to consume the marzipan over a few days. Leftover marzipan is delicious with chocolate or melted into a hot drink such as coffee, hot tea, or cocoa, in place of sugar or honey.

Citrus Herb Couscous

Makes 2 servings

This recipe uses candied citrus peels that have been dehydrated and ground to a fine powder. This adds sweetness and flavor. The addition of herbs makes this an unusual couscous breakfast.

AT HOME

Place the couscous; half the candied lemon, lime, and orange powder; and herbs in a medium-size ziplock freezer bag. Wrap the milk powder in a piece of plastic wrap and place in the couscous bag. Do the same for the other half of the candied lemon, lime, and orange powder.

AT CAMP

Bring 1 cup water to a boil. Meanwhile make ½ cup of soy milk. Remove the bundle of candied lemon, lime, and orange powder from the freezer bag and set aside. Very carefully add the water to the bag with the couscous. Let stand 5 minutes. Scoop it into bowls, top with milk, and sprinkle with the powder.

Tip

While the flavor isn't as nice, you can use a little True Lime and True Lemon powder with a bit of sugar in place of the candied citrus powder. A little lemonade powder works here too.

1 cup instant couscous

1–2 tablespoons candied lemon, lime, and orange powder to taste

⅛ teaspoon dried thyme, dried basil, or dried rosemary, crumbled

Enough soy milk powder to make ½ cup of milk

1 cup water, plus enough to reconstitute the milk

Quinoa Berry Muffins

Dehydration Time: 7–12 hours
Makes 6 muffins

¼ cup quinoa, uncooked (or 1 cup cooked)

½ cup water, plus enough water to rehydrate quinoa, plus 3 tablespoons plus ⅓ cup

1 tablespoon chia seeds

⅛ cup vegetable or grapeseed oil

½ teaspoon pure almond extract

½ cup unbleached all-purpose flour

½ cup whole wheat flour

¾ teaspoon baking powder

½ teaspoon salt

⅛ teaspoon cardamom

¼ teaspoon cinnamon

1½ tablespoons soy milk powder

⅓ cup brown sugar or maple sugar

¼ cup dried mixed berries

⅓ cup walnuts, chopped

Parchment paper

These are a moist, dense muffin that we've enjoyed on many a trip. The most memorable was on the private beach of a secluded lake in Ontario, Canada's Algonquin Provincial Park. Most canoeists will avoid what amounted to be 10 kilometers of portages to get to this spot, but the backpacker in me didn't mind in the least.

At Home

Place the quinoa in a fine sieve and rinse for at least 3 minutes to remove the bitter coating. Drain, place in a nonstick frying pan, and toast the quinoa, stirring frequently. As soon as some of the seeds start to pop, remove the quinoa from the pan. Put the toasted quinoa and ½ cup water into a pot. Bring the mixture to a boil; cover and simmer for 10 minutes. Remove from the heat and leave the lid on for an additional 10 minutes. Fluff with a fork as you would for rice and let cool. Once the quinoa has cooled, measure the mixture and write this measurement on a sticky note. Spread on lined dehydrator trays and dry for 7 to 12 hours or until no moisture remains. Put the sticky note and dried quinoa in a medium-size ziplock freezer bag.

Wrap the chia seeds in a small piece of plastic wrap and put it in the bag with the dried quinoa. Mix the oil and extract together and place in a small leakproof container; put this in the quinoa bag. Mix flours, baking powder, salt, cardamom, cinnamon, and soy milk powder together and place in a small ziplock bag. Place the brown sugar in a separate snack-size ziplock bag. Mix the dried berries and walnuts together in a snack-size ziplock as well and put all the remaining bags in with the quinoa.

At Camp

Remove the bundles from the bag of dry ingredients. Rehydrate the quinoa by adding enough boiling water with the quinoa to equal the measurement on your sticky note. Add 3 tablespoons of water to the chia seeds and let them sit until the mixture is thick and gelatinous. Add the oil–almond extract mixture to the chia mixture. Stir in ⅓ cup water and when well combined add the brown sugar. Then add the chia mixture to the bag of dry ingredients and the rehydrated quinoa and stir to combine. Gently add the dried berries and nuts.

Put the batter into silicone muffin cups placed in your baking pan or pour directly into a parchment paper–lined baking pan. Bake for 25 to 30 minutes or until a toothpick or knife inserted in the center comes out clean.

Sweet Apricot Pistachio Nut Muffins

⅔ cup almond flour (also called almond meal)

½ cup sorghum flour

¼ cup tapioca flour

¼ teaspoon salt

½ teaspoon baking powder

¼ teaspoon baking soda

½ scant teaspoon xanthan gum

⅛ teaspoon dried lemon zest

1 tablespoon chia seeds

⅔ cup brown sugar

¼ cup dried apricots, chopped

¼ cup pistachio nuts, coarsely chopped

1 tablespoon olive oil

¾ cup water

Parchment paper

Makes 6 muffins

Almond flour adds a nutty sweetness to these muffins. I used dried apricots and pistachios here, but this recipe works well with any dried fruit and nut combination. Dried pineapple and macadamia nuts, dried pears and walnuts, cranberries and pecans, blueberries and hazelnuts—the only limit is your imagination.

AT HOME

Mix the almond flour with the other flours, salt, baking powder, baking soda, xanthan gum, and lemon zest together with a whisk and place in a large ziplock freezer bag. Wrap the chia seeds in a small piece of plastic wrap and put it in the bag with the dried ingredients. Do the same with the brown sugar. Mix the apricots and pistachio nuts together in a snack-size ziplock and place it in the bag with the dry ingredients. Add the oil to the other olive oil you will take on your trip.

AT CAMP

Remove the bundles from the bag of dry ingredients. Add 3 tablespoons of water to the chia seeds and let them sit until the mixture is thick and gelatinous. Add 1 tablespoon olive oil to the chia mixture. Stir in ½ cup of brown sugar. Add ½ cup water to the liquid ingredients; then stir the mixture into the dry ingredients. Combine well. Add an extra tablespoon of water, if needed, until the muffin batter is evenly and well moistened but still remains fairly thick. Stir in the apricots and pistachio nuts.

Put the batter into silicone muffin cups placed in your baking pan or pour directly into a parchment paper–lined baking pan. Bake for 30 to 35 minutes or until a toothpick or knife inserted in the center comes out clean. The tops will be firm and golden. Remove the muffins from the pan immediately and let them cool for 10 minutes in the silicone cups before removing. If you leave them in the baking pan, they will sweat and become soggy, and if you take them out of the cups too soon, you'll be left with half the muffin stuck in the bottom of the muffin cup.

Pumpkin Pecan Breakfast Muffins

Makes 6 muffins

This moist muffin has the subtle flavor of pumpkin pie but isn't overly sweet. While I used raisins, you can easily substitute any dried fruit, candied ginger pieces, or even chocolate or carob chips. The pecans can be replaced by your favorite nut or pepitas. The best thing about this recipe is that you'll forget they are gluten free. You can make this more decadent with a drizzle of maple syrup over the top.

At Home

Mix the flours, soy milk powder, baking powder, baking soda, salt, xanthan gum, and spices together and place in a large ziplock freezer bag. Wrap the chia seeds in a small piece of plastic wrap and put it in the bag with the dried ingredients. Mix the raisins and pecans together in a snack-size ziplock and place it in the bag with the dry ingredients. Mix the oil, vanilla extract, and maple syrup together and place in a small leakproof container.

At Camp

Remove the bundles from the bag of dry ingredients. Add 3 tablespoons of water to the chia seeds and let them sit until the mixture is thick and gelatinous. Stir in the oil-extract-syrup mixture. Then add the mixture plus 1 cup water to the bag of dry ingredients and gently mix to combine. Stir in the raisins and nuts.

Put the batter into silicone muffin cups placed in your baking pan or pour directly into a parchment paper–lined baking pan. Bake for 25 to 30 minutes or until a toothpick or knife inserted in the center comes out clean.

½ cup sorghum flour

⅙ cup coconut flour

¼ cup tapioca flour

¼ cup almond flour

⅛ cup pumpkin flour, made from pumpkin meat (see page 36)

⅛ cup soy milk powder

¾ teaspoon baking powder

½ teaspoon baking soda

¼ teaspoon salt

½ teaspoon xanthan gum

½ teaspoon cinnamon

½ teaspoon ground ginger

⅛ teaspoon nutmeg

1 tablespoon chia seeds

¼ cup sultanas or dark raisins

¼ cup pecans, chopped

⅙ cup canola or vegetable oil

1 teaspoon pure vanilla extract

⅓ cup maple syrup

1 cup water plus 3 tablespoons

Parchment paper

Blueberry Lavender Biscuits

1 recipe Basic Biscuits (page 220) or Gluten-free Biscuits (page 221)

⅛ cup dried blueberries

3 teaspoons fine granulated sugar or organic cane sugar

⅛ teaspoon dried lavender to taste

Parchment paper

Makes 2–3 servings

Lavender imparts a slightly floral note to these breakfast biscuits, but be sure to use food-grade lavender as some garden varieties are not edible. You can now find lavender in most spice shops as it is an ingredient in the popular herbes de Provence spice blend. If you eat honey, a little clover or apple blossom honey goes nicely with these biscuits.

At Home

Combine the ingredients for your choice of biscuit recipe and place in ziplock freezer bag. Wrap the dried blueberries in plastic wrap and add this to the bag. Mix the sugar and the lavender together in a snack-size ziplock bag and put that in with the biscuit mix. Pack the vegetable shortening or butter, as indicated in the biscuit recipe, with what you will take on your trip.

At Camp

Add 2 teaspoons of the lavender sugar mixture to the dry biscuit mix and combine well. Follow the "At Camp" instructions for the biscuits. When you place them on the parchment paper–lined pan, sprinkle the remaining lavender sugar on top of each biscuit. Bake as indicated in the instructions for the biscuit recipe. Serve warm with butter or vegan butter substitute.

Herb and Cheese Biscuits

Makes 2–3 servings

If you are using vegan cheese, make sure you choose one that melts well. These hearty biscuits can be served on their own or as a side to scrambled tofu or scrambled eggs.

AT HOME

Combine the ingredients for your choice of biscuit recipe and place in a ziplock freezer bag. Wrap the herbs in plastic wrap and place the bundle in the bag with the biscuit mix. Wrap the cheese. Pack the vegetable shortening or butter, as indicated in the biscuit recipe, with what you will take on your trip.

AT CAMP

Remove the herb bundle from the bag and mix the herbs with the dry ingredients. Follow the "At Camp" instructions for the biscuits. Break up the cheese into small pieces and place it into the mix before you add the water. Bake as indicated in the instructions for the biscuit recipe. Serve warm with butter or vegan butter substitute.

1 recipe Basic Biscuits (page 220) or Gluten-free Biscuits (page 221)

⅛ teaspoon dried thyme

⅛ teaspoon dried oregano

1-by-1-by-3-inch block of Cheddar or Cheddar flavor vegetarian cheese

Fruit and Nut Breakfast Cookies

⅓ cup almonds, skins removed

⅓ cup sunflower seeds, hulls removed

½ cup shredded coconut, toasted if desired

½ teaspoon cinnamon

¼ teaspoon cloves

⅛ teaspoon cardamom

A pinch of kosher salt

½ teaspoon fresh orange zest

¼ cup dried goji berries or cranberries

¼ cup dried blueberries

¼ cup dried apricots

¼ cup dried dates

⅓ cup dried apples

¼ cup dried black Mission figs

Dehydration Time: 7–10 hours
Makes about 30 cookies

When I made this recipe, I put a call out on a popular Appalachian Trail hiking forum for recipe testers because I was off the trail awaiting the birth of our daughter, Kaia. Mike Mullen from Texas graciously stepped forward and made these cookies for one of his backpacking trips. When his darling wife taste tested the cookies, she remarked, "Mmmm, these would be great to give at Christmas!"

AT HOME

Soak the almonds and sunflower seeds overnight in just enough cold water to cover them. Drain well. Toast the coconut, if desired, in a nonstick frying pan just until you start to see a little color. Grind the nuts and seeds in a food processor until you have a coarse grind. Put the mixture into a bowl and stir in the coconut, spices, salt, and orange zest. Put the dried fruit into the food processor and pulse until the mixture is sticky but still somewhat chunky. Add the nut mixture to the fruit in the food processor and mix well.

Line your food dehydrator with fruit leather trays, plastic wrap, or parchment paper. Drop the fruit cookie mixture by heaping tablespoons and press flat until about ¼-inch thick. If your unit has a temperature control, set it for 110°F and dry for 6 to 8 hours and then remove the cookies from the liners and place them on the mesh. Allow them to dry for 1 to 2 hours or until they are a texture that you like. Wrap the finished cookies individually in plastic wrap and then place them in a ziplock freezer bag.

Green Tea and Ginger Quinoa Pancakes

Makes 2 servings

This is a recipe we enjoy both at home and in the backcountry. The flavor is much different than a traditional pancake.

At Home

Mix the quinoa flour, baking powder, salt, and sugar together in a large ziplock freezer bag. Wrap the chopped ginger in plastic wrap and place, along with the green tea bag, in the freezer bag with the dry ingredients. Add vegetable oil and butter or substitute to what you will take with you on your trip. Pack the syrup in a leakproof bottle. If you decided to use loose tea, remember to pack a paper tea filter, tea ball, or piece of cheesecloth.

At Camp

Add ½ cup very hot water, preferably water that has been off the boil for a few moments, to the green tea and let steep for 3 to 5 minutes, being sure not to let it get too strong. Remove the tea bag. Allow the tea to cool for a few minutes and then add ½ cup cool water. Add the chopped candied ginger to the dry ingredients in the ziplock bag. Combine well. Add ¾ cup of the tea mixture to the dry ingredients in the ziplock bag. Stir to moisten and add extra tea as necessary to obtain a pancake batter consistency.

Place a little vegetable oil in a frying pan and heat over a medium flame. Pour in one-fourth of the batter and cook until the edges appear dry. Then flip and cook until the underside is golden. Repeat until you have 4 pancakes, adding more oil to the pan between each pancake as necessary. Serve with a little butter and your favorite syrup.

Tip

The batter is easy to manage if you make it in the ziplock freezer bag. Then simply cut off a corner of the bag and squeeze the batter into the pan. Between pancakes, be careful to situate the bag so that the batter doesn't spill out of the cut corner.

1 cup quinoa flour

2 teaspoons baking powder

¼ teaspoon salt

1 tablespoon sugar

⅛ cup candied ginger, finely chopped

1 green tea bag or enough loose tea to make 1 cup

2 tablespoons vegetable oil for frying

Butter or vegan butter substitute (optional)

Maple syrup (optional)

1 cup water

Earl Grey and Apple Pancakes

Makes 2 servings

1 cup unbleached all-purpose flour

2 tablespoons soy milk powder

2 teaspoons baking powder

¼ teaspoon salt

2 tablespoons sugar

Egg replacer equivalent to 1 egg

⅛ cup dried apples or ½ small fresh apple, finely chopped

1 Earl Grey tea bag

2 tablespoons vegetable oil for frying

Butter or vegan butter substitute (optional)

Maple syrup or apple syrup (optional)

1 cup water, plus enough to rehydrate dried apples

There is something about the scent of bergamot, one of the main components of Earl Grey and the flavoring for these pancakes, that is comforting to me. It reminds me of my first days at university. It was January and the winter was particularly nasty. I spent relaxing times curled up with Wuthering Heights *or* Jane Eyre *from my English literature class and a steaming cup of Earl Grey to take the chill off.*

AT HOME

Mix the flour, soy milk powder, baking powder, salt, sugar, and egg replacer together in a large ziplock freezer bag. Wrap the dried apples in plastic wrap, if you are using them, and place them, along with the Earl Grey tea bag, in the freezer bag with the dry ingredients. Add vegetable oil and butter or substitute to what you will take with you on your trip. Pack the syrup in a leakproof bottle. If you decided to use a fresh apple, remember to pack it before your trip.

AT CAMP

Add some boiling water to the dried apples so they can rehydrate a bit. Add ½ cup boiling water to the Earl Grey tea bag and let steep for 3 minutes, being sure not to let it get too strong. Remove the bag. Allow the tea to cool for a few minutes; then add ½ cup cool water. Drain the apples well, or if you are using fresh, chopped apple, add it to the dry ingredients in the ziplock bag. Combine well. Add ¾ cup of the tea mixture to the dry ingredients in the ziplock bag. Stir to moisten and add extra tea as necessary to obtain a pancake batter consistency. Do not overmix or the pancakes will be tough.

Place a little vegetable oil in a frying pan and heat over a medium flame. Pour in one-fourth of the batter and cook until the edges appear dry. Then flip and cook until the underside is golden. Repeat until you have 4 pancakes, adding more oil to the pan between each pancake as necessary. Serve with a little butter and your favorite syrup.

Tips

When brewing the tea, don't let it get too strong and don't squeeze the tea bag, as this will make it bitter.

The batter is easy to manage if you make it in the ziplock freezer bag. Then simply cut off a corner of the bag and squeeze the batter into the pan. Between pancakes, be careful to situate the bag so that the batter doesn't spill out of the cut corner.

Cinnamon Griddle Toast

Makes 2 servings

4 slices bread

Enough soy milk powder to make ⅔ cup

⅛ cup chickpea flour

½ teaspoon cinnamon

⅛ teaspoon nutmeg

Syrup or other suitable topping

1 teaspoon pure maple syrup or agave nectar

Vegetable oil

⅔ cup water

This griddle toast is the vegan version of French toast. I have fond memories of serving this to my husband and seeing how surprised he was that it was egg and dairy free. No worries if the bread gets a little flattened in your pack; it will come back when cooked.

At Home

Put the bread in a large ziplock freezer bag and compress the slices until they are somewhat flattened. Mix the soy milk powder, chickpea flour, cinnamon, and nutmeg together in a smaller ziplock freezer bag. Put your desired topping into a small plastic bag and put that and the bag of soy milk and chickpea flour in the larger bag with the bread. Add the syrup and vegetable oil to the other syrup and oil you will take on your trip.

At Camp

Remove the bag with the milk and chickpea flour mixture from the large ziplock freezer bag and dump it in a pot. Add ⅔ cup of water and 1 teaspoon of maple syrup or agave nectar, and combine well. Put a little vegetable oil in your frying pan and preheat it over medium heat. Dip a piece of bread into the mixture and fry it, flipping once, until golden. Repeat with the remaining slices. Garnish with dried-fruit compote, freeze-dried berries, a drizzle of your favorite syrup, or a freshly sliced banana and a handful of toasted pecans.

Tips

Use your favorite bread and let it get a day or two old before making this, as fresh bread doesn't work quite as well. Using a loaf that you slice yourself gives better results.

It is important to use a stove with the ability to simmer or to raise the pan from the flame so that you don't scorch the toast.

Potato Spinach Hash Browns

**Dehydration Time: 6–10 hours
Makes 2–3 servings**

I've experimented with hash browns on our backcountry trips and could never get the crispness I wanted. One morning I was at the ophthalmologist, and to say the wait was long would be an understatement. I made small talk with the Indian lady next to me about the Hindu festival of Diwali, which had just passed. She graciously shared stories about the vegetarian foods she makes for the holiday and told me about the crispness that chickpea flour lends to fried foods. I decided to try it with these hash browns and voila! Wonderful, crispy hash browns.

AT HOME

Dehydrate the potatoes, onions, and spinach separately on lined dehydrator trays for 6 to 10 hours. The spinach will likely be done long before the potatoes. When the potatoes are fully dried, run them through a blender or coffee grinder until they are broken into very small flakes. Mix the dried spinach, onion, potatoes, and chia seeds together and place in a medium-size ziplock freezer bag. Put the chickpea flour in a second bag and put that bag into the bag with the potatoes. Pack 2 pieces of parchment paper. Pack the oil with the other oil that you will be taking on your trip.

AT CAMP

Add equal amounts of potato-spinach mixture and boiling water and let reconstitute for 10 to 15 minutes, adding a little more water as necessary but maintaining a thick consistency. Pour the chickpea flour onto a piece of parchment paper. If it is windy, weight the corner with something heavy such as a small rock. Lay the other piece of parchment paper on a plate or rock. While you heat the oil in a frypan over medium heat, make little patties about ¼-inch thick and 3 inches in diameter. Dip each side in chickpea flour and lay in a single layer on

1 cup cooked, mashed russet potatoes

¼ red onion, minced

¼ cup cooked spinach, chopped

2 tablespoons chia seeds

¼ cup chickpea flour

Vegetable oil for frying

Salt and pepper to taste

Parchment paper

the second piece of parchment paper. Fry in hot oil until each side is a deep golden brown. Season the hash browns immediately with salt and pepper. Serve hot.

Tips

If you have a stove that runs too hot on medium, then carefully use your pot lifter to hold the frying pan an inch or so above the flame.

These are great with a dollop of salsa, salsa verde, chili sauce, or tomato chutney.

Asparagus and Cheese Frittata

Dehydration Time: 6–10 hours
Makes 2 servings

Spring in my neck of the woods is filled with the sound of wildlife, the sight of blooming lilacs, and the appearance of one of my favorite veggies, asparagus. It grows wild in some areas, but I prefer buying from the local farmers' market. While this is a breakfast recipe, it would also be great for brunch on a rest day or for a nice dinner with a side of biscuits.

At Home

Steam the asparagus over boiling water until tender-crisp, about 3 to 5 minutes. Remove from heat and let cool. Then cut the asparagus into 1-inch pieces and place on mesh-lined dehydrator trays, leaving space between them. Dehydrate for 6 to 10 hours or until completely dry and place in a ziplock freezer bag. Put the scrambled egg mix in a ziplock freezer bag with a note about how much water to add to reconstitute. Add the package of powdered scrambled egg mix to the bag containing the asparagus. Wrap the Swiss cheese in plastic wrap. Add the butter or oil to what you will take on your trip.

At Camp

Combine equal parts of boiling water and dried asparagus to reconstitute. Let sit for about 15 to 20 minutes. In a separate container, mix scrambled egg powder with water as indicated on the note you enclosed and beat well with a fork.

Put a little butter or oil in the bottom of a pot or frying pan. Add ¼ cup of grated Swiss cheese to the egg mixture and pour into the preheated pan. Top with the rehydrated asparagus and cook on medium to low heat until the egg mixture is cooked. Add salt and pepper. Remove the frittata from the pan, cut into 2 servings, and sprinkle each with 1 tablespoon of Swiss cheese while the frittata is still hot.

1 cup fresh asparagus, bottoms removed

2 servings powdered scrambled egg mix, plus water as necessary

¼ cup grated Swiss cheese, plus 2 tablespoons for topping

Butter or vegetable oil

Salt and pepper to taste

Tips

If a little egg mixture remains uncooked in the center, just tilt the pan slightly and let the uncooked egg move to the outer edges.

If you plan to have this more than a few days into your trip, keep the Swiss cheese in a block and cut it thin with a knife or use a grater designed for backpacking when you are at camp.

Pumpkin Breakfast Bars

Makes 14 bars

*This make-at-home recipe is a favorite around here. Some-
times I have to pop them into the freezer or the guys will
devour them before we leave on our backcountry adventure.
Be sure to use plain pumpkin and not pumpkin pie filling for
these. A drizzle of chocolate on the top would make these into
a yummy dessert bar.*

AT HOME

Preheat oven to 350°F. Lightly oil a 9-inch square baking
pan or line with parchment paper and oil the paper. Mix the
ground flaxseeds and whole flaxseeds together; then add ½
cup water. Set aside for a minimum of 5 minutes. Mix the
stewed pumpkin with the brown sugar and vanilla extract
and set aside. Mix the remaining dry ingredients together in a
large mixing bowl. Combine the flax mixture with the pumpkin mixture and pour into the dry ingredients. Mix well and
press into the prepared baking pan. Bake for 30 to 40 minutes.
Remove from the oven and let cool completely before removing from the pan and cutting into 14 bars. Wrap tightly in
plastic wrap and use within 1 week.

Vegetable oil

4½ teaspoons ground flaxseeds
or flax meal

1 teaspoon whole flaxseeds

½ cup water

¾ cup canned stewed pumpkin
or puréed roasted pumpkin

⅛ cup brown sugar

½ teaspoon pure vanilla extract

¾ cup old-fashioned rolled oats,
coarsely ground

¼ cup whole wheat or
unbleached all-purpose flour

½ teaspoon cinnamon

¼ teaspoon ground ginger

⅛ teaspoon nutmeg

⅓ cup walnuts

⅓ cup raw pepitas

⅓ cup dried cherries

⅓ cup dried peaches or plums,
diced

⅓ cup dried pears, diced

⅓ cup dried apples, diced

Polentina with Stone Fruit Compote

⅛ cup dried sweet black cherries

⅛ cup dried peaches, chopped

A pinch of allspice

2 teaspoons sugar

¼ cup plus 2 tablespoons instant polenta

1 tablespoon brown sugar or maple sugar

⅛ teaspoon salt

Enough soy milk powder to make ¾ cup

½ teaspoon pure vanilla extract (optional)

1 teaspoon butter or vegan butter substitute

1¼ cups water, plus enough to reconstitute the milk

Makes 2 servings

Polentina is an Italian form of polenta that is a camp-worthy breakfast to warm you on a snowy morning. In summer I dry cherries and peaches for compote to serve atop the polentina. Of course, you can use any combination of dried fruit that you like. You could even use a generous dollop of strawberry preserves, warmed up and spiked with a little allspice or cinnamon.

AT HOME

Put the cherries, dried peaches, allspice, and sugar in a piece of plastic wrap. Mix the instant polenta, 1 tablespoon brown sugar or maple sugar, and salt in a medium-size ziplock freezer bag. Add a note with the cooking time from the polenta package. Put the soy milk powder in another ziplock bag, seal, and place in the bag with the polenta. Put the vanilla extract, if using, in a small leakproof container and add it to the polenta bag. Pack the butter or vegan butter substitute with the butter that you will take with you on your trip.

AT CAMP

Remove the bags from the polenta bag. Put ¼ cup water in a pot with the fruit mixture. Heat until boiling, add 1 teaspoon butter or vegan butter substitute, and set aside to rehydrate. Make ¾ cup soy milk. Add the milk with 1 cup of water in pot. Bring to a boil, being careful not to burn the milk, and slowly stir in the polenta mixture a bit at a time so that it doesn't lump. Cook while stirring constantly for 1 to 5 minutes depending on the note you made about the cooking time. Add the vanilla extract if you are using it. Divide into 2 servings and top with fruit compote.

Roasted Sweet Potato Breakfast Bread

Dehydration Time: 8–10 hours
Makes 3–4 servings

The addition of sweet potatoes creates this moist and dense breakfast bread that is reminiscent of a scone. It pairs nicely with a hot cup of camp coffee or spicy chai tea. You can also substitute a squash, such as butternut, for the sweet potatoes in this recipe and add a pinch of ginger to switch things up. The addition of pepitas or pecans adds a nice bit of crunch. I used Bob's Red Mill Gluten Free All Purpose Baking Mix for the gluten-free flour blend in this recipe, but feel free to use your favorite gluten-free mix.

At Home

Spread the sweet potatoes on lined dehydrator trays and dry for 8 to 10 hours. When the mashed sweet potatoes are dry, they will be leathery with some brittle spots. Break the dried mixture into small pieces by hand and run it through a blender or coffee grinder until it becomes a powder. Package ¼ cup of the sweet potato powder in a ziplock freezer bag. Mix the flours, baking powder, sugar, salt, egg replacer, and cinnamon together in a ziplock freezer bag. Wrap the raisins, if using, in a piece of plastic wrap and put it and the bag of sweet potato powder into the bag with the dry ingredients. Pack the shortening with the other shortening that you will take on your trip. Pack a little extra gluten-free flour blend.

At Camp

Rehydrate ¼ cup of the sweet potato mixture by adding ¼ to ⅓ cup boiling water. It is best to start with the smaller amount and add more water as needed. Mix 2 tablespoons of shortening with the flour mixture using your fingertips until the mixture looks like small beans. Add the raisins to the dry ingredients.

1 cup sweet potatoes, cooked and mashed

¼ cup potato flour (not potato starch)

¾ cup gluten-free flour blend

1 teaspoon baking powder

¼ cup brown sugar

¼ teaspoon salt

Egg replacer equivalent to 1 egg

1 teaspoon cinnamon

¼ cup raisins (optional)

2 tablespoons shortening

⅔ cup water plus 2 tablespoons

Parchment paper

Mix the cooled and rehydrated sweet potatoes and ⅓ cup water together and add to the flour mixture, combining until you have very soft dough. Add more water by the tablespoon, if necessary, to bring the dry ingredients together. Bake in a parchment paper–lined pan for 20 to 30 minutes or until a toothpick inserted in the center comes out clean.

Tip

If the sweet potato mixture rehydrates too wet, add 1 tablespoon or so of flour to thicken it.

Lentil Cakes

Dehydration Time: 5–7 hours
Makes 2 servings

These lentil cakes are slightly reminiscent of spicy Italian sausage because of the anise flavor that fennel seeds bring and the spice from the crushed red chilies. They are tasty served in a biscuit with a relish of chopped plum tomatoes and basil.

AT HOME

Dry the lentils on lined dehydrator trays for 5 to 7 hours or until dried through. Place the lentils in a ziplock freezer bag along with the mustard powder and dried onion. Bundle the fennel seeds, dried parsley, and crushed red chilies in a piece of plastic wrap and put the bundle in with the lentils. Measure the oats into a ziplock freezer bag and put that bag inside the lentil bag. Add the oil to the other olive oil that you will take on your trip.

AT CAMP

Remove the bundles from the bag of lentils. Add boiling water to the lentil mixture, in a ziplock bag, using a little less than 1 part water to 1 part dried ingredients. Let sit for 5 to 10 minutes and add a little more water if necessary. Add the spices and oats to the lentil mixture in the freezer bag. Be careful as the liquid may still be hot. Let the air out of the bag, close it tightly, and knead it to mix everything together.

Heat the olive oil in a frying pan. Cut one corner off the bag. Squeeze one-fourth of the mixture into the frying pan and then flatten into a patty with your spoon or spatula. Fry the patties for approximately 4 minutes, turning occasionally. Season with salt and pepper to taste.

1 cup canned green lentils, rinsed and drained

½ teaspoon dry mustard powder

1 tablespoon dried onion

¼ teaspoon aniseed or fennel seeds, crushed

½ teaspoon dried parsley

¼ teaspoon crushed red chili peppers (optional)

½ cup rolled oats

2 tablespoons olive oil

Salt and pepper to taste

Spiced Breakfast Dal

Dehydration Time: 5–8 hours
Makes 2–3 servings

1 cup dried red lentils

½ teaspoon vegetable oil

2 teaspoons ground coriander

1 teaspoon cumin to taste

1¼ cups water

2 cardamom pods

A pinch of salt

2–3 heaping tablespoons
coconut cream powder
to taste

Spicy lentils for breakfast—why not? The aroma of this savory recipe will wake up your senses, and the hearty lentils will warm your tummy on a cold morning.

AT HOME

Pick over the lentils to remove any foreign matter and put them in a fine strainer. Rinse with cold water and let drain. Heat the vegetable oil on medium heat in a pan large enough to cook the lentils in. Add the coriander and cumin. Let the spices cook for a minute, being careful not to burn them. Add 1⅛ cups of water, the lentils, and cardamom pods. Let simmer until tender, adding water as necessary and stirring occasionally, for about 20 minutes. Add a pinch of salt and remove the cardamom pods.

Measure the lentils and write this measurement on a sticky note. Pour onto lined dehydrator trays and dry for 5 to 8 hours. Place the dried lentil mixture, coconut cream powder, and the sticky note in a ziplock freezer bag.

AT CAMP

Add enough boiling water to the lentil mixture to equal the measurement on your sticky note. Be sure to account for and add your dried ingredients to the rehydration container prior to adding the water. You can always add more water if you need to.

Spreads for Breakfast

How bored of peanut butter we've become. I came up with these spreads when trying to add a little variety to what we put on our toasted bagels at breakfast.

Maple Vanilla Almond Butter

Makes 8 servings

1 cup roasted almond butter, at room temperature

1 tablespoon maple syrup or agave nectar

½ teaspoon pure vanilla extract

¼ teaspoon kosher salt

Combine all ingredients together in a blender. Transfer to a leakproof container.

At Camp

Serve on toasted bagels or biscuits, or heat as a dip for fresh apple slices. This will keep for several weeks without refrigeration except in extreme heat.

Agave Orange Almond Butter

Makes 8 servings

1 cup roasted almond butter, at room temperature

1 tablespoon agave nectar

⅛ teaspoon pure orange extract

⅛ teaspoon candied orange powder

¼ teaspoon kosher salt

Combine all ingredients together in a blender. Transfer to a leakproof container.

At Camp

Serve on toasted bagels, biscuits, or muffins, or put a dollop in with your favorite hot cereal. This will keep for several weeks without refrigeration except in extreme heat.

Chocolate Chickpea Butter

Dehydration Time: 5–7 hours
Makes 4 packages containing 2–3 servings each

1 cup canned chickpeas, rinsed and drained

¼–½ teaspoon pure almond extract to taste

Water

¼ cup carob or cocoa powder

¼ cup maple sugar or brown sugar

½ teaspoon instant espresso powder

A pinch of cinnamon

A pinch of salt

1 tablespoon peanut or other nut butter per package

A drizzle of olive oil

At Home

Purée the chickpeas with the almond extract and a few tablespoons of water until you have a smooth paste. Spread on lined dehydrator trays and dry for 5 to 7 hours. In a bowl combine the dried chickpea mixture with the carob or cocoa powder, sugar, espresso powder, cinnamon, and salt. Divide into 4 ziplock freezer bags. Pack the peanut butter and olive oil with what you will already be taking with you on your trip.

At Camp

Rehydrate the chickpea mixture in the ziplock bag using a formula of 1½ parts dried mix to 1 part water. Wait 5 or 10 minutes and then add a little more water if needed. Once rehydrated, add 1 tablespoon of peanut butter and a drizzle of olive oil. Knead the bag until well combined. Serve as a spread for baguette slices, bagels, croissants, digestive-style cookies, or biscuits.

Breakfast Syrups

Sometimes we like to switch up traditional things such as maple syrup on our pancakes. The following syrup recipes might seem a little fussy, and they will take some effort, so they aren't for everyone. That said, these can be a nice addition to glam up a breakfast of pancakes or biscuits. You can also use the syrups on other foods such as hot cereal, fresh fruit, cornbread, or a toasted bagel. Use leftover syrup at home for a weekend brunch, as an addition to oil and vinegar for a unique salad dressing, or on vanilla ice cream.

End quantities and times may vary slightly, so you may have to reduce or increase the cooking time accordingly. This takes a little practice and a close eye. If you let it cook too long or on too low heat, it will tighten up like a thick caramel.

APPLE CINNAMON SYRUP

This syrup packs a strong apple punch, and the natural pectin in the apples means that you don't need the help of lemon juice. It is great on pancakes, especially if you put some rehydrated apple pieces in the batter. You can also use it with oil and vinegar to make a nice salad dressing.

4 cups pure, unsweetened apple juice

2 cinnamon sticks, broken in half

AT HOME

In a heavy-bottomed saucepan bring the juice to a simmer over medium heat and then turn the burner down to medium-low. Add the cinnamon sticks. Stir frequently to keep the mixture from scorching. Remove the cinnamon sticks halfway through cooking. Let cook for 30 to 35 minutes or until the mixture has reduced and the consistency becomes slightly syrupy. Keep in mind that the mixture will thicken quite a bit as it cools. Let cool for 30 minutes in the pot. Store in a glass jar and refrigerate for up to 6 weeks. Before your trip, transfer the amount of syrup that you will use into a small leakproof container.

Blueberry Lavender Syrup

This is nice served with toasted walnuts as a topper for hot cereal or as syrup for rehydrated dried fruits such as peaches and pears. You could even use it on fresh fruit if you were inclined to carry some in your pack. Be sure to use food-grade lavender in this recipe.

3 cups unsweetened white grape juice

1 cup unsweetened blueberry juice

1 teaspoon lemon juice

½ cup sugar

2 pieces ¼-by-3-inch fresh lemon rind

⅛–¼ teaspoon dried lavender to taste

At Home

Mix the juices and sugar in a heavy-bottomed saucepan over medium heat until the sugar dissolves completely. Add the lemon rind. Bring the juice to a simmer and then turn the burner down to medium-low. Stir frequently to keep the mixture from scorching. Add the lavender during the last 15 minutes of cooking. Let cook for 30 to 35 minutes or until the mixture has reduced and the consistency becomes slightly syrupy. Keep in mind that the mixture will thicken quite a bit as it cools. Let cool for 30 minutes in the pot. Store in a glass jar and refrigerate for up to 6 weeks. Before your trip, transfer the amount of syrup that you will use into a small leakproof container.

Earl Grey and Orange Syrup

This idea happened purely by accident. I love making jams and jellies and thought I'd try my hand at an Earl Grey tea jelly. Well, I didn't use enough lemon or pectin and the jelly never set. We used it on pancakes and griddle toast. At camp I like to rehydrate peaches in boiling water, drain them, add the syrup, and pour it over the griddle toast. It's quite decadent. It can also be used to drizzle over pound cake or biscuits, or as an addition to salad dressing.

3 cups Earl Grey tea, made from 3 tea bags

1 cup unsweetened orange juice

1 teaspoon lemon juice

2/3 cup sugar

2 pieces ¼-by-3-inch fresh lemon rind

At Home

Mix the brewed tea, juices, and sugar in a heavy-bottomed saucepan over medium heat until the sugar dissolves completely. Add the lemon rind. Bring the liquid to a simmer and then turn the burner down to medium-low. Stir frequently to keep the mixture from scorching. Let cook for 30 to 35 minutes or until the mixture has reduced and the consistency becomes slightly syrupy. Keep in mind that the mixture will thicken quite a bit as it cools. Let cool for 30 minutes in the pot. Store in a glass jar and refrigerate for up to 6 weeks. Before your trip, transfer the amount of syrup that you will use into a small leakproof container.

Pomegranate Syrup

Pomegranate syrup not only has a beautiful color, but also the taste is wonderful with the right balance of tart and sweet. It is a refreshing change to maple syrup or agave nectar. You can cook the syrup a little longer to make pomegranate molasses for use in salads and baking.

4 cups unsweetened pomegranate juice

2 teaspoons lemon juice

⅔ cup sugar

At Home

Mix the juices and sugar in a heavy-bottomed saucepan over medium heat until the sugar dissolves completely. Bring to a simmer and then turn the burner down to medium-low. Stir frequently to keep the mixture from scorching. Let cook for 30 to 45 minutes or until the mixture has reduced and the consistency becomes slightly syrupy. Keep in mind that the mixture will thicken quite a bit as it cools. Let cool for 30 minutes in the pot. Store in a glass jar and refrigerate for up to 6 weeks. Before your trip, transfer the amount of syrup that you will use into a small leakproof container.

Chapter 6

Lunches

The type of lunch fare you choose will depend on what outdoors activity you are participating in. Thru-hikers tend to be grazers, and some backpackers and paddlers opt for a more leisurely lunch. There are many snack recipes in this book to suit those who like to eat while they are walking or paddling. This chapter is for the backpacker or paddler who would like to have a more substantial lunch or for those days where one can take a little more time to stop and smell the pine trees. Although we tend to stop for a rest and a relaxed lunch, there are days where we graze instead. This happens when we are trying to reach a certain campsite and the day's travel is going to be long and arduous or when the weather is on the verge of getting bad and we want to get to camp ahead of a storm. Whichever your preference, it is important that you eat during the day to keep your body fueled. I know I tend to get crabby when I haven't eaten—it's merely my body's way of reminding me that it needs some sustenance.

A lunch stop can be beneficial when you are traveling in a group with novices. It gives everyone a chance to catch up and to chat about the next leg of the journey while taking some time to rest. Having a chance to recharge can keep spirits up. Stopping also gives you a few moments to add water to that ingredient you are planning to rehydrate for supper or to check for blisters.

I mentioned weather earlier. It is a good idea to pack a few extra snacks in your pack in case the weather is bad enough that stopping for lunch would be undesirable. Speaking of which, seasons also come into play. In winter, you'll want warmer fare and in summer you'll probably enjoy a trail salad more.

Uncooked Fare

Sometimes it is nice to avoid cooking for lunch. I, quite often, try to have lunch without the use of my stove. The following items make for great uncooked lunches:

- Bagels
- Coleslaw
- Crackers
- Cream cheese
- Dips
- Fruit
- Gazpacho
- Hard cheese (for the ovo-lacto vegetarians)
- Honey
- Hummus
- Jam
- Leftovers
- Nut butters
- Pickles
- Pita bread
- Preserves and chutneys
- Salsas
- Spreads
- Tortilla chips
- Trail sprouts
- Vegetable antipasto
- Vegetables (choose sturdy types)
- Wraps

Dried fruit or vegetable antipasto mixed with cream cheese could be put on a bagel, or you could have cream cheese topped with hot pepper jelly on crackers. Apples are great with dip or nut butter or even in coleslaw. Vegetables are a tasty alternative for dipping in hummus. Add trail sprouts to a wrap or nut butter to a bagel. Leftover biscuits from dinner the night before or breakfast are good with a variety of toppings. Gazpacho with leftover focaccia bread makes a nice treat for lunch.

Cooking on the Go

It is not a wise idea to plan a cooking fire for lunch, as day hikers on the Booth's Rock Trail in Algonquin Provincial Park discovered on July 13, 1998. A couple cooked their lunch atop the cliff at the highest point of the trail. It gets pretty windy up there and I suppose they didn't douse the fire properly. To make a long story short, their cooking fire caused a forest fire that wasn't completely out until 8 days later, and it all could have been avoided with the use of a backpacking stove. If you do decide to have a hot lunch, here are some tips:

- Keep your pots and stove accessible so that you don't have to root through your pack.
- Start rehydrating your meal at breakfast so that you merely have to reheat it at lunch.

* If you have a Thermos, fill it with boiling water in the morning for a hot drink or instant soup.

* Do not block the trail or portage.

* Make sure you have enough water for cooking and cleanup.

* Bring extra ziplock bags in case you have leftovers.

* Be sure to clean up any garbage from your lunch spot and practice Leave No Trace principles.

It is best to plan lunches that require the least amount of dishes and cleanup. One-pot meals such as soups or stews are preferred. Sometimes it is nice to toast pitas or your bagel or the filling for your wrap. You might want to consider lighter fare so that you aren't hiking on too full of a stomach.

Jicama, Savoy Cabbage, and Mango Slaw

Dehydration Time: 5–10 hours
Makes 3–4 servings

⅔ cup carrot, coarsely grated

1 cup jicama, coarsely grated

⅔ cup mango, julienned

1¼ cup Savoy cabbage, shredded

¼ cup celery leaves (optional)

¼ cup red onion, minced

⅓ cup red pepper, julienned

2 tablespoons white balsamic or white wine vinegar

2½ tablespoons olive oil

Kosher salt to taste

Jicama (pronounced "hick-a-ma") has a slightly nutty and sweet flavor with the texture of a water chestnut. Although it looks like a turnip and is often referred to as Mexican turnip or Mexican potato, jicama is actually a legume. I first made this slaw for a backpacking trip along the rugged coastline of Georgian Bay in Ontario, Canada.

At Home

Grate the carrot and jicama on a coarse grater. Place on dehydrator trays to dry. Dry the mango on a separate dehydrator tray. Shred the cabbage, mix it with the celery leaves, if using, and dry the mixture on separate dehydrator trays lined with parchment paper or an additional mesh screen. Dry the minced red onion and red pepper on separate mesh-lined trays. When all the ingredients are dry, place them together in a ziplock freezer bag. Put the vinegar in a leakproof container and put that in the bag with the cabbage and jicama mixture. Add the olive oil to the other oil you will take with you on the trip.

At Camp

Shortly before you plan to eat the salad, rehydrate the dried ingredients with cold water using a ratio of 1 part dried mix to ⅔ part water. Check the salad after a few minutes and add a little more water as necessary. Drain any excess water once the cabbage and jicama have reconstituted and dress with a mixture of 2 tablespoons white balsamic vinegar and 2½ tablespoons olive oil. Adjust to suit your taste. Season the slaw with salt and pepper.

Tip

Don't let the slaw rehydrate in too much water or for too long or it will become soggy.

Jicama and Red Cabbage Slaw

Dehydration Time: 5–10 hours
Makes 4–6 servings

One unseasonably warm September weekend we were headed up a creek on the first day of a weeklong wilderness canoe trip. What was supposed to be a long leisurely paddle became more of a hike as low water levels forced us to wade for several miles. To my surprise it was a lot of fun. We stopped at a nice spot on shore and enjoyed a lunch of this salad with biscuits. I had to smile when I saw the vibrant pink color that the jicama took on from the red cabbage during rehydration.

At Home

Grate the jicama on a coarse grater. Place on dehydrator trays to dry with the cilantro. Shred the cabbage and dry it on separate dehydrator trays lined with parchment paper or an additional mesh screen. Dry the minced jalapeño pepper and corn on separate mesh-lined trays. When the jicama, cabbage, and jalapeño pepper are dry, place them together in a ziplock freezer bag. Add cumin and chili powder to the bag. Place the corn in a separate ziplock freezer bag. Put the vinegar in a leakproof container and put that in the bag with the cabbage and jicama mixture. Add the vegetable oil to the oil you will take with you on the trip and do the same with the agave nectar. Pack a fresh lime right before your trip.

At Camp

Add boiling water to cover the corn and let it rehydrate for about 30 minutes. Shortly before you plan to eat the salad, rehydrate the remaining dried ingredients with cold water using a ratio of 1 part dried mix to ⅔ part water. Check the salad after a few minutes and add a little more water as necessary. Drain any excess water once the cabbage and jicama have reconstituted and dress with a mixture of 1 tablespoon vinegar, 1 to 2 tablespoons fresh lime juice, ½ teaspoon agave

3 cups jicama, peeled and coarsely grated

1½ tablespoons fresh cilantro

3 cups red cabbage, shredded

1 jalapeño pepper, minced

½ cup corn

½ teaspoon cumin

½–1 teaspoon chili powder

1 tablespoon mango or red wine vinegar

3 tablespoons vegetable oil

½ teaspoon agave nectar

Juice of 1 lime

Salt and pepper to taste

nectar, and 3 tablespoons vegetable oil. Adjust to suit your taste. Season the slaw with salt and pepper.

Tips

Don't let the slaw rehydrate in too much water or for too long or it will become soggy.

You could use freeze-dried corn in place of the home-dehydrated corn to reduce rehydration time or you can start the rehydration process at breakfast so that you don't have to take your stove out at lunch.

If you aren't vegan, honey can be used as a substitute for the agave nectar.

Mushroom Salsa

Dehydration Time: 7–10 hours
Makes 2–3 servings

There is something about the earthiness of mushrooms and how wonderful they taste with the complex acidity of aged balsamic vinegar. I like to use a combination of portobello, shitake, cremini, and white button mushrooms for this recipe. Serve with bagel crisps, rusks, melba toast, or crackers. For a hearty lunch or dinner, serve it over pasta or potato gnocchi and top with a little drizzle of olive oil.

At Home

Heat ½ tablespoon of olive oil in a skillet over medium heat and then add the jalapeño pepper and onion. When the onion starts to soften, add the balsamic vinegar and simmer until the onion starts to caramelize and the vinegar starts to thicken. Then add the dried thyme and mushrooms and cook for a few minutes until the mushrooms are warmed through. Season the salsa to taste with salt and pepper.

Measure the mushroom mixture and write this measurement on a sticky note. Dehydrate on lined dehydrator trays for 7 to 10 hours. Add the extra olive oil to the other oil that you will take on your trip.

At Camp

Add enough boiling water to the salsa to equal the measurement on your sticky note. Be sure to account for and add your dried ingredients to the rehydration container prior to adding the water. You can always add more water if you need to. Once the salsa has rehydrated, you might have to reheat it. Drizzle with a little olive oil.

Tip

You can also use cold water to rehydrate this by adding water at breakfast and letting it rehydrate as you hike.

½ tablespoon olive oil, plus 1 tablespoon

½ jalapeño pepper, minced

½ cup red onion, minced

2 tablespoons balsamic vinegar

¼ teaspoon dried thyme

1¾ cups mixed mushrooms, chopped

Kosher salt to taste

Freshly ground black pepper to taste

Caribbean Hummus

Dehydration Time: 5–7 hours
Makes 2–4 servings

¼ cup banana, sliced

⅛ cup lime juice

⅔ cup mango, chopped

1 19-ounce can chickpeas

2 tablespoons cashew butter

A pinch of kosher salt

2–3 teaspoons Jamaican jerk
seasoning paste to taste

East meets the Caribbean in this play on hummus. It has a sweeter flavor than traditional hummus, which makes it perfect for younger adventurers. The heat of Jamaican jerk seasoning can vary by brand so adjust accordingly.

At Home

Cut up the banana and let the pieces sit in the lime juice while you chop the mango. Place the mango in a food processor and purée. Add the banana and lime mixture and process until smooth. Then add the chickpeas, cashew butter, and salt. Process again. Add the jerk seasoning 1 teaspoon at a time, blending between teaspoons until it suits your taste. Spread evenly on lined dehydrator trays, keeping the mixture about ¼-inch thick. Dry for 5 to 7 hours or until the mixture crumbles and is thoroughly dry. Store in a medium-size ziplock freezer bag.

At Camp

Rehydrate the hummus using a formula of 1½ parts dried mix to 1 part water. Wait 5 to 10 minutes and then add a little more water if it's too dry. Serve as a dip with Greek pitas or your favorite crackers or use as a spread in a wrap. This is also nice served with plantain or cassava chips.

Smoky Lentil Pâté

Dehydration Time: 5–7 hours
Makes 2–4 servings

Sometimes I crave foods that have a combination of smokiness and earthiness. This recipe hits the mark with the use of mushrooms and smoked paprika. I like to reconstitute it with hot water so I can enjoy the dip while it is warm, which is especially nice on a cold day, but it will rehydrate well with cool water too.

At Home

Heat the olive oil in a frying pan and then add in the mushrooms. Sauté the mushrooms for 5 to 7 minutes and then add the chives and garlic. Cook for 2 minutes more and then add the spices, stirring to coat the mushrooms. Add the apple juice and gently scrape the bottom of the pan to loosen any mushroom bits. Simmer until the juice reduces by half and then remove from the heat. Add the lentils and salt and stir to combine. Let cool. Place the mixture in a food processor or blender and blend until nearly smooth. The texture should be similar to hummus. Spread evenly on lined dehydrator trays, keeping the mixture about ¼-inch thick. Dry for 5 to 7 hours or until the mixture crumbles and is thoroughly dry. Store in a medium-size ziplock freezer bag.

At Camp

Rehydrate the lentil pâté using a formula of 1½ parts dried mix to 1 part water. Wait 5 or 10 minutes and then add a little more water if needed. Serve the dip warm or cold with crackers, Greek pita wedges, or tortilla chips or use as a spread in a vegetable wrap.

Tip

If you are using canned lentils, be sure to rinse and drain them first.

1 tablespoon olive or vegetable oil

1 cup fresh cremini mushrooms, coarsely chopped

⅛ cup fresh chives or green onions, chopped

2 cloves garlic, finely chopped

1 tablespoon fresh oregano or 1 teaspoon dried oregano

1 teaspoon smoked paprika

½ teaspoon freshly ground black pepper

½ cup apple juice or apple cider

2 cups cooked red or green lentils

A pinch of kosher salt

Olive Tapenade

Dehydration Time: 8–10 hours
Makes 3–4 servings

1 cup pimento-stuffed green olives, drained

1 cup pitted black olives, drained

1 cup marinated artichoke hearts, drained

1 hot banana pepper, coarsely chopped

½ sweet red pepper, coarsely chopped

1 clove garlic, minced

¼ teaspoon dried basil

1 tablespoon capers, minced

1 tablespoon lemon or lime juice

1 tablespoon extra virgin olive oil

I first had this tapenade at an autumn gathering being hosted in Ontario, Canada's Algonquin Provincial Park. The recipe came from my friend Alison Delmage, and it was her contribution to an impromptu potluck. I have modified the dish to suit backcountry trips, and although it is great as a spread, it can double as a refreshing addition to pasta for dinner.

At Home

Put the olives and artichokes in a food processor and pulse to chop the mixture. It should be finely chopped, but not to the point of being a purée. Put the olive mixture in a bowl and set aside. Next, put the peppers in the food processor and pulse until the peppers are the same consistency as the olive mixture. Add the peppers to the olive mixture along with the garlic, basil, capers, and lemon juice. Stir until well combined.

Measure the tapenade and write this measurement on a sticky note. Spread onto lined dehydrator trays and dry for 8 to 10 hours. Package the tapenade in a medium-size ziplock freezer bag and add the olive oil to the other olive oil you are taking on your trip.

At Camp

Add enough water to the tapenade mix to equal the measurement on your sticky note. Be sure to account for and add your dried ingredients to the rehydration container prior to adding the water. You can always add more water if you need to. Let rehydrate for 10 to 15 minutes and add more water if needed. Stir in 1 tablespoon of olive oil and serve with your favorite cracker or flatbread.

Tip

If you don't have a food processor, you can chop the ingredients by hand. It's a little more work but the results will be just as good.

Pumpkin Hummus

Dehydration Time: 5–8 hours
Makes 2–4 servings

This play on hummus doesn't contain any chickpeas or tahini, but it is still packed with flavor. It makes a great no-cook lunch and is delicious in a wrap with spiced black beans. Our favorite is to serve this with a cornbread, jalapeño cracker.

AT HOME

Combine all ingredients in a food processor or large bowl if using a hand blender. Process them until you have a thick paste. Spread evenly on lined dehydrator trays, keeping the mixture about ¼-inch thick. Dry for 5 to 8 hours or until the mixture is thoroughly dry. Grind into a powder in a spice grinder or blender. Store in a medium-size ziplock freezer bag.

AT CAMP

Rehydrate the pumpkin mixture using a formula of 1½ parts dried mix to 1 part water. Wait 5 to 10 minutes and then add a little more water if it's too dry.

Tip

You may use fresh pumpkin that has been roasted or stewed for this but canned pumpkin is easier. Do not use pumpkin pie filling, as it has other ingredients that would be unwanted in this recipe.

2 cups cooked canned pumpkin

¼ cup lime juice

1 heaping teaspoon lime zest

2 tablespoons pumpkin seed butter

1 tablespoon chipotle pepper, finely chopped

1–2 cloves roasted garlic

¼ teaspoon ancho chili powder

¼ teaspoon black pepper

A pinch of kosher salt

Roasted Corn and Ancho Salsa

1 cup roasted corn

2 teaspoons ancho chili powder

¾ cup plum tomatoes, drained and chopped

¼ cup red onion, minced

2 tablespoons lime juice

⅛ teaspoon black pepper

¼ teaspoon kosher salt

2 tablespoons fresh cilantro

Dehydration Time: 7–12 hours
Makes 2–3 servings

Our small city is surrounded by miles and miles of farmland, and in August there are many roadside stands selling cobs of sweet corn by the dozen. If you don't feel like grilling the corn, you can just use it plain, but the grilling really does add a wonderful smoky flavor and it brings out the natural sweetness.

At Home

Grill the peeled corn cobs over high heat on a barbeque or under the broiler until they start to take on color. Let cool and cut the corn from the cobs. Combine all the ingredients together in a large bowl. Dry on lined dehydrator trays for 7 to 12 hours or until the pieces are dried through. Break the salsa into small pieces and place it in a ziplock freezer bag.

At Camp

Add hot water to the salsa mixture using a little less water than dried mix. Add more water if necessary. Serve with tortilla chips, crackers, bagel crisps, or in a wrap with beans.

Tip

If you are planning to have this for lunch on the trail, add hot water to the salsa mixture at breakfast, and it will be ready by the time you stop for lunch.

Greek Red Pepper Dip

Dehydration Time: 5–7 hours
Makes 2–4 servings

*This hummus-like recipe was originally created for a
wilderness-cooking workshop. I often create several dips
and dry them. This way I can illustrate how easy it is to
rehydrate this type of fare as a trail lunch without having to
use a stove. The participants pass the dip around to munch
on and this particular one always gets rave reviews.*

AT HOME

Roast the red peppers according to the instructions on page
7. Once they've cooled, peel them and chop them into ¼-inch
pieces. Combine all the ingredients in a food processor or
large bowl if using a hand blender. Process them until you
have a thick paste.

Spread evenly on lined dehydrator trays, keeping the
mixture about ¼-inch thick. Dry for 5 to 7 hours or until the
mixture crumbles and is thoroughly dry. Store in a medium-
size ziplock freezer bag.

AT CAMP

Rehydrate the dip using a formula of 1½ parts dried mix to
1 part water. Wait 5 to 10 minutes and then add a little more
water if it's too dry. Serve as a dip with Greek pitas or your
favorite crackers or use as a spread in a wrap.

Tips

If you need to increase your fat intake for cold-weather hiking,
drizzle a little olive oil on the hummus just before you eat it.

Fresh vegetables also make a great accompaniment for
this dip.

⅓ cup roasted red peppers

1 19-ounce can chickpeas,
rinsed and drained

3 tablespoons lime juice

2 cloves garlic

2 tablespoons tahini

¼ cup Feta cheese or 1½
tablespoons capers

¼ teaspoon dried oregano

A pinch of kosher salt

Grilled Strawberry Jalapeño Salsa

Dehydration Time: 7–12 hours
Makes 2–3 servings

2 cups fresh whole strawberries (1 cup after grilling)

¾ cup plum tomatoes, drained and chopped

1–2 jalapeño peppers, seeds removed and minced

¼ cup red onion, minced

2 tablespoons lime juice

¼ teaspoon black pepper

¼ teaspoon kosher salt

2 tablespoons fresh cilantro

Every June we are overrun with local strawberries, so I am always looking for different ways to use them. As strange as it sounds, grilled strawberries are gorgeous in both sweet and savory dishes. The sweetness of the strawberries balances the heat of the jalapeño peppers in this salsa. You can use balsamic vinegar instead of lime juice if you prefer.

At Home

Grill the whole strawberries on a barbeque over high heat or under the broiler until they start to take on color. Alternatively, you may roast them in a 350°F oven for 30 minutes. Combine all the ingredients together in a large bowl. Dry on lined dehydrator trays for 7 to 12 hours or until the pieces are dried through. Break the salsa into small pieces and place them in a ziplock freezer bag.

At Camp

Add warm water to the salsa mixture using a little less water than dried mix. Add more water if necessary. Serve with tortilla chips, crackers, or bagel crisps.

Tip

If you are planning to have this for lunch on the trail, add warm water to the salsa mixture at breakfast, and it will be ready by the time you stop for lunch.

Pear and Fennel Slaw

Dehydration Time: 8–10 hours
Makes 2–4 servings

Fennel is a neat vegetable with the slight flavor of anise. What I appreciate about fennel, besides the flavor, is that it can be used cooked or raw and that all parts of the vegetable can be used. The bulb is used in this salad, and you can use the stalks and fronds for other dishes. Even the seeds can be used as a spice. This slaw combines fennel with pear and has a dressing that will make your tongue tingle just a little.

At Home

Prepare the fennel and set aside. Grate the pears and soak them in water treated with Fruit Fresh or lime juice. Drain and combine with the fennel, lime juice, and lime zest. Place on dehydrator trays that have been lined with a mesh screen and dry for 8 to 10 hours. Put the dried fennel and pear mixture in a medium-size ziplock freezer bag.

Mix the dressing ingredients together in a pot. Place over medium-high heat and bring to a boil. Let the mixture simmer for 3 minutes, and then remove it from the stove and let cool before packaging in a leakproof container for your trip.

At Camp

Add just enough water to the fennel and pears to cover them. Allow to rehydrate for 15 to 30 minutes. Once the mixture has rehydrated, drain off any excess water and add the dressing.

Tip

If you are planning to have this for lunch on the trail, add cold water to the slaw mixture at breakfast, and it will be ready by the time you stop for lunch.

Slaw

3 cups fennel bulb, cored and julienned

3 cups pears, coarsely grated

Fruit Fresh or lime juice

1 tablespoon lime juice

¼ teaspoon lime zest

Dressing

¼ cup white wine or white balsamic vinegar

1 tablespoon agave nectar

¼ teaspoon Dijon mustard

¼ teaspoon celery salt

¼ teaspoon black pepper

Very small pinch of cayenne pepper

Roasted Tomato Dip

Dehydration Time: 5–7 hours
Makes 2–4 servings

1 small shallot

¼ cup onion

1 clove garlic

2 cups grape or cherry
   tomatoes

1 tablespoon olive oil

Kosher salt to taste

Black pepper to taste

¼ teaspoon cayenne pepper

½ teaspoon dried ancho chile

1 teaspoon fresh cilantro

1 tablespoon lime juice

1 teaspoon lime zest
   (optional)

1 cup cannellini beans or
   white kidney beans

This dip wasn't initially created for the trail. I'm part Scottish, and New Year's, or Hogmanay as we call it, is always a big deal in our family. I made this dip as part of a feast of munchables for the first New Year's celebration in our new home. It went over well, so the next time I made it for one of our wilderness trips. It's great on toasted Greek-style pitas.

At Home

Preheat oven to 350°F. Mince the shallot and onion. Cut the garlic and tomatoes in half. Put the shallot, onion, garlic, and tomatoes in a shallow baking dish and drizzle with the olive oil. Season the mixture with salt and pepper, to taste. Bake for 45 minutes, stirring occasionally. The tomatoes will start to caramelize and become very soft. Remove from the oven and let the mixture cool.

   Place the tomato mixture in a blender or food processor with the remaining ingredients and pulse until well combined. Spread evenly on lined dehydrator trays, keeping the mixture about ¼-inch thick. Dry for 5 to 7 hours or until the mixture is thoroughly dry and resembles fruit leather. Store in a medium-size ziplock freezer bag.

At Camp

Rehydrate the tomato dip using a formula of 1½ parts dried mix to 1 part water. Wait 5 or 10 minutes and then add a little more water if necessary. When you reach your lunch stop, you can warm the dip or enjoy it cold with crackers, bagel crisps, breadsticks, Greek pita wedges, or tortilla chips. It is also good in a wrap with vegetables or used as a sauce.

Balsamic French Lentil Salad with Walnuts and Chevré

Dehydration Time: 5–7 hours
Makes 3–4 servings

Many of my readers know of my love affair with lentils and trail salads. This French-inspired dish is best served warm, but it will do cold as well. If you use goat cheese in this, you'll need to have it on the first day or two of your trip.

AT HOME

Check the lentils over and remove any debris. Rinse them in a fine strainer and set aside to drain. Heat 1 to 2 teaspoons olive oil in a medium-size pot over medium heat. Add the onion and sauté until softened, being careful not to brown them. Add 2 cloves garlic and sauté for 1 minute. Remove the onions and garlic and set aside. Add the lentils, water, and bay leaf. Simmer for 30 to 40 minutes, stirring occasionally. Add the thyme during the last 10 minutes of cooking. Remove from heat, discard the bay leaf, and stir in the onion mixture. Measure the mixture and write this measurement on a sticky note. Spread on lined dehydrator trays and dry for 5 to 7 hours at 135°F. Toast the walnuts in a dry frying pan until they start to become fragrant. Remove from the pan to cool. Put the dried lentils in a ziplock freezer bag with the sticky note. Wrap the walnuts in a piece of plastic wrap and add to the bag. Mix the olive oil and balsamic vinegar together and put in a leakproof container and place in the bag with the lentils. Wrap the goat cheese, if you are using it, in plastic wrap right before your trip.

AT CAMP

Rehydrate the lentil mixture by adding enough boiling water to equal the measurement on your sticky note. Be sure to account for and add your dried ingredients to the rehydration container prior to adding the water. You can always add more

1 cup du Puy or green lentils

1–2 teaspoons olive oil

1 large red onion, diced

2 cloves garlic, minced

1⅓ cups water

1 bay leaf

¼ teaspoon dried thyme

¼ cup walnuts, toasted and coarsely chopped

2½ tablespoons olive oil

1½ tablespoons balsamic vinegar

¼ cup goat cheese (optional)

Salt and pepper to taste

water if you need to. Once the lentils are rehydrated, about 15 to 20 minutes, drain off any excess water, reheat if desired, and lightly dress with the mixture of 2½ tablespoons of olive oil and 1½ tablespoons balsamic vinegar using just enough to coat. Crumble the goat cheese on top and season with salt and pepper to taste. Serve with pieces of baguette or Greek-style pitas.

Tip

You can also start this rehydrating at breakfast with cool water. Then simply reheat or serve cold at lunch.

White Bean and Artichoke Dip

Dehydration Time: 5–7 hours
Makes 2–4 servings

I like to use marinated artichokes for this recipe if I can keep my husband from eating them right out of the jar. Of course, you can remove the hearts from the artichokes yourself, but it can be fiddly and the marinated ones are yummy. Lemon and fresh rosemary are delicious additions to this dip, but you can easily change the herb to create different flavor combinations.

AT HOME

Purée the beans, artichoke hearts, rosemary, garlic, lemon juice, salt, and pepper in a blender or food processor. Dehydrate on lined dehydrator trays as you would for fruit leather. The dip takes 5 to 7 hours to dry. Once it is dry, place it in a medium-size ziplock freezer bag. Wrap the crushed red chilies and Parmesan cheese, if using, in a piece of plastic wrap and place the bundle in the bag with the dried ingredients.

AT CAMP

Remove the crushed red chili and cheese bundle, if using. Rehydrate the dip using a formula of 1½ parts dried mix to 1 part water. Wait 5 to 10 minutes and then stir in the contents of the bundle and add a little more water if the dip is too dry. Serve warm or cold, as a dip with your favorite crackers or pita wedges or as a spread in a wrap.

Tip

If you need to increase your fat intake on cold-weather hikes, simply add some olive oil to the dip before serving.

1½ cups cannellini or white kidney beans, drained and rinsed

¾ cup marinated or water-packed artichoke hearts

½ sprig fresh rosemary, stem removed

2 cloves garlic, minced

⅛ cup lemon juice to taste

¼ teaspoon kosher salt

¼ teaspoon white pepper

A pinch of crushed red chilies (optional)

3 tablespoons Parmesan cheese, grated (optional)

Five-spice Pineapple Slaw

4 fresh pineapple rings or 4 canned pineapple rings packed in juice

3 cups Savoy cabbage

2 medium carrots

¼ teaspoon five-spice powder

2 tablespoons macadamia nuts, chopped

1½ tablespoons apple cider vinegar

3 tablespoons vegetable oil

Salt and pepper to taste

Dehydration Time: 5–10 hours
Makes 3–4 servings

Chinese five-spice powder pairs nicely with the sweet flavor of grilled pineapple in this unusual slaw. This also makes a great filling for a wrap or pita with a little peanut butter and crushed red chili peppers added to the dressing.

AT HOME

Preheat the grill to 350°F. Grill the pineapple until it softens and you have grill marks. Shred with two forks and set aside to cool. Shred the cabbage and the carrots and dry them on separate dehydrator trays that have been lined or include an additional mesh screen. Do the same with the shredded grilled pineapple.

When the cabbage, carrots, and pineapple are dry, place them in a ziplock freezer bag. Wrap the five-spice powder and macadamia nuts in separate pieces of plastic wrap and put the bundles in with the dried cabbage mixture. Place the cider vinegar in a leakproof container and put that in the bag with the cabbage. Add the vegetable oil to the other oil you will take with you on your trip.

AT CAMP

Shortly before you plan to eat the salad, remove the spice and nut bundles. Then rehydrate the dried ingredients with cold water using a ratio of 1 part dried mix to ⅔ part water. Check the salad after a few minutes and add a little more water as necessary.

Drain any excess water once the cabbage has reconstituted and then add the five-spice powder, apple cider vinegar, and vegetable oil to suit your taste. Season the coleslaw with salt and pepper and sprinkle the chopped macadamia nuts on top.

Tip

Don't let the slaw rehydrate in too much water or for too long or it will become soggy.

Harvest Hummus with Roasted Pepitas

Dehydration Time: 5–7 hours
Makes 2–4 servings

⅓ cup walnuts, chopped

1½ tablespoons balsamic vinegar

1 19-ounce can chickpeas, rinsed and drained

1 hot banana pepper, seeds removed

3 tablespoons lemon juice

2 tablespoons pumpkin seed butter

¼–½ teaspoon cumin

½ teaspoon dried cilantro

A pinch of kosher salt

¼ teaspoon cracked black pepper

¼ cup pepitas, toasted

As we were doing preparations for a last-minute trip, I realized that I was out of tahini. I wanted to make hummus but didn't have time to go to the grocery store, so I used ground walnuts and pumpkin seed butter instead.

AT HOME

Toast the walnuts in a dry frying pan until fragrant. Set aside to cool. Grind the nuts in a food processor for about 5 minutes until they are very fine. Add the balsamic vinegar and pulse again. Then add the remaining ingredients (except the pepitas) and blend until you have a thick paste. Spread evenly on lined dehydrator trays, keeping the mixture about ¼-inch thick. Dry for 5 to 7 hours or until the mixture crumbles and is thoroughly dry. Store in a medium-size ziplock freezer bag. Wrap the pepitas in a piece of plastic wrap and put it in the freezer bag with the hummus.

AT CAMP

Remove the pepitas from the freezer bag. Rehydrate the hummus using a formula of 1½ parts dried mix to 1 part water. Wait 5 to 10 minutes, and then add a little more water if it's too dry. Sprinkle with the pepitas and serve as a dip with Greek pitas or your favorite crackers or use as a spread in a wrap.

Tip

If you need to increase your fat intake on cold-weather hikes, simply add some olive oil to the hummus before serving.

Ginger, Wasabi, Edamame Spread

1 teaspoon lime zest

½ teaspoon wasabi powder

2 tablespoons lime juice

1½ teaspoons fresh ginger, finely grated

2 cups edamame beans, cooked

1 teaspoon tamari or soy sauce

1 clove garlic, minced

⅛ teaspoon cayenne pepper

¼ teaspoon kosher salt

½ teaspoon finely ground black pepper

Dehydration Time: 5–7 hours
Makes 2–4 servings

Edamame means "twig bean" or "bean on a branch," and these young green soybeans are a nutritious addition to your menu whether at home or on the trail. It is best to buy edamame that have been taken out of the pods and flash frozen. This spread is infused with the Japanese flavors of ginger and wasabi.

At Home

Remove the zest from a lime and set aside. Mix the wasabi powder and lime juice together until the powder is fully dissolved. Using a food processor or hand blender, combine all of the ingredients until you have a thick, smooth paste. Spread evenly on lined dehydrator trays, keeping the mixture about ¼-inch thick. Dry for 5 to 7 hours or until the mixture crumbles and is thoroughly dry. Store in a medium-size ziplock freezer bag.

At Camp

Rehydrate the spread using a formula of 1½ parts dried mix to 1 part water. Wait 5 to 10 minutes and then add a little more water if it's too dry. Serve as a dip with your favorite crackers or pita wedges or use as a spread in a wrap.

Tips

If you are gluten intolerant, be sure to read the label when buying tamari sauce. True tamari sauce is gluten free, but some less expensive varieties contain gluten.

If you need to increase your fat intake on cold-weather hikes, simply add some olive oil to the spread before serving.

Indian Carrot Salad

Dehydration Time: 6–10 hours
Makes 3–4 servings

Our friend Chander Bhardwaj is from India. Chander introduced Bryan to many interesting foods when they would lunch together at a little Indian restaurant. Bryan would sometimes bring home meals from the restaurant for us to try, and I was compelled to delve more into creating other Indian-inspired meals on my own. Moong dal, or yellow split lentils, are now a staple in our house, and they make this carrot salad a little heartier. The addition of black mustard seeds gives this flavorful dish a slight pungency. If you don't like black mustard seeds, omit them.

AT HOME

Soak the dal in 2 cups of boiling water for 3 hours. Drain the dal and then mix with the carrots, mango, coconut, and cilantro. Spread on lined dehydrator trays and dry for 6 to 10 hours. Place the mixture into a medium-size ziplock freezer bag. Wrap the garam masala in a bit of plastic wrap and add the bundle to the bag with the carrot mixture. Heat the oil in a pot over medium heat. Add the *chile de arbol* and cook until the chili peppers start to darken slightly. Remove the chili from the pan and the pan from the heat immediately. Let the oil cool and then pour the infused oil into a leakproof container. Place the black mustard seeds in a piece of plastic wrap if you plan to use them and add the bundle to the carrot bag. Pack a fresh lime right before your trip.

AT CAMP

Remove the spice bundle and mustard seeds from the freezer bag and set aside. Rehydrate the salad mixture in the plastic bag by using a formula of 1½ parts dried mix to 1 part water. Wait 5 to 10 minutes and then add a little more water if needed. If you accidentally use too much water, be sure to drain the salad well before serving.

⅓ cup *moong dal*

2 cups boiling water

2 cups carrots, coarsely grated

⅓ cup mango, coarsely grated

⅓ cup unsweetened coconut

2 tablespoons fresh cilantro, chopped

½ teaspoon garam masala

2 tablespoons vegetable oil

1–2 dried *chile de arbol*

¼ teaspoon black mustard seeds (optional)

Juice of 1 lime

A pinch of kosher salt

When the salad has rehydrated, dress it with the infused oil, garam masala, 2 tablespoons of lime juice, and a pinch of salt.

Tip

If desired, toast ¼ teaspoon black mustard seeds in 1 teaspoon of the heated infused oil and add to the salad with the garam masala, lime juice, and salt. Don't do this at home, as the black mustard seeds will make the salad really pungent when they've sat in the dressing too long. It should be done right before you serve the dish.

Mediterranean Garbanzo Bean Salad

Dehydration Time: 8–12 hours
Makes 2 servings

I like to think of this salad as a little trip around the Mediterranean because it combines ingredients common in Spain, Italy, Greece, Israel, and Egypt. Za'atar is a flavorful spice blend available through Middle Eastern specialty stores and online spice retailers. This salad can be served cold but is especially delicious when served warm. You can even serve it over cooked quinoa or couscous for a nice dinner.

AT HOME

Heat the oil in a frying pan over medium to medium-high heat. Add the shallots and sauté for a few minutes. Add the crushed red chilies, orange zest, orange juice, and orange segments. Cook for a few more minutes and then add the lemon juice, chickpeas, olives, and *za'atar* spice blend. Simmer for a few minutes and then remove from the heat. Stir in the pepper and salt.

Allow the mixture to cool and then measure the amount you will dry. Write this measurement on a sticky note. Spread the salad on lined dehydrator trays to dry. When the salad is dry, package it in a ziplock freezer bag along with your note.

AT CAMP

Rehydrate the salad by adding enough boiling water to the mix to make it equal to the measurement on your sticky note. Be sure to account for and add your dried ingredients to the rehydration container prior to adding the water. You can always add more water if you need to. Once the salad has rehydrated, reheat it if desired.

Tips

If you can't find *za'atar*, then use a combination of thyme and basil, as they will pair nicely with this salad as well.

1½ tablespoons olive oil or vegetable oil

⅓ cup shallots, finely chopped

¼ teaspoon crushed red chilies (optional)

1 teaspoon orange zest

2 tablespoons fresh orange juice

Segments of 1 large orange

1 teaspoon lemon juice

2 cups canned chickpeas (garbanzo beans), drained and rinsed

½ cup green olives, pitted and chopped

½ teaspoon *za'atar* spice blend

1 teaspoon black pepper, freshly ground

⅛ teaspoon kosher salt

If you'd like to have this recipe for lunch, you can add cold water to the mixture at breakfast and let it rehydrate in your pack as you travel.

This is also good for dinner served on couscous or quinoa that has been cooked with a little vegetable stock or orange juice or with pitas that have been toasted, drizzled with a little olive oil, and sprinkled with a bit of the *za'atar* spice.

Toasted Quinoa Tabbouleh with Black Lentils

Dehydration Time: 7–12 hours
Makes 3–4 servings

Tabbouleh is usually made with bulgur wheat, but I'm not a big fan when it comes to the texture of bulgur and it's not gluten free. So this is my take on the traditional tabbouleh with the optional addition of black beluga lentils—a small legume with an earthy flavor.

At Home

Place the quinoa in a fine sieve and rinse for at least 3 minutes to remove the bitter coating. Drain and place in a nonstick frying pan to toast the quinoa, stirring frequently. As soon as some of the seeds start to pop, remove the quinoa from the pan. Put the toasted quinoa and 2 cups water into a pot. Season the water with ¼ teaspoon salt. Bring the mixture to a boil; cover and simmer for 10 minutes. Remove from the heat and leave the lid on for an additional 10 minutes. Fluff with a fork as you would for rice and let cool. Combine the tomatoes, red onion, parsley, and mint with the quinoa; measure the mixture and write this measurement on a sticky note. Spread on lined dehydrator trays and dry for 7 to 12 hours or until no moisture remains. Put the sticky note and dried tabbouleh in a medium-size ziplock freezer bag. If you are using the lentils, cook them in ¾ cup unsalted water until tender, about 15 to 20 minutes. Drain any excess water, measure the lentils, and add that measurement to the sticky note about the quinoa. Spread on lined dehydrator trays to dry for 7 to 10 hours. Add the olive oil to any other olive oil that you will take on your trip. Pack a fresh lemon and a fresh English cucumber the day before you leave.

1 cup quinoa

2 cups plus ¾ cup water

¼ teaspoon kosher salt

3 fresh plum tomatoes, seeded and chopped

⅛ cup red onion, minced

⅓ cup fresh Italian parsley, chopped

2 tablespoons fresh mint, chopped

¼ cup black lentils (optional)

⅓ cup extra virgin olive oil

1 fresh lemon

1 fresh English (seedless) cucumber

Freshly cracked or ground black pepper to taste

Salt to taste

At Camp

Add boiling water to the quinoa mixture and to the lentils, separately, if using, to equal the measurement on your sticky note. Be sure to account for and add your dried ingredients to the rehydration containers prior to adding the water. You can always add more water if you need to. Drain any excess water. Chop the cucumber into ½-inch pieces and stir into the quinoa mixture. Juice the lemon with a fork and mix well with ⅓ cup of olive oil. Pour over the tabbouleh and let sit for 5 to 10 minutes to let the flavors combine. Season with pepper and salt.

Tips

Always check lentils carefully for foreign matter before cooking and don't salt them until they are finished cooking, as it will make them tough.

You could rehydrate the lentils and quinoa mixture together, but sometimes the lentils will turn the quinoa a muddy color, so I like to reconstitute them separately.

If you will be using this early in your trip, you could use fresh tomatoes instead of drying them with the quinoa.

Gazpacho

Dehydration Time: 8–12 hours
Makes 3–4 servings

The first time I had this cold Spanish soup was at a little café in the heart of Toronto. The day was so hot that you could fry an egg on the sidewalk. I fell in love with the dish and discovered that it makes a yummy trail lunch with crackers or pita or light dinner with flatbread or biscuits, especially on an excruciatingly scorching day when your appetite might be diminished.

At Home

Coarsely chop the tomatoes, half of a red and a green pepper, half of the cucumber, and the garlic. Purée in a blender or food processor with the vinegar until smooth. Stir in the vegetable cocktail, hot pepper sauce, salt, and pepper. Measure the soup and write this measurement on a sticky note. Spread on lined dehydrator trays and dehydrate at 135°F for 8 to 12 hours or until completely dry and leathery. Dry the chopped green onions on a separate lined tray. Grind the dried leather in small batches in a coffee grinder or in a blender. Place the dried soup mixture and the sticky note in a ziplock freezer bag and add in the dried onions. Add the oil to the other olive oil that you will take on your trip. Before you leave, carefully pack a cucumber and a small sweet yellow pepper.

At Camp

At breakfast add enough cool water to the soup to equal the measurement on your sticky note. Be sure to account for and add your dried ingredients to the rehydration container prior to adding the water. You can always add more water if you need to. When you stop for lunch, stir in ⅛ cup each diced cucumber and diced sweet yellow pepper. Drizzle with a little olive oil, if desired, and serve with your favorite bread, crackers, or pita.

3 fresh plum tomatoes, peeled and seeded

½ sweet red pepper, seeded

½ green pepper, seeded

½ English cucumber, peeled and chopped

1 garlic clove, minced

1 tablespoon red wine vinegar

1¾ cups vegetable cocktail

⅛ teaspoon hot pepper sauce

⅛ teaspoon kosher salt

Freshly ground pepper to taste

1 green onion, chopped

1–2 teaspoons olive oil (optional)

1 fresh English or seedless cucumber

1 small fresh sweet yellow pepper

Tips

This recipe requires that you pack in a cucumber and a pepper. Look for organic peppers, as they tend to be smaller and will fit better into a container. You won't use all of the pepper or cucumber, so I usually plan to use the rest for a simple cucumber salad at supper and to snack on the leftover pepper while I hike.

To save time at lunch, you can dice the pepper and the cucumber at breakfast while your camp mates break down camp. Put them in a spare ziplock freezer bag and pack them carefully in the top of your pack.

Grilled Vegetable and Sprout Wrap

Dehydration Time: 6–12 hours
Makes 2 large wraps or 4 small ones

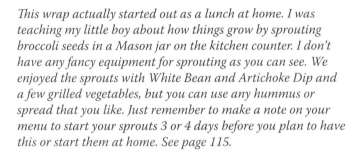

This wrap actually started out as a lunch at home. I was teaching my little boy about how things grow by sprouting broccoli seeds in a Mason jar on the kitchen counter. I don't have any fancy equipment for sprouting as you can see. We enjoyed the sprouts with White Bean and Artichoke Dip and a few grilled vegetables, but you can use any hummus or spread that you like. Just remember to make a note on your menu to start your sprouts 3 or 4 days before you plan to have this or start them at home. See page 115.

AT HOME

Prepare the vegetables and mix the vinegar, olive oil, and garlic together. Add the vegetables (except the carrot) and let marinate for 30 minutes or so. Preheat the barbeque, remove the vegetables from the marinade, and grill until they are cooked through. Remove and let cool. Cut the mushroom and red pepper into small ½-inch pieces. Grate the carrot on the coarse side of a box grater. Dry the carrots on a lined dehydrator tray and dry the remaining vegetables separately on mesh-lined dehydrator trays for 6 to 10 hours or until leathery. Place the vegetables, except for the carrots, together in a medium-size ziplock freezer bag. Pack the carrots and dried dip or hummus separately in small freezer bags and then put those in the bag with the vegetables. Wrap 2 tablespoons of sprouting seeds in plastic wrap and put the bundle in with the vegetables. Bring a copy of the Water Bottle Sprout Garden instructions from pages 115–116 and pack a water bottle, piece of cheesecloth, and a rubber band unless you've already started your sprouts at home. In that case, don't forget to bring the sprouts with you. Package the wraps in a large ziplock freezer bag with a layer of parchment paper between each one to prevent them from sticking together.

1 small zucchini, sliced lengthwise

1 red pepper, quartered

1 portobello mushroom, stem removed

⅛ cup white balsamic vinegar or aged balsamic vinegar

2 tablespoons olive oil

1 clove garlic, minced

⅛ cup carrot, coarsely grated

3 tablespoons White Bean and Artichoke Dip (see page 101), dried measurement

2 tablespoons broccoli sprouting seeds

2 large or 4 small wraps

Salt and pepper to taste

At Camp

Rehydrate the main bag of vegetables with cool water at breakfast using a ratio of 1 part dried vegetables to ⅔ part water. When you stop for lunch, check the vegetables and add the carrots to the rehydration container with the rehydrated vegetables. If you have excess water in the container, it will rehydrate the carrots. If not, add a little more water. Add 2 tablespoons of water to the dip in the bag. Wait 5 minutes and add a little more water if necessary. Cut a slit in the bag and squeeze some dip out on each wrap. Spread. Drain the vegetables well and add some to each wrap. Add a few table-spoons of the trail-grown sprouts. Season the wrap to taste with salt and pepper.

Tips

You'll likely have leftover sprouts. Use them to garnish a soup for dinner, to top gazpacho or a wrap the next day, or for a little salad. If you plan to keep them for a day or two, don't forget to water them.

Water Bottle Sprout Garden

Makes 4–5 servings

Even though this technique appeared in my first book, I felt it important to include it in this second volume as well. Sprouts are full of nutrients and flavor, and they add that fresh crunchiness that I start to miss after a few days in the wilds. Among our favorites are broccoli, adzuki beans, peas, lentils, and alfalfa. You can make a little sprout salad or use them as an addition to wraps, sandwiches, and salads, and as delicious garnish on soups and stews. You'll want to start your sprouts 3 to 4 days before you plan to eat them.

2 tablespoons organic
  sprouting seeds

Potable water

AT HOME

Pack a wide-mouth 32-ounce Nalgene water bottle with a small carabiner attached to the lid strap. Place a few rubber bands and four layers of cheesecloth cut about 2 inches larger than the size of the top of the bottle in a ziplock freezer bag. Pack the sprouting seeds in another ziplock freezer bag and place that in with the rubber bands and cheesecloth.

AT CAMP

One morning about 3 or 4 days before you want to eat the sprouts, place 2 tablespoons of sprouting seeds in your water bottle and add a cup of filtered water to the seeds. Seal the bottle and let the seeds soak for 4 to 6 hours.

Open the bottle and place two layers of cheesecloth over the opening. Secure with a rubber band. Drain the seeds well, and if you are still on the move, attach the bottle to the outside of your pack with the carabiner.

For the next few days all you need to do is rinse the seeds/ sprouts at breakfast and dinner. To rinse just pour in about 1 cup of potable water and gently swirl the sprouts in the bottle. Then drain well. Carry the bottle with the top open and the cheesecloth in place; replace the cloth if it gets dirty. By the third or fourth day, depending on the type of seeds you're growing, you will have crunchy sprouts.

Tips

If you will be going on a short trip, you can start the sprouts at home a day or two before you leave. If you have leftover sprouts, keep watering them and save them for the next day.

Chapter 7

SNACKS

T here are times on the trail or on a paddling trip where stopping for a full lunch just isn't feasible. Other times you just aren't all that hungry. It is those times that grazing on snacks throughout the day can be an effective way to keep you fueled. Sometimes a snack is as simple as a handful of trail mix, nuts, or dried fruit. Other times it is something more elaborate such as a homemade energy bar or savory roasted chickpeas. You can even save leftover baking from the night before to have as a snack the following day. Snacks can range from the sweet to the savory and from store-bought to homemade. No matter what you choose, consider storage carefully.

Snack Storage

Storing snacks in individual serving-size packages is useful for many reasons. First of all, it ensures that you will have enough to last through your trip. Second, it prevents contamination, especially when traveling in a group where you might not know how clean your camp mates' hands really are. It also prevents camp mates from gold mining the GORP (good ol' raisins and peanuts). When you take fresh fruits for your snacks, you can prevent them from bruising by wrapping the fruit in a few paper towels or placing the fruit in a hard-sided container. If you do use a hard-sided container, open it at camp to release some of the humidity. Containers such as the Froot Guard and Banana Guard from **bananaguard.com** are vented and do not need to be opened. Use fresh fruit early in your trip to prevent spoilage and to get rid of a little pack weight.

Chocolate snacks such as bark are best stored in the middle of your pack and used for cool-weather trips. Dark chocolate doesn't melt as easily as other types and is better in hotter weather. Wrap chocolate in waxed or parchment paper so that it is easy to deal with in the event that it softens in the heat.

Maple Sugared Walnuts

Makes 6–8 servings

Often, on our way to a favorite trailhead, we would stop at a little gourmet shop in the outskirts of a close-by town to purchase a package of sugared walnuts. Unfortunately there isn't a little gourmet shop on the way to every trailhead or access point, so I was inspired to create my own version of maple sugared walnuts.

AT HOME

Line a cookie sheet with parchment paper and set aside. Melt the butter or butter substitute over medium heat in a heavy-bottomed skillet. Add the maple syrup and heat, stirring constantly with a wooden spoon, until the mixture starts to bubble, foam, and becomes slightly opaque. You'll feel the syrup tightening up. Reduce the heat to low. Then add the salt, cardamom, and wasabi powder to taste, stirring to combine well. Add the nuts and continue stirring for about 2 minutes to coat evenly. As soon as the mixture coating the nuts seems dry and sugary, remove the pan from the heat and spread the nuts in a single layer on the parchment paper–lined cookie sheet. Use two forks to separate the nuts. Allow to cool for at least an hour before packaging and store in an airtight container until you leave for your trip. Then, transfer the nuts to a ziplock freezer bag and remove as much of the air as possible.

Tips

It is important to use a heavy-bottomed skillet or frying pan for this recipe so that you do not scorch the syrup mixture. You must stir the mixture constantly or it will burn.

Use only Grade A light or medium pure maple syrup for this recipe, as anything else will give poor results.

1 tablespoon butter or vegan butter substitute

⅓ cup pure maple syrup

¼ teaspoon kosher salt

¼ teaspoon ground cardamom

½–¾ teaspoon wasabi powder to taste

2 cups walnuts

Vanilla Sugared Almonds with Dried Berries

2 cups raw whole almonds

1 tablespoon butter or vegan butter substitute

⅓ cup maple syrup

2½ teaspoons pure vanilla extract

¼ teaspoon kosher salt

½ cup dried cranberries

½ cup dried blueberries

Makes 8–10 servings

I love the flavor of vanilla and almonds and it seems that my family does too. When I make this snack, I have to hide it from friends and family or I end up having to make another batch before our trip. It is best to have your ingredients measured and ready to go before you start making the coating.

At Home

Line a cookie sheet with parchment paper and set aside. Lightly toast the almonds in a dry frying pan over medium heat, until fragrant, being careful not to scorch the nuts. Set aside. Melt the butter or butter substitute over medium heat in a heavy-bottomed skillet. Add the maple syrup and heat, stirring constantly with a wooden spoon, until the mixture starts to bubble, foam, and becomes slightly opaque. Add the vanilla extract and stir to combine. You'll feel the syrup tightening up. Reduce the heat to low. Add the nuts and continue stirring for about 2 minutes to coat evenly. As soon as the mixture coating the nuts seems dry and sugary, remove the pan from the heat and spread the nuts in a single layer on the parchment paper–lined cookie sheet. Sprinkle with kosher salt and then use two forks to separate the nuts. Allow to cool for at least an hour before packaging and store in an airtight container until you leave for your trip. Then, transfer the nuts to a ziplock freezer bag, add the berries, and remove as much of the air as possible.

Tips

It is important to use a heavy-bottomed skillet or frying pan for this recipe so that you do not scorch the syrup mixture. You must stir the mixture constantly or it will burn.

Use only Grade A light or medium pure maple syrup for this recipe, as anything else will give poor results.

Maple Balsamic Walnuts with Apples and Dates

Makes 8–10 servings

Maple and balsamic make a great pair and is often a combination I use for salad dressings. The addition of red chili flakes adds just a touch of heat and complements the sweetness of the maple sugar and the fruit.

AT HOME

Line a cookie sheet with parchment paper and set aside. Heat the olive oil and balsamic vinegar over medium heat in a heavy-bottomed skillet until the mixture thickens and reduces. Add the maple syrup and heat, stirring constantly with a wooden spoon, until the mixture starts to bubble, foam, and becomes slightly opaque. You'll feel the syrup tightening up. Reduce the heat to low. Then add the crushed red chili peppers and salt, stirring to combine well. Add the nuts and continue stirring for about 2 minutes to coat evenly. As soon as the mixture coating the nuts seems dry and sugary, remove the pan from the heat and spread the nuts in a single layer on the parchment paper–lined cookie sheet. Use two forks to separate the nuts. Allow to cool for at least an hour before packaging and store in an airtight container until you leave for your trip. Then, transfer the nuts to a ziplock freezer bag, add the chopped apples and dates, and remove as much of the air as possible.

Tips

It is important to use a heavy-bottomed skillet or frying pan for this recipe so that you do not scorch the syrup mixture. You must stir the mixture constantly or it will burn.

Use only Grade A light or medium pure maple syrup for this recipe, as anything else will give poor results.

1 tablespoon olive oil

2 tablespoons balsamic vinegar

⅓ cup pure maple syrup

¼–½ teaspoon crushed red chili peppers

¼ teaspoon kosher salt

2 cups walnuts

⅓ cup dried apples, chopped

⅓ cup Medjool or honey dates, chopped

Spiced Date, Cherry, Almond, and Carob Bars

Makes 8–10 bars

1 cup dates such as Medjool or honey dates

½ cup dried cherries

⅛ cup carob or cocoa powder

⅛ teaspoon cinnamon

Tiny pinch of cayenne pepper to taste

¾ cup whole salted almonds

This version of my date bars was inspired by the Mayan Hot Chocolate in my first book, A Fork in the Trail. *I love the little bit of background spice from the cayenne. Just make sure you use it sparingly or your camp mates may be in for a surprise!*

At Home

Pulse the dates in a food processor with ¼ cup of the dried cherries, carob powder, and spices until the mixture is ground to a thick paste. Toast the almonds, if desired, in a dry nonstick frying pan over medium heat just until they start to become fragrant. Be careful that you do not burn them. Add to the dates and pulse to chop the nuts. Remove the container from the food processor and take out the blade. Stir in the remainder of the dried cherries. Line a square baking pan with plastic wrap and press the mixture firmly into the pan. Refrigerate for an hour and then turn out onto a cutting board. Remove the wrap and cut into 8 to 10 bars. Wrap each bar in plastic wrap and reshape by pressing each side on a flat surface if desired.

Tips

Wipe your knife with a hot water–soaked paper towel between cuts to prevent it from sticking. You can reuse the piece of wrap you lined the pan with to wrap your bars.

Date, Pecan, Blueberry, and Ginger Bars

Makes 8–10 bars

I was a young girl taking a 4-H outdoor living course the first time I made date bars. As an adult, I wanted to add a little something to the recipe and I've always loved candied ginger. It gives these a nice bite that awakens the taste buds.

At Home

Pulse the dates in a food processor until ground to a thick paste. Toast the pecans, if desired, in a dry nonstick frying pan over medium heat just until they start to become fragrant. Be careful that you do not burn them. Add to the dates and pulse to chop the nuts. Remove the container from the food processor and take out the blade. Stir in the dried blueberries and candied ginger. Line a square baking pan with plastic wrap and press the mixture firmly into the pan. Refrigerate for an hour and then turn out onto a cutting board. Remove the wrap and cut into 8 to 10 bars. Wrap each bar in plastic wrap and reshape by pressing each side on a flat surface if desired.

Tips

Wipe your knife with a hot water–soaked paper towel between cuts to prevent it from sticking. You can reuse the piece of wrap you lined the pan with to wrap your bars.

1 cup dates such as Medjool or honey dates

¾ cup pecans

¼ cup dried blueberries

⅛ cup candied ginger, chopped

Tropical Kiwi Trail Cookies

1 cup dates such as Medjool or honey dates

½ cup almonds

½ cup cashews

2 kiwi fruit, peeled and quartered

3 tablespoons fresh lime juice

¼ teaspoon lime zest

½ cup shredded coconut

**Dehydration Time: 5–8 hours
Makes about 18–20 cookies**

Kiwi is a favorite around here. I first made these because we were going day hiking with a friend who is a raw foodie and I volunteered to make the snacks. I'm still torn as to whether these should be considered a snack or dessert.

AT HOME

Pulse the dates in a food processor until ground to a thick paste. Toast the almonds, if desired, in a dry nonstick frying pan over medium heat just until they start to become fragrant. Be careful that you do not burn them. Add the almonds and cashews to the dates and pulse to chop the nuts. Add the kiwi fruit, lime juice, and lime zest, and then pulse again until well combined. Remove the container from the food processor and take out the blade. Toast the coconut, if desired, in a dry frying pan until golden and then stir into the date and kiwi mixture.

Line your food dehydrator with fruit leather trays, plastic wrap, or parchment paper. Drop the fruit cookie mixture by heaping tablespoons and press flat until about ¼-inch thick. If your unit has a temperature control, set it for 104°F and dry for 5 to 8 hours or until the cookies are dry and firmed up. Wrap the cookies in waxed paper and store in ziplock bags. These cookies will keep in the freezer for up to 3 months.

Almond, Carob, Flax Balls

Makes 4 balls

This simple recipe can be put together on the trail or you can make it ahead of time. It makes a great treat for kids on the trail.

At Home

Mix the flax meal and carob powder together and pour into a ziplock freezer bag. Put the almond butter and maple syrup into separate small leakproof containers or add to the other almond butter and maple syrup you will take on your trip.

At Camp

Mix 2 tablespoons of almond butter, 1 teaspoon of maple syrup, and 1 tablespoon of water with the ingredients in the freezer bag. Knead to combine. Make into 4 balls.

Tips

Cashew butter can be substituted for the almond butter, and ground pepitas or popped amaranth for the flax meal.

You can also make this ahead of time. Just follow the "At Camp" instructions to make it at home and roll it into a log and wrap in waxed paper. Then break pieces off when you plan to eat it and roll them into a ball.

2 tablespoons flax meal

1 tablespoon carob powder

2 tablespoons almond butter

1 teaspoon maple syrup

1 tablespoon water

Black Cherry Apple Leather

1 cup fresh ripe sweet black cherries, pitted

½ cup unsweetened applesauce

Dehydration Time: 6–15 hours
Makes 4 servings

Not only is the Niagara Escarpment in Ontario, Canada, beautiful for day hikes, but it is also a prime area for growing fruit. When cherries are in season, I often go a little overboard, so to keep the fruit from going bad, I break out the dehydrator. I often dry a tray of pitted and halved black cherries at the same time. This sweet fruit leather has a bold flavor.

At Home

Purée the pitted cherries until they are the consistency of applesauce. If they are overripe and very juicy, you can drain off a little of the liquid. Stir in the applesauce. Spread the purée about ¼-inch thick on lined dehydrator trays.

Let the fruit dry for 6 to 15 hours (depending on the moisture content and ripeness of the fruit) until it is pliable like leather. Cut it into pieces, wrap it in plastic wrap, and refrigerate it until your trip. This snack will keep for up to 6 months if refrigerated and for 6 to 8 weeks without refrigeration.

Tip

For a real calorie boost, roll out marzipan until it is ⅛-inch thick and lay a piece on top of the dried cherry leather. Roll the leather up and then slice into pinwheels using a very sharp knife. Wrap each pinwheel separately in plastic wrap or waxed paper.

Carrot Muffin Leather

Dehydration Time: 6–15 hours
Makes 4 servings

This whole carrot leather idea of mine started as a way to sneak some extra vegetables into my son's school lunches. When my son, Tobias, first tried the vegetable leather, he exclaimed, "This tastes like carrot muffins, Mom!"

AT HOME

Use a food processor or blender to purée the carrots. Mix all of the ingredients together except the walnuts and coconut. Spread the purée about ¼-inch thick on lined dehydrator trays. Sprinkle sparingly with finely chopped walnuts and coconut, if desired. Let the fruit dry for 6 to 15 hours (depending on the moisture content) until it is pliable like leather. Cut it into pieces, wrap it in plastic wrap, and store it in the refrigerator until your trip. This snack will keep for up to 6 months if refrigerated and for 6 to 8 weeks without refrigeration.

Tips

Steam the carrots rather than boiling them in order to retain nutrition. You can also use leftover carrots for this.

If you don't have orange extract, then substitute with ½ teaspoon pure vanilla extract.

2½ cups carrots, cooked

½ cup unsweetened applesauce

2 tablespoons dark brown sugar

½–¾ teaspoon cinnamon

¼ teaspoon nutmeg

⅛ teaspoon pure orange extract

1½ tablespoons walnuts, finely chopped (optional)

1 tablespoon coconut (optional)

Poached Vanilla Pear Leather

1 cup water

2 cups white wine

1 vanilla bean, split lengthwise and scraped,
reserving the seeds
and pod

¾ cup granulated sugar

1 tablespoon lemon zest

5 ripe pears (Anjou, Bosc, or
Bartlett), peeled, cut in
half, and seeds removed

Dehydration Time: 6–15 hours
Makes 4 servings

*I love serving poached pears for dessert. One day I was look-
ing for some inspiration for a new fruit leather recipe when I
remembered that some leftover poached pears from a dinner
party we hosted the evening before were still in the fridge. I
thought I'd give it a try, and the results were delicious. There
is no need to pretreat the pears as you normally would for
leather, as the cooking does that for you.*

At Home

Combine the water, wine, vanilla bean pod and seeds, sugar,
and lemon zest in a medium saucepan. Bring the mixture to
a boil and stir until the sugar is dissolved. Add the pears and
poach over medium-low heat until the pears are fork-tender
but not starting to fall apart, about 10 minutes. Remove the
pears and let them cool.

Purée the cooked pears until they are the consistency of
applesauce. Spread the purée about ¼-inch thick on lined
dehydrator trays.

Let the fruit dry for 6 to 15 hours (depending on the moisture content and ripeness of the fruit) until it is pliable like
leather. Cut it into pieces, wrap it in plastic wrap, and refrigerate it until your trip. This snack will keep for up to 6 months if
refrigerated and for 6 to 8 weeks without refrigeration.

Tip

Save the liquid from the pears and reduce it to make syrup to
use on pancakes, crepes, or fruit salad.

Cinnamon Apple Crisps

Dehydration Time: 8–10 hours
Makes 1 bag

This recipe always reminds me of fall hikes in apple country and the view of rolling farmland from the trail on the top of the escarpment. The smell of apples, sprinkled with cinnamon, scents the house with the comforting smells of fall. I like to use Royal Gala or Granny Smith apples for this purpose.

AT HOME

Mix the water and lemon juice together in a large bowl. Peel the apples if desired. Slice the apples into rings that are ³⁄₁₆- to ¼-inch thick. Put the slices in the bowl with the lemon juice and water mixture. Separate the apple slices to ensure both sides get treated with the liquid. Drain the apples and remove any excess moisture with a paper towel or clean tea towel. Place on lined dehydrator trays and sprinkle lightly with cinnamon. Dry the apples at 135°F, for 8 to 10 hours, until they are crispy, like a potato chip. Let cool and pack in a sturdy airtight container. These will keep for up to 6 months in a cool dry place before flavor loss occurs.

1½ cups water

3 tablespoons lemon juice

6 apples, cored

1 teaspoon cinnamon

Citrus Seed Balls with Figs and Agave

Makes 10 balls

1 cup sunflower seeds

1 cup dried Turkish or Calimyrna figs

½ teaspoon each of lemon or lime and orange zest

A pinch of salt

3 tablespoons agave nectar

¼ cup pecans, very finely chopped (optional)

⅓ cup carob or cocoa powder, finely ground nuts, or coconut milk powder

The combination of figs and citrus zest make this a yummy energy source for a long day of backpacking or paddling.

At Home

Using a food processor, grind the sunflower seeds for about 5 minutes until they are very fine and stick to the outside of the container. Add the figs, citrus zest, and salt and pulse until well combined. Then add 1 tablespoon of the agave nectar and process again. Repeat with the second and third tablespoons of agave nectar, adding 1 tablespoon at a time until the mixture is just sticky enough to hold its shape. Mix in the pecans, if using. Form into 10 balls and roll each ball in carob, cocoa, finely ground nuts, or coconut milk powder.

Garam Masala Roasted Chickpeas

Makes 1½ cups

My husband, Bryan, always complained about there not being enough savory snacks when it comes to munchables for our wilderness camping trips. He loves Indian food, so I made this Indian-inspired chickpea snack for him. He was a happy camper.

At Home

Preheat the oven to 425°F and line a baking sheet with parchment paper or foil. Set aside. Lay the chickpeas in a single layer on paper towels and use another paper towel to dry them. As you are drying them you will notice that some will lose their skins. Pick out and discard the skins and then put the chickpeas on the lined cookie sheet. Mix the olive oil, garam masala, ginger, and coriander together in a small bowl. Pour over the chickpeas and stir to coat evenly. Bake for 35 to 50 minutes, stirring every 10 minutes. The chickpeas will be done when they are crispy and dried through. Sprinkle with salt the moment the mixture is removed from the oven. Allow to cool completely before packaging in an airtight container.

2 cups canned chickpeas, rinsed and drained

2 teaspoons olive oil

1 teaspoon garam masala

A pinch of ground ginger

A pinch of ground coriander seed

½ teaspoon kosher salt

Lime and Black Pepper Roasted Chickpeas

2 cups canned chickpeas, rinsed and drained

2 teaspoons olive oil

¼–½ teaspoon finely ground black pepper

1½ tablespoons fresh lime juice

1 teaspoon fresh cilantro, finely chopped

½ teaspoon kosher salt

Makes 1½ cups

This crunchy chickpea snack has a nice hint of lime combined with the bite of black pepper. I like to use the full amount of black pepper but you can adjust to suit your tastes. You can switch up the flavor by using an herb other than cilantro. Now, if only I could keep my husband from eating these right off the baking sheet.

At Home

Preheat the oven to 425°F and line a baking sheet with parchment paper or foil. Set aside. Lay the chickpeas in a single layer on paper towels and use another paper towel to dry them. As you are drying them you will notice that some will lose their skins. Pick out and discard the skins and then put the chickpeas on the lined cookie sheet. Mix the olive oil, black pepper, lime juice, and cilantro together in a small bowl. Pour over the chickpeas and stir to coat evenly. Bake for 35 to 50 minutes, stirring every 10 minutes. The chickpeas will be done when they are crispy and dried through. Sprinkle with salt the moment the mixture is removed from the oven. Allow to cool completely before packaging in an airtight container.

Sun-dried Tomato Flax Crackers

Dehydration Time: 18–20 hours
Makes 30 crackers

I took these to an annual gathering of backpackers and paddlers that I host up north. Everyone must have liked them, because in the time it took for me to set up my tent, they had all been devoured. The flavor of these crackers is reminiscent of pizza.

AT HOME

Place the sun-dried tomatoes in a bowl. Take ½ cup water and pour just enough of it over the tomatoes to cover them. Let soak for an hour or more. Place the flaxseed in a large bowl. Cover the seeds with enough water to immerse them completely. Let soak for 2 or 3 hours, stirring occasionally and adding as little water as needed to prevent them from clumping. The seeds will release a gel-like substance, making the mixture thick and gooey.

Pulse the tomatoes, garlic, crushed red chilies, basil, and olive oil together in a blender or food processor until you have a thick paste that is slightly coarse. Pour the tomato mixture into a large bowl and stir in the flaxseed, ground sunflower seeds, kosher salt, and pepper.

Spread the mixture on lined dehydrator trays. Dry at 105°F for 4 hours then cut into cracker-size pieces. Dry for another 6 hours, then flip the crackers over and dry for an additional 8 to 10 hours or until they are fully dried and crisp. Store the crackers in an airtight container.

Tip

Leftover crackers are great broken up as a garnish for soup or salad.

½ cup sun-dried tomatoes, chopped

1½–2 cups water

½ cup flaxseed

2 cloves garlic, minced

⅛ teaspoon crushed red chili pepper

¾ teaspoon dried basil

1 tablespoon olive oil

¼ cup ground sunflower seeds

1 teaspoon kosher salt

½ teaspoon fresh black pepper

Roasted Pumpkin and Squash Seeds

1¾ cups fresh pumpkin or squash seeds

1 tablespoon olive oil

¼ teaspoon garlic powder

⅛–¼ teaspoon cayenne pepper

¼ teaspoon smoked paprika

¼ teaspoon dried onion flakes

¼ teaspoon allspice

¼ teaspoon freshly ground black pepper

¼ teaspoon kosher salt

Makes 1¾ cups

When I was little, I used to love getting a pumpkin at Halloween just so I could have roasted pumpkin seeds to share with my friends. Now that I am a grown-up, every time I cook a squash or make a jack-o'-lantern with my kids, I save the seeds to make this tasty treat for the trail. The seeds can be eaten on their own, used as an ingredient in GORP, or used as a garnish for savory muffins, breads, soups, and salads.

At Home

Preheat the oven to 350°F. Line a baking sheet with parchment paper and set aside. Remove all pulp from the seeds, rinse them well, and pat dry with a clean tea towel or paper towels. Combine the oil and spices in a bowl large enough to accommodate the pumpkin seeds. Add the seeds and stir well so that all the seeds are evenly coated. Spread the pumpkin seeds on the baking sheet in a single layer, making sure that the seeds do not overlap each other. Roast for 20 minutes, then stir the seeds and roast until they become crispy. The length of time will depend on the type and size of seeds that you have used. When the seeds are toasted, remove them from the oven and let cool before packaging them in a ziplock freezer bag. The seeds will keep for 1 to 2 weeks.

Veggie Chips

Dehydration Time: 6 hours and up
Quantities vary

For my first backpacking trip I visited a local bulk foods store to purchase ingredients for GORP. While wandering the aisles, I discovered veggie chips. Of course, they were fried and over-salted for my tastes, plus they didn't really taste like vegetables, so I started making my own with the food dehydrator. I use a variety of vegetables, including potatoes, sweet potatoes, jicama, radishes, beets, parsnips, carrots, zucchini, kale, and green beans.

3 cups vegetables, sliced paper thin (if using green beans, leave them whole)

1 tablespoon olive or vegetable oil

Kosher salt to taste

Your choice of seasonings to taste

AT HOME

Fill a large bowl with ice water. Put a pot of water on to boil and put the vegetable slices into a fine strainer or sieve. When the water begins to boil, dunk the sieve into the water for 60 seconds and then put the strainer full of vegetables into the ice water for 1 minute to stop any cooking. Drain well and pat dry with paper towels.

Toss the vegetables in the oil and then arrange them about ½ inch apart on lined dehydrator trays. Sprinkle with salt and desired seasonings. Dry at 125°F to 135°F for 6 to 12 hours. Some vegetables may take even longer, up to 24 hours. Flip the vegetables over a few times during the drying process. When the chips are crisp, let cool and pack in a sturdy airtight container. These will keep for up to 3 months in a cool dry place before flavor loss occurs.

Here are some seasoning ideas:

* rosemary, lemon juice, lemon zest, and garlic powder

* black pepper, lime juice, lime zest, and coarse salt

* chili powder and cumin

* garam masala

* balsamic vinegar and coarse sea salt

* herbes de Provence

* nutritional yeast (this gives a cheesy flavor) and black pepper

* nutritional yeast and smoked paprika

* *za'atar* spice blend

Grilled Cinnamon Pineapple

Fresh pineapple, peeled, cored, and cut into rings or canned pineapple rings packed in juice, drained

Cinnamon to taste

Dehydration Time: 10–15 hours
Quantities vary

I love grilling fruit because the natural sugars caramelize slightly, which enhances the flavor. Pineapple works wonderfully for this dried-fruit snack, as do peaches or nectarines. You can use as little or as much fruit as you want for this recipe as there really aren't any measurements.

AT HOME

Preheat the grill to 350°F. Meanwhile, prepare the fruit and sprinkle, to taste, with cinnamon. Grill the fruit until it softens and you have grill marks. Let cool.

Dry on lined dehydrator trays for 10 to 15 hours or until leathery but dry all the way through. Place in a ziplock freezer bag and store the bag in the refrigerator until your trip. This snack will keep for up to 6 months if refrigerated and for 6 to 8 weeks without refrigeration.

Roasted Nut and Mango Energy Bars

Makes 10 bars

This is a sweet and easy to make energy bar recipe that is based on a recipe from my first book, A Fork in the Trail. *I've modified the original, which used honey, to suit the vegan lifestyle. If you have celiac disease, look for a gluten-free cereal with a heavy flake.*

AT HOME

Toast the almonds and peanuts in a dry frying pan over medium heat until fragrant. Set aside to cool. Heat the agave nectar and brown sugar in a large pot and let simmer for 1 minute. (Boiling too long will make the bars brittle.) Remove the pan from the heat and add the peanut or almond butter. Stir until the peanut or almond butter is well incorporated. Add the crushed cereal, roasted nuts, mango, and carob chips. Combine well.

Coat the bottom and sides of an 8-inch square pan with vegetable oil. Scoop the mixture into the pan and pack down evenly. Freeze for 30 minutes. Transfer the pan contents to a cutting board. Allow to return to room temperature and then cut into 10 bars. Wrap the bars in waxed paper and store in ziplock bags. The bars will keep in the freezer for up to 3 months.

Tips

The agave nectar can be replaced with honey or maple syrup. If you do use maple syrup, be careful not to cook it too much or the bars will be crumbly.

½ cup raw almonds and peanuts, coarsely chopped

⅓ cup agave nectar

¼ cup brown sugar

¼ cup peanut butter or almond butter

2 cups cereal made of strong flakes, crushed

¼ cup dried mango, finely chopped

¼ cup carob chips

Cherry and Almond Energy Bars

⅓ cup agave nectar

¼ cup brown sugar

¼ cup almond butter

2 cups cereal made of strong flakes, crushed

½ cup dried cherries

½ cup slivered almonds

Makes 10 bars

There is something I find very comforting about the flavor of cherries and almonds together. This recipe was a happy accident that happened when I thought I was using cranberries. These bars pair well with a hot cup of chocolate in the evening. If you have celiac disease, look for a gluten-free cereal with a heavy flake.

AT HOME

Heat the agave nectar and brown sugar in a large pot and let simmer for 1 minute. (Boiling too long will make the bars brittle or sugary.) Remove the pan from the heat and add the almond butter. Stir until the almond butter is well incorporated. Add the crushed cereal, dried cherries, and slivered almonds. Combine well.

Coat the bottom and sides of an 8-inch square pan with vegetable oil. Scoop the mixture into the pan and pack down evenly. Freeze for 30 minutes. Transfer the pan contents to a cutting board. Allow to return to room temperature and then cut into 10 bars. Wrap the bars in waxed paper and store in ziplock bags. The bars will keep in the freezer for up to 3 months.

Tips

The agave nectar can be replaced with honey or maple syrup. If you do use maple syrup, be careful not to cook it too much or the bars will be crumbly.

Balsamic and Basil Bagel Crisps

Makes 4–6 servings

Back when I was a young student in university, money was pretty tight. At holiday time I would make baskets of home-made goodies for my family and close friends. I'd stay up late on Christmas Eve and the house would be filled with the wonderful aromas as I was packaging these flavorful bagel crisps. The intensity of the balsamic comes out as these bake.

AT HOME

Preheat the oven to 350°F and place the rack in the middle. Slice the bagels ⅛-inch thick so that you have thin rounds the shape of large coins. You can also cut them horizontally into large rings; however, they pack better if cut crosswise.

Mix the olive oil, balsamic vinegar, basil, thyme, and black pepper together in a small bowl or ramekin. Let sit for 10 minutes so that the flavors can infuse into the oil. Brush one side of each bagel slice with the oil mixture and place in a single layer, seasoned side up, on a nonstick baking sheet. Be sure to stir the mixture frequently between brushings so that the spices don't settle to the bottom. Sprinkle with kosher salt. Bake the slices for 10 to 15 minutes or until crispy. Let cool completely before storing the bagel crisps in an airtight container for up to a week.

2 large bagels

3 tablespoons olive oil

1 ½ tablespoons balsamic vinegar

½ teaspoon dried basil

¼ teaspoon dried thyme, crumbled

¼ teaspoon freshly ground black pepper

Kosher salt to taste

Mole Spiced Bagel Crisps

Makes 4–6 servings

2 large bagels

4 tablespoons olive oil

½–¾ teaspoon chili powder

½ teaspoon cocoa or carob powder

Very tiny pinch of cayenne pepper

A pinch of cinnamon

A pinch of ground coriander

Kosher salt to taste

This bagel crisp recipe has a flavor reminiscent of Mexican mole sauce with a bit of background heat. They taste good with salsa or salsa verde, as a side for Black Bean, Corn, and Sweet Potato Soup or chili, or on their own as a snack. The flavors intensify as the bagels crisp up in the oven, so go easy on the cayenne unless you like it really spicy.

At Home

Preheat the oven to 350°F and place the rack in the middle. Slice the bagels ⅛-inch thick so that you have thin rounds the shape of large coins. You can also cut them horizontally into large rings; however, they pack better if cut crosswise.

Mix the olive oil, chili powder, cocoa powder, cayenne, cinnamon, and ground coriander together in a small bowl or ramekin. Let sit for 10 minutes so that the flavors can infuse into the oil. Brush one side of each bagel slice with the oil mixture and place in a single layer, seasoned side up, on a nonstick baking sheet. Be sure to stir the mixture frequently between brushings so that the spices don't settle to the bottom. Sprinkle with kosher salt. Bake the slices for 10 to 15 minutes or until crispy. Let cool completely before storing the bagel crisps in an airtight container for up to a week.

Bagel Crisps with Herbes de Provence

Makes 4–6 servings

Herbes de Provence is a classic French herb mixture that usually contains rosemary, thyme, tarragon, basil, savory, cracked fennel, lavender, and marjoram. I've always made my own blend using dried lavender and other herbs from my kitchen garden. Now, one can find it at most larger grocery chains with a good spice and herb selection or from online spice merchants.

2 large bagels

3 tablespoons olive oil

1½ teaspoons herbes de Provence

Kosher salt to taste

At Home

Preheat the oven to 350°F and place the rack in the middle. Slice the bagels ⅛-inch thick so that you have thin rounds the shape of large coins. You can also cut them horizontally into large rings; however, they pack better if cut crosswise.

Mix the olive oil and herbes de Provence together in a small bowl or ramekin. Let sit for 10 minutes so that the flavors can infuse into the oil. Brush one side of each bagel slice with the oil mixture and place in a single layer, seasoned side up, on a nonstick baking sheet. Be sure to stir the mixture frequently between brushings so that the spices don't settle to the bottom. Sprinkle with kosher salt. Bake the slices for 10 to 15 minutes or until crispy. Let cool completely before storing the bagel crisps in an airtight container for up to a week.

Tip

If you don't have herbes de Provence or you want to switch things up a bit, you can use any spice blend that you have on hand. Just stick to the 1½ teaspoon quantity for herbs and spice.

Dark Chocolate Bark with Blueberries and Candied Lemon

⅓ cup whole almonds or cashews, unsalted

1 cup dark chocolate, broken into pieces

⅙ cup dried blueberries

⅙ cup candied lemon, finely chopped (see pages 7–8)

Makes 3–4 servings

A few years ago a fellow backpacker and foodie wrote me to see if I could find a North American source for a lemon chocolate bar. The bar was from Ghana, and I was never able to source the product for him. His request became the inspiration for this unique bark recipe. Be sure to use a good-quality dark chocolate such as Côte d'Or or Lindt.

AT HOME

Toast the nuts, if desired, in a dry frying pan over medium heat until fragrant. Set aside. Heat water in double boiler, making sure it doesn't touch the top section. If you don't have a double boiler, fill a pot about half of the way with water and place a heatproof glass or metal bowl on top. The bowl should fit snugly. Make sure that the water does not touch the bottom of the bowl. Bring the water to a boil and reduce the heat to medium-low to keep the water simmering.

Put the chocolate in the top section or bowl and stir until it has melted. Shut the heat off and add the blueberries, candied lemon, and nuts, stirring to coat. Spread the mixture on a cookie sheet lined with waxed paper and let set. When it has hardened, break it into large pieces and pack them in a ziplock freezer bag.

Tip

Substitute the blueberries with candied ginger to give it a little bite.

Chocolate-covered Wasabi Peas with Pomegranate

**Dehydration Time: 10–15 hours
Makes 3–4 servings**

This all started in my quest to make homemade wasabi peas. To say that experiment was disastrous is an understatement. I finally was successful but the outcome just wasn't worth the effort. It is a bit of an unusual combination but one that I find addictive. It's really no surprise, as I adore dark chocolate, and the complexity of flavor works well with the spiciness of the wasabi. The dehydrated pomegranate adds a hint of fruitiness.

⅙ cup wasabi peas

1 cup dark chocolate, broken into pieces

⅙ cup dried pomegranate gems

AT HOME

Put the wasabi peas in a ziplock bag. Whack the bag a few times with a rolling pin or the bottom of a pot in order to break up the wasabi peas a little. Set aside. Heat water in a double boiler, making sure it doesn't touch the top section. If you don't have a double boiler, fill a pot about half of the way with water and place a heatproof glass or metal bowl on top. The bowl should fit snugly. Make sure the water does not touch the bottom of the bowl. Bring the water to a boil and reduce the heat to medium-low to keep the water simmering.

Put the chocolate in the top section or bowl and stir until it has melted. Shut the heat off and add the wasabi peas and pomegranate, stirring to coat. Spread the mixture on a cookie sheet lined with waxed paper and let set. When it has hardened, break it into large pieces and pack them in a ziplock freezer bag.

To Dry Pomegranate

Cut a fresh ripe pomegranate in half. Remove the seeds while keeping the pomegranate under water in a large bowl. This helps in a few ways. First of all it keeps the juice from splattering and second it keeps the pith and seeds separate. The seeds will sink and the pith will float to the top.

Spread the pomegranate gems in a single layer on a lined dehydrator tray. Dehydrate at 135°F for 10 to 15 hours. Depending on the size of the gems, it may even take a little longer.

Tip

If you are ovo-lacto vegetarian, consider melting half dark and half white chocolate and swirling them together to make this bark.

Walnut and Anise Stuffed Figs

Makes 12

½ teaspoon aniseed or fennel seed

12 Turkish or Calimyrna figs

12 walnut halves

This is a quick and easy to make snack that is great for day hikes and for a handy little snack on longer trips. You could precut the figs and let the children help. If you don't care for the flavor of anise or fennel, you could substitute with a little orange zest or a little grating of nutmeg. I used Turkish or Calimyrna figs for this because they aren't quite as sweet as black Mission figs.

At Home

Crush the aniseed or fennel seed in a mortar and pestle. Cut a slit in the fig large enough to accommodate a walnut half. Put a very tiny pinch of the crushed aniseed in the slit and then push in the walnut. Squeeze to close and wrap in a small piece of plastic wrap or waxed paper. Put the wrapped, stuffed figs in a ziplock freezer bag.

Tips

If you don't have a mortar and pestle, you can use the heel or bottom of a heavy pot to crush the seeds. Place the seeds on a cutting board and then use pressure on the pot to crack the seeds. A quick pulse in a coffee grinder reserved for spices works well too—just be careful not to pulverize them.

These will keep for weeks in your pack, but you should check them periodically to ensure that they aren't drying out.

Alegria Trail Candy

Makes 12 pieces

Vegetable oil for popping
amaranth

½ cup popped amaranth
(about ¼ cup before
popping)

⅓ cup pure maple syrup

⅙ cup pepitas, flaxseed, or
sunflower seeds

*This Mexican candy made from popped amaranth is said
to date back to the time of the Aztecs. The great thing about
amaranth is that it is a good source of protein and has other
important nutrients. My version of Alegria veers from the
traditional because I used maple syrup and added pepitas.
Don't worry too much if every single grain of amaranth fully
pops as the toasted grains add a wonderful bit of crunch.*

AT HOME

Line a plate with waxed paper. Heat 1 tablespoon of oil in a
wok or deep skillet that has a lid over medium-high to high
heat. Add 1 tablespoon of amaranth seeds and cook, moving
constantly so they don't scorch, until they start to pop and
turn white. This happens very fast; about 15 to 20 seconds.
Remove them from the pan immediately and set aside to
cool. Repeat until you have ½ cup. Heat the maple syrup over
medium-high heat, stirring constantly, for 5 minutes or until it
darkens a shade and starts to thicken. If you are using a candy
thermometer, look for a temperature of 244°F. Stir in the
popped amaranth and pepitas. Immediately spread the mixture on the waxed paper–covered plate with a wooden spoon
that has been lightly oiled or with a silicone spatula. Press the
mixture down until it's about ¼- to ½-inch thick. Let cool for
10 to 15 minutes and cut into 12 pieces. Wrap individually in
waxed paper and store in a ziplock freezer bag.

Tofu Jerky

Dehydration Time: 8–10 hours
Makes 4 servings

Pressing some of the moisture out of the tofu before marinating turns it into a bit of a sponge, allowing more of the flavor to be absorbed.

At Home

Press the tofu in a tofu press or by placing the tofu on a plate and putting a cutting board on top of it. Put something heavy like a pot on top of the cutting board. Let press for 30 minutes. Slice the tofu into pieces about ¼-inch thick. Mix the tamari or soy sauce with the lime juice, lime zest, minced onion, garlic, black pepper, plum sauce, and crushed red chilies. Dip each piece in the marinade to ensure that the tofu is well coated and leave all the tofu in the marinade overnight or for 12 to 24 hours. Place the marinated tofu on lined dehydrator trays. Dehydrate for 8 to 10 hours or until the tofu is dry and chewy but still pliable. Place the tofu in a ziplock freezer bag.

Tip

If you are gluten intolerant, be sure to read the label when buying tamari sauce. True tamari sauce is gluten free, but some less expensive varieties contain gluten.

1 pound of extra firm or firm tofu

½ cup tamari or soy sauce

1 tablespoon lime juice

1 teaspoon lime zest

2 tablespoons red onion, minced

1 clove garlic, minced

1 tablespoon fresh fine ground black pepper

1 tablespoon plum sauce or maple syrup

½–1 teaspoon crushed red chilies to taste

Chapter 8
DINNERS

When you've been backpacking or paddling for an entire day, you are apt to be pretty hungry by the end of it. Some wilderness travelers I've spoken with say that their appetite is diminished the first night or two out but then comes back, full force. I find that mine is also reduced when it is very hot out; I tend to graze more on those days, often having a lunch for dinner. My husband and I opt for the teamwork approach when it comes to arriving in camp and making dinner. Often, especially if the weather is bad or we get to camp late in the day, he'll set up the shelter and I'll get dinner rehydrating. Sometimes, if the weather is particularly nasty, I'll look at my menu and switch to an easier dinner if I had planned something a little more elaborate. I usually keep a written copy of my meal plan in my map case or the top of my pack so that I can keep track of the food inventory. This negates having to search through our packs to see what we have left.

It is important to get all of the food-related activities over and done with, and your pack hung, before dark if at all possible. First of all, cleanup is much easier to expedite with some daylight, and second, little critters such as mice and raccoons can be bothersome once the sun sets. Plus, it's really quite cumbersome to try and hang your food in the dark. If you are in an area that requires it, you must use an approved bear canister.

If you are making a soup, ragout, stew, or chili at home, drying the leftovers can be a great way to make meals for the trail. You'll just need to make sure that the vegetables are chopped small and uniformly to aid with drying. Consider doubling the dinner recipes from this book, having some for dinner at home, then drying the rest. This saves time by not having to cook twice. Hot spices and peppers will lose a bit of their heat during the dehydration process, so you may want to pack a little extra of the spice in your dish to use at camp. Nutritional yeast is great to pack as an alternative to cheese. It imparts a cheesy-like flavor when sprinkled on pasta dishes and soups.

Vegetables and Side Dishes

Vegetables are very simple to dehydrate for reheating as a side in the backcountry. Frozen or canned vegetables that have been drained can be dried without blanching. Just place them on the screens or fruit roll trays of your dehydrator. Don't use canned peas unless you like mush. Frozen peas and canned or frozen corn can dehydrate beautifully, but there is a bit of a trick to rehydrating them. Rehydrate them in a container such as a wide-mouth Nalgene water bottle. Add boiling water, seal the container, and place it in a cozy. The steam seems to create a little pressure in the container, and the vegetables will take on the water. Be patient, as this can take anywhere from a half hour to 45 minutes. Sometimes, if we are having corn or peas as part of a dinner meal, I will start the rehydration at lunch, but only if we are having a cooked lunch and I have the stove out anyway. Alternatively, you can purchase freeze-dried versions of these vegetables from places such as **justtomatoes.com.** I still prefer to dry my own because of the convenience and cost savings. Squash, pumpkin, and turnips are best when cooked thoroughly and mashed before drying. You can make your own potato and sweet potato flakes by drying mashed versions of these and running them through a spice or coffee grinder after drying. Fresh vegetables such as corn, green or yellow beans, asparagus, carrots, parsnips, broccoli, cauliflower, or Brussels sprouts need to be blanched in boiling water for a few minutes before dehydrating. Refer to your dehydrator user manual for more information on times. The more delicate produce such as spinach, mushrooms, peppers, and tomatoes do not need to be blanched first. I wouldn't recommend taking fresh mushrooms, as they go off pretty quickly. If you don't want to dry your own, you can find all sorts of varieties, already dried, in most large supermarkets or Asian markets. Don't be alarmed if they seem a bit pricey—a little goes a long way. Shredded vegetables such as carrots, fennel, and cabbage do not need to be blanched and can go straight on the dehydrator trays. Frozen baby lima beans are one of my favorite vegetables to dry as a side dish, as are frozen hash browns. Artichokes, canned or jarred in water, also dry beautifully.

Grains and Starches

There are no hard-and-fast rules for these recipes. If you don't like the texture or can't have couscous due to celiac disease, then feel free to substitute rice, quinoa, amaranth, or pasta. If quinoa isn't your cup of tea, you can use Israel couscous, kasha (buckwheat groats), or small pasta. There are no limitations. I've included some serving suggestions with many of the recipes in order to give you some options. Some larger and thicker pasta shapes don't cook well at higher altitudes. As an example, angel hair is a good substitute for spaghetti in this situation. Smaller pasta shapes designed for soups are a great alternative too. Rice pasta cooks very quickly and is great at high altitude. You can also precook and dehydrate pasta, rice, and other grains such as quinoa. Cook rice or pasta as you normally would but remove it from the heat a minute or two earlier than normal. For pasta, pour a glass of ice cold water into the pot to stop the cooking. For rice, sit the pot in a sink of cold water, being sure that the water is only as high as the rice in the pot. Spread your pasta or rice on dehydrator trays and dry for 6 to 10 hours or until thoroughly dry. At camp add hot or boiling water and let the food sit in a pot cozy for about 15 minutes or until reconstituted.

Dried garlic, peppers, tomatoes, olives, and herbs make wonderful additions to sides such as biscuits and add great flavor to pizza crusts.

Packaging Meals

Each recipe includes guidelines for packaging the meals. Keep in mind that if you are not using the sauces and such right away then you should freeze them. Do not freeze the pastas, rice, tortillas, pitas, couscous, or such—only freeze the items that you have dehydrated. Be sure to write the name of the recipe, number of servings, date, and predehydration measurements on a note and put it inside the bag. You might also write the page number of the recipe on the note as well— that will make it easy for you to find the camp instructions when you are getting ready for your trip. "At Camp" instructions can also be found for download at **aforkinthetrail.com.** Pastas such as fusilli (corkscrews), farfalle (bow ties), or penne lisce (lined tubes) travel best and stand up to quite a bit of abuse. If you do take spaghetti or angel-hair pasta, wrap it tightly with plastic wrap and place it in an empty paper towel tube to prevent the noodles from breaking.

If you will be traveling in a situation where you won't use all the servings in a single meal, simply split the recipe into single-serving portions when packaging it. Be sure to label the packages and insert a note with each serving so that you know how much water to add back into the food. If you forget to add the note, add just enough water at camp to barely cover the ingredients.

Other Meal Ideas

Lunch recipes, such as Roasted Tomato Dip, Olive Tapenade, Mediterranean Garbanzo Bean Salad, and any of the salsas, can be easily converted to dinner fare by serving with a grain or starch such as a pasta or bread.

½ cup quinoa, rinsed and drained

1 tablespoon olive oil

½ cup onion, chopped

¼ cup celery, finely diced

1 clove garlic

½ cup frozen spinach, thawed (measure after squeezing out the excess liquid)

½ cup canned tomatoes, drained and liquid reserved

¼ cup reserved tomato liquid

½ teaspoon dried basil

½ teaspoon dried oregano

¼ teaspoon dried crushed red chilies

1 cup black beans

1 cup carrots, coarsely grated

1¾–2 cups vegetable stock

Salt and pepper to taste

2 medium sweet peppers, chopped

2–3 tablespoons nutritional yeast or a small block of vegetarian or regular mozzarella

Unstuffed Peppers with Quinoa

Dehydration Time: 6–10 hours
Makes 4–6 servings

I remember the first time I had stuffed peppers. I was about 8 and an Italian neighbor lady made them once when I was visiting her granddaughter. I was fascinated with her picking the red and yellow peppers from the garden, cutting them in half with the stems still on, and stuffing them before they went into the oven. I've used quinoa instead of rice, black beans instead of ground meat, and nutritional yeast in place of cheese.

At Home

Place the quinoa in a fine sieve and rinse for at least 3 minutes to remove the bitter coating. Drain and set aside. Heat the olive oil in a saucepan and sauté the onions and celery until the onions are translucent. Add the garlic and sauté for 1 minute. Stir in the spinach, tomatoes, and reserved tomato liquid. Simmer for 5 minutes or until most of the liquid has evaporated. Add the basil, oregano, dried crushed red chilies, quinoa, black beans, carrots, and 1¾ cups vegetable stock. Bring to a boil and simmer for 15 minutes on medium-low heat. Season with salt and pepper to taste. Check partway through cooking and if necessary add a bit more stock.

Meanwhile, preheat the oven to 350°F. Place the peppers in a single layer in a baking dish. Top with the quinoa and vegetable mixture, cover with foil, and bake for 20 to 30 minutes or until the peppers are tender. Let cool.

Measure the unstuffed pepper mixture and write this measurement on a sticky note. Dry the mixture on lined dehydrator trays for 6 to 10 hours. Put the pepper mixture and the sticky note in a ziplock freezer bag. If you are using nutritional yeast, wrap it in plastic wrap and place it in the bag with the pepper mixture. If you are using cheese, wrap the cheese before you leave for your trip.

At Camp

Add enough boiling water to the dried mixture to equal the measurement on your sticky note. Be sure to account for and add your dried ingredients to the rehydration container prior to adding the water. You can always add more water if you need to. Once the unstuffed peppers have rehydrated, you might have to reheat the mixture. Sprinkle with nutritional yeast and serve.

If you are using cheese, put the hot pepper mixture into your backpacking pot, stir in ½ cup grated cheese, and then top it with the remaining ½ cup cheese. Cover it and let sit until the cheese melts.

Butter Bean and Kale Ragout

1 bunch or 8–10 cups kale

1 tablespoon olive oil

¾ cup onion, chopped

¼ cup shallots, minced

2 cloves garlic

1¾ cups canned, diced tomatoes

1–2 teaspoons Mexican green chilies or jalapeños, to taste, minced

1 bay leaf

¼ teaspoon cumin

½ cup water

2 cups butter beans or baby lima beans, canned or frozen

½ teaspoon dried basil

½ teaspoon dried oregano

Salt and pepper to taste

Dehydration Time: 5–10 hours
Makes 4–6 servings

This recipe was inspired by a backpacker named Carrie Fink from Minnesota. After a fall day of preparing her backyard for the upcoming winter, she made a similar dish to use up kale from her garden. She served it with cornbread that night, and it was a delicious way to warm up. This is my take on it.

AT HOME

Wash and drain the kale. Remove the stems and any questionable leaves, and then give the greens a coarse chop. Heat the oil in a large pot on medium heat. Add the onions and cook until they start to turn translucent. Add the shallots and cook for 1 minute. Stir in the kale and cook for 5 minutes until the greens are wilted. Add the garlic and cook for 2 minutes, then add the tomatoes, green chilies or jalapeños, bay leaf, cumin, and water. Simmer for an hour and then add the beans. If you are using canned beans, rinse and drain them. If using frozen, just put them in the pot. Let the pot return to a simmer and continue to cook for 10 minutes or until the beans are heated through. Add the basil, oregano, salt, and pepper. Remove the bay leaf and allow the ragout to cool.

Measure the ragout and write this measurement on a sticky note. Place the ragout onto lined dehydrator trays and dry for 5 to 10 hours or until no moisture remains. Put the dried ragout in a ziplock freezer bag along with the sticky note.

AT CAMP

Add enough boiling water to the soup mix to equal the measurement on your sticky note. Do not add the water first or you will have too much liquid. Once the ragout has rehydrated, heat it through and serve.

Tip

If you can't find butter beans or lima beans, white kidney beans will also do fine in this recipe.

Chana Masala

Dehydration Time: 6–10 hours
Makes 4–6 servings

This recipe makes me think fondly of two Fork in the Trail *readers, James Nelson and Amber Leberman of Chicago, Illinois. They sent me a photo of this recipe, which first appeared in an online backpacking publication from Ohio called* GetOut! *They enjoyed the Chana Masala at the Lake Richie campsite on Michigan's Isle Royale. This beautiful spot was one of their favorite places to camp. They spent hours there watching adult loons teaching juveniles to dive and listening to the Chippewa Harbor wolf pack howling in the distance.*

AT HOME

It is helpful to prepare and measure all the ingredients before you start. Heat the oil in a heavy-bottomed pot over medium-high heat. Add the cumin seeds, and once they start popping, about 25 seconds, add the onion. Sauté the onion until it starts to brown slightly. Then add the chili pepper, garlic, and ginger and stir well. Quickly add the tomatoes and let simmer for about 5 minutes. Meanwhile cut the potatoes into bite-size pieces. Reduce the heat to medium. Add the salt, coriander, garam masala, and turmeric and stir well. Then add the potatoes stirring to coat with the onion, tomato, spice mixture. Add 1 cup of water and bring to boil. Reduce the heat to low, cover, and simmer for 20 minutes or until the potatoes are soft. Add the chickpeas and more water if necessary and let simmer for another 20 minutes. Remove the chana masala from the heat and add the cilantro. Let the mixture sit with the lid on for 15 to 20 minutes before dehydrating. Allow to cool.

Measure the soup and write this measurement on a sticky note. Spread the soup on lined dehydrator trays and dry for 6 to 10 hours. Put the soup and the sticky note in a ziplock freezer bag.

2–3 tablespoons canola oil

1 teaspoon cumin seeds

1 large onion, thinly sliced

1 green chili pepper, finely minced

2 teaspoons fresh garlic, minced

2 teaspoons fresh ginger, minced

1¼ cups canned diced tomatoes

3 medium potatoes, washed, peeled, and diced

2 teaspoons salt

2 teaspoons ground coriander seed

2 teaspoons garam masala

1½ teaspoons turmeric

1 cup water

3 cups canned chickpeas, rinsed and drained

2 tablespoons fresh cilantro, chopped

At Camp

Add enough boiling water to the dried soup to equal the measurement on your sticky note. Be sure to account for and add your dried ingredients to the rehydration container prior to adding the water. You can always add more water if you need to. Once the soup has rehydrated, you might have to reheat it. Serve with chapati, naan bread, or pitas, if desired.

Note

James went missing on a solo backpacking trip in Colorado's Holy Cross Wilderness in October 2010. He was never found. It is a risk we all face when we go into the wilderness. This recipe is dedicated to his memory, to the Search and Rescue people who risked their own lives trying to find him, and to those he left behind.

Roasted Ratatouille

Dehydration Time: 7–10 hours
Makes: 3–4 servings

I'll never forget my son watching the Disney movie Ratatouille *for the first time. I was in the kitchen preparing food to be dehydrated for spring trips and I could hear Tobias exclaim, "He's just like my Mom!" Every time I make this dish I think of that winter afternoon. Roasting the vegetables for this ratatouille adds so much to the flavor and makes it easy to prepare. I've used an Italian pepper called pepperoncini that can be found in jars in most large grocery stores. This is a yellowish pepper with a bit of heat; you could substitute a small amount of minced banana pepper if you can't find them.*

AT HOME

Roast the peppers according to the directions on page 7. Set the oven to broil. Place a wire rack over a baking pan. Slice the eggplant into circles and lay in a single layer on the wire rack. Sprinkle with 2 teaspoons coarse salt and let sit for 30 minutes. This will help remove some of the moisture. After 30 minutes rinse off the salt and dry the slices with paper towels. Chop the roasted peppers and put them into a large bowl. Set aside. Spread the diced zucchini in a single layer on a baking sheet. Drizzle with just enough olive oil to coat the zucchini, about 1 tablespoon, and stir to ensure the oil is well distributed. Broil for 10 minutes and then remove them from the oven and add them to the peppers. Cut the eggplant into dices about the same size as the zucchini. Put the eggplant on the baking sheet and oil as you did for the zucchini. Broil for 15 minutes and then add to the peppers and zucchini.

Heat a skillet over medium heat and add a small amount of olive oil. Sauté the onions until they are soft. Add the garlic, pepperoncini, bay leaf, and rosemary. Cook for 1 minute, then season with salt and pepper, and add the tomatoes. Simmer for 15 minutes until the tomatoes start to break down and the mixture thickens. You can do this while you are roasting the vegetables. Remove the bay leaf and rosemary sprig.

1 sweet red pepper and 1 sweet yellow pepper, roasted

1 large eggplant

2 teaspoons coarse salt

2 small zucchini, diced

2 tablespoons olive oil

1 onion, diced

1 clove garlic

1 pepperoncini or Tuscan pepper, minced

1 small bay leaf

½ rosemary sprig

A pinch of salt and pepper

4 medium tomatoes, seeded and roughly chopped

3 tablespoons fresh basil

Pour the sauce over the vegetables and toss to coat. Gently stir in the basil.

Measure the ratatouille and write this measurement on a sticky note. Dry on lined dehydrator trays for 7 to 10 hours. Put the mixture in a medium-size ziplock freezer bag with your sticky note.

AT CAMP

Add enough boiling water to the dried ratatouille to equal the measurement on your sticky note. Be sure to account for and add your dried ingredients to the rehydration container prior to adding the water. You can always add more water if you need to. Once the mixture has rehydrated, you might have to reheat it. Serve with rice, pasta, focaccia, or your favorite trail bread.

Pasta alla Puttanesca

Dehydration Time: 7–10 hours
Makes 3–4 servings

There is a bit of mystique and legend surrounding puttanesca sauce. One story tells of the sauce being made by the ladies of the night in Naples. This is a sultry, spicy, and slightly salty pasta sauce that is traditionally made with anchovies. Of course, that wouldn't be vegetarian, so I've substituted capers, which are the brined bud from a bush. I've also used black garlic, a fermented product that has a slight molasses flavor, to add a bit of sweetness, but if you can't find it, use whole cloves of roasted garlic.

AT HOME

Heat 1½ tablespoons of olive oil in a large pot on medium heat. Squeeze the black garlic out of the skin and onto your cutting board. Run the side of your knife over the cloves a few times to mush the fermented garlic into a paste. Set aside. Add the raw garlic and cook for 1 minute, being careful that it doesn't brown. Stir in the black garlic and heat through. Add the tomatoes (including the purée from the can), olives, capers, and crushed red chilies. Simmer for about 10 minutes until the sauce starts to thicken and break the tomatoes up with a spoon. Season with black pepper and add the fresh herbs. Stir until combined. Let the sauce cool.

Measure the sauce and write this measurement on a sticky note. Pour onto lined dehydrator trays and dry for 7 to 10 hours. Put the uncooked pasta in a large ziplock freezer bag. Place the dried sauce and the sticky note in a ziplock freezer bag and put that in the bag with the pasta. Wrap the Parmesan cheese, if using. Add the rest of the olive oil to the other oil you will take on your trip.

AT CAMP

Add enough boiling water to the sauce to equal the measurement on your sticky note. Be sure to account for and add your

1½ tablespoons plus 2 tablespoons olive oil

2 cloves black garlic

3 cloves garlic, minced

1 28-ounce can plum tomatoes

½ cup Kalamata olives, pitted and quartered

2 tablespoons capers, rinsed and drained

½ teaspoon dried crushed red chilies

Freshly ground black pepper to taste

2 tablespoons fresh Italian or flat leaf parsley, chopped

1 tablespoon fresh basil leaves, chopped

¾ pound spaghetti or linguine (uncooked measurement)

1-by-1-by-3-inch block Parmesan cheese (optional)

dried ingredients to the rehydration container prior to adding the water. You can always add more water if you need to. Once the sauce has rehydrated, reheat if necessary and serve over linguine or spaghetti. Drizzle each serving with ½ tablespoon olive oil before eating.

Tip

The day you plan to have the sauce for dinner, start rehydrating it at lunchtime by mixing the dried sauce with cool water in a leakproof container. The sauce will be fully rehydrated at dinnertime.

Gnocchi with Brown Butter and Balsamic

Makes 4–6 servings

Gnocchi is an Italian potato dumpling that is usually served with a sauce. If you have celiac disease, you can sometimes find gnocchi that is made from rice. Gnocchi often comes in shelf-stable packages, but it is weightier than pasta. You can also use your favorite shelf-stable cheese tortellini in this recipe.

AT HOME

Package the butter with any other butter that you will take on your trip. Put the balsamic vinegar in a small leakproof bottle. Toast the walnuts in a dry nonstick frying pan for a few minutes. Let cool and wrap in plastic wrap. Put the gnocchi package in a large ziplock bag. Place the bottle of balsamic and the walnuts in with the gnocchi. Wrap the cheese and add it to the bag when you are ready to leave on your trip.

AT CAMP

Shave the Parmesan cheese and set aside. Boil salted water and cook the gnocchi or tortellini according to the package directions. Drain the water, put the pot in a cozy, and set it aside. In another pot or frying pan melt ½ cup butter over medium-low heat, stirring frequently. When the foam subsides, and the butter begins to turn golden brown, remove the pot from the heat. This will take about 2 to 3 minutes. Let it cool for a minute and then add 2 tablespoons plus 1 teaspoon balsamic vinegar and season with salt and pepper. Pour over the gnocchi or tortellini and top with the walnuts and Parmesan cheese shavings.

Tip
If your stove doesn't have a low setting, just lift the pan by the pot grip and hold it a small distance from the flame.

½ cup butter

2 tablespoons plus 1 teaspoon balsamic vinegar

⅓ cup walnuts, chopped

1 package shelf-stable potato gnocchi (about 1 pound) or shelf-stable cheese tortellini

1-by-1-by-3-inch block Parmesan cheese

¼ teaspoon kosher salt

Black pepper to taste

Arugula and Baby Spinach Pesto

Dehydration Time: 5–7 hours
Makes 4–6 servings

2 tablespoons walnuts, coarsely chopped

2 cloves garlic, minced

1½ cups arugula

½ cup baby spinach

¼ teaspoon kosher salt to taste

¼ teaspoon freshly ground black pepper

1 teaspoon red wine vinegar

1-by-1-by-3-inch block Parmesan cheese (optional)

¼ cup extra virgin olive oil

This recipe was one of those happy accidents that happened when I was trying to use up some fresh greens prior to one of our longer trips. The peppery flavor of the arugula is great on pasta or gnocchi, tossed with tofu and vegetables, or used as a pizza sauce. I prefer walnuts in this pesto but you can substitute pine nuts.

At Home

Toast the walnuts in a dry frying pan until they become fragrant. Let the nuts cool and then wrap half of them in plastic wrap. Mince the garlic and set aside.

Fill a large bowl with ice water. Put a pot of water on to boil and put the arugula and spinach into a fine strainer or sieve. When the water begins to boil, dunk the sieve into the water for 10 to 15 seconds and then put the strainer full of greens into the ice water to stop any cooking. Drain well. Add garlic and 1 tablespoon of the walnuts to the food processor and pulse until the nuts resemble a fine meal. Add greens, salt, pepper, and vinegar. Blend well. Spread the mixture on lined dehydrator trays and dry for 5 to 7 hours. Allow to cool and place the mix in a ziplock bag. Put the walnut bundle in the bag with the dried greens. Wrap the Parmesan cheese, if using. Add the olive oil to the other oil you will take on your trip.

At Camp

Add ½ part water to 1 part dried mix and allow to rehydrate, adding water a little at a time if necessary. Add ¼ cup of olive oil to the bag, close the bag, and knead with your hands until combined. Shave the Parmesan cheese, if using, with your knife or cut into small pieces and crumble with your fingers. Add the cheese and nuts to the bag and mix again, or, if you are having this with pasta, toss the pasta with the pesto and sprinkle the cheese and nuts on top.

Bruschetta Pasta with Goat Cheese

Dehydration Time: 7–10 hours
Makes 2–3 servings

This recipe came together by mere chance near Matagamasi Lake in the beautiful Chiniguchi region of Temagami, Ontario, Canada. At the beginning of our trip, our friend Bill slipped in boot-sucking mud and sprained his ankle, which meant we needed to stay put for a few days until he could walk again. The weather was miserable—we didn't think it would ever stop raining. I went to rehydrate our spaghetti sauce only to realize that I didn't have it. What I did have was some dehydrated bruschetta topping and a bit of leftover goat cheese. So I improvised and it was a hit.

AT HOME

Mix the tomatoes, onions, garlic, thyme, and basil together in a bowl. Let sit for 30 to 40 minutes so that the flavors infuse. Spread the mixture on lined dehydrator trays and dry for 7 to 10 hours. Put the pasta in a large freezer bag. Package the bruschetta mixture into a medium-size ziplock freezer bag and put the bag in with the pasta. When you are ready to leave for your trip, wrap the goat cheese in a piece of plastic wrap and place that in a separate freezer bag and store in an insulated cooler bag or cozy. Package the olive oil with the other olive oil you will take on your trip.

AT CAMP

Add warm water to the bruschetta mixture using a little less water than dried mix. Add more water if necessary. Boil salted water and cook the pasta until al dente. Drain the water, drizzle with 2 tablespoons olive oil, put the pot in a cozy, and set it aside. In another pot or frying pan, heat the bruschetta mix and add the goat cheese over low heat. If your stove doesn't have a low setting, just lift the pan by the pot grip and hold it a small distance from the flame. Stir gently until the goat cheese

1¼ cups fresh plum tomatoes, diced

2–3 green onions, sliced

1 clove garlic, minced

¼ teaspoon dried thyme

1 tablespoon fresh basil, chopped

½ pound pasta such as penne, fusilli, or farfalle (uncooked measurement)

¼ cup fresh goat cheese or herbed goat cheese

2 tablespoons olive oil

Salt and pepper to taste

melts. Add the bruschetta and cheese mixture to the pasta in the pot and stir to coat. Season to taste with salt and pepper.

Tips

Plum tomatoes are also known as Roma or Italian tomatoes.

This meal is best for cooler weather or the first few days of a trip, as goat cheese will not last over the long term. A cooler bag or cozy will help keep the cheese cool. You can substitute shelf-stable Brie or Camembert or even use a bit of Parmesan.

If you will be at higher altitudes, choose a smaller pasta shape such as tripolini (a small bow tie shape) or angel hair.

Polenta with Sage e'Fagioli

Dehydration Time: 6–8 hours
Makes 4–6 servings

Fagioli *means "beans" in Italian. This peasant dish tradition-ally incorporates beans, tomato sauce, broth, and pasta. I thought it would be yummy to have the beans atop a sage-infused polenta instead of pasta.*

At Home

Heat the olive oil and sauté the garlic in a skillet over medium heat for 1 minute. Add the tomatoes and simmer for 15 minutes. Then add the beans, sage, salt, and pepper and simmer for another 10 minutes. Remove from the heat and let cool. Measure the bean mixture and write this measure-ment on a sticky note. Dry on lined dehydrator trays for 6 to 8 hours. Put the bean mixture in a medium-size ziplock freezer bag with your sticky note. Mix the instant polenta, powdered vegetable stock, roasted garlic powder, and dried rubbed sage in a medium-size ziplock freezer bag. Add a note with the amount of water needed and cooking time from the polenta package. Wrap the nutritional yeast, if using, in plastic wrap and place that in the bag with the bean mixture along with the polenta bag. Pack the butter, olive oil, or vegan butter substi-tute with the butter that you will take with you on your trip.

At Camp

Add enough boiling water to the dried bean mixture to equal the measurement on your sticky note. Be sure to account for and add your dried ingredients to the rehydration container prior to adding the water. You can always add more water if you need to. Once the bean mixture has rehydrated, you might have to reheat it. Set aside in a cozy.

Make the polenta according to the package directions you included in the bag and slowly stir in the polenta a bit at a

1 teaspoon olive oil

1 garlic clove, minced

1¼ cups canned diced tomatoes

2 cups canned cannellini beans or white kidney beans, rinsed and drained

1 tablespoon fresh sage, chopped

Salt and pepper to taste

½ cup plus 2 tablespoons instant polenta

2 teaspoons powdered vegetable stock

½ teaspoon roasted garlic powder

¼ teaspoon dried rubbed sage (not ground sage)

1 tablespoon nutritional yeast (optional)

2 tablespoons butter, olive oil, or vegan butter substitute

time so that it doesn't lump. Cook while stirring constantly for 1 to 5 minutes depending on the note you made about the cooking time. Divide the cooked polenta into servings and top with the rehydrated bean and tomato mixture. Sprinkle with nutritional yeast if desired.

Tip

You can use the bean and tomato mixture over pasta, rice, or quinoa or add a little extra stock and tubetti noodles to make the more traditional pasta e'fagioli.

Four Pepper Chili

**Dehydration Time: 6–8 hours
Makes 4–6 servings**

This hearty, flavorful chili is a little bit sweet and a little bit spicy. Serve with Masa Dumplings (see page 215) and garnish with cheddar-flavored soy cheese or nutritional yeast if desired.

At Home

Heat the vegetable oil in a large pot over medium heat. Add the onion and sauté until it starts to soften and become translucent. Add the garlic and peppers to the pot and cook for 5 minutes until softened. Then add the tomatoes, chili sauce, vegetable stock, chili powder, cumin, oregano, cayenne pepper, and black pepper and simmer over low heat for 25 minutes. Stir in the beans and heat for an additional 5 minutes, then add the cilantro. Allow the chili to cool.

Measure the chili and write this measurement on a sticky note. Pour onto lined dehydrator trays and dry for 6 to 8 hours. Place the dehydrated chili and the sticky note in a ziplock freezer bag. Package the Masa Dumplings, if you are using them, according to the recipe on page 215.

At Camp

Add enough boiling water to the chili mix in a pot to equal the measurement on your sticky note. Be sure to account for and add your dried ingredients to the pot prior to adding the water. You can always add more water if you need to. Once the chili has rehydrated, you may have to reheat it. If you are using the Masa Dumplings, follow their instructions to cook them in the chili.

1 tablespoon vegetable oil

1½ cups red onion, chopped

4 cloves garlic, minced

¾ cup each yellow and green sweet peppers, chopped

1½ tablespoons banana pepper, minced

2 jalapeño peppers, minced

2 cups canned diced tomatoes

1 cup tomato-based chili sauce (not hot sauce)

1½ cups vegetable stock

1½ tablespoons chili powder

2 teaspoons cumin

1 teaspoon dried oregano

¼ teaspoon cayenne pepper

¼ teaspoon black pepper

1 15-ounce can red kidney beans, drained and rinsed

1 15-ounce can white kidney beans, drained and rinsed

1½ tablespoons fresh cilantro, chopped

1 tablespoon vegetable oil

½ cup onion, chopped

1½ cups sweet potatoes, diced

1 clove garlic

3½ cups vegetable stock

Harvest Spice Blend (see below)

3 cups canned stewed pumpkin

½ cup red peppers, chopped

½–1 whole jalapeño, minced

3 cups dark red kidney beans

Juice of half a lime

1½–2 tablespoons cilantro

Kosher salt to taste

¼ cup roasted pepitas

Harvest Spice Blend

1 teaspoon carob powder

1½ teaspoons dried ancho chile pepper, ground

½ teaspoon cumin

¼ teaspoon smoked paprika

⅛ teaspoon cinnamon

⅛ teaspoon dried oregano

⅛ teaspoon freshly ground black pepper

⅛ teaspoon cayenne pepper

Autumn Harvest Chili

Dehydration Time: 5–8 hours
Makes 4–6 servings

This harvest-inspired chili reminds me of those fall hikes in Ontario, Canada's Algonquin Provincial Park when the air is cool and crisp and the sugar maple canopy is a brilliant color. An herbaceous focaccia or cornbread makes a wonderful side for this dish.

At Home

Heat the oil in a large pot over medium heat. Sauté the onion and the sweet potatoes until they start to caramelize, then add the garlic and cook for 1 minute. Add the vegetable stock and let simmer for 10 minutes before adding the Harvest Spice Blend and pumpkin. Simmer for another 10 minutes and then add the peppers and beans. Let the chili cook for 15 minutes. Stir in the lime juice and cilantro and salt, to taste. Remove from the heat and let cool.

Measure the chili and write this measurement on a sticky note. Pour onto lined dehydrator trays and dry for 5 to 8 hours. Place the dried chili and the sticky note in a ziplock freezer bag. Wrap the pepitas in a piece of plastic wrap and place the bundle in the bag with the chili.

At Camp

Add enough boiling water to the chili mix to equal the measurement on your sticky note. Be sure to account for and add your dried ingredients to the rehydration container prior to adding the water. You can always add more water if you need to. Once the chili has rehydrated, you might have to reheat it. Sprinkle with pepitas before serving.

Tip

If you can't find roasted pepitas, simply place raw pepitas on a cookie sheet, sprinkle with a little salt and pepper, and roast at 350°F, stirring frequently, until they start to become fragrant and take on a little bit of color.

Mushroom Burgundy

Dehydration Time: 7–10 hours
Makes 4–5 servings

They say opposites attract and nothing could be truer about my husband and me. When I first met Bryan, he was a die-hard meatatarian and I was a vegetarian. I wanted to cook a special dinner for him that was reminiscent of beef Bourguignonne— one of his favorite dishes. He loved the meat-free version I created for him and to this day asks me to make it. This recipe is perfect for a special occasion, such as an anniversary, being celebrated in the wilds.

AT HOME

Heat 1 tablespoon olive oil and 1 tablespoon butter together in a Dutch oven or large heavy-bottomed saucepan over medium-high heat. Add the mushrooms and cook for 4 to 5 minutes until they begin to take on color but aren't releasing any juices. Transfer the mushrooms to a plate and set aside.

Turn the heat down to medium and add 1 teaspoon of olive oil. Cook carrots and onion until the onions are golden brown. Add the garlic and sauté for 1 minute.

Add the wine and scrape the bottom of the pot with a wooden spoon. This will deglaze the pot. Turn the heat back up to medium-high and reduce the liquid by half to concentrate the flavors. Stir in the vegetable stock and tomato paste. Bring the mixture back to a boil and add the mushrooms along with any juices that have accumulated on the plate. Reduce the heat to medium-low and let the mixture simmer for 20 minutes or until the mushrooms are tender. Add the pearl onions and let simmer for 5 more minutes.

Mix the remaining tablespoon of butter with the potato flour until well combined and then stir it into the pot. Add the thyme. Reduce the heat to low and simmer for 10 minutes or until it reaches a thick stewlike consistency. Season the stew with salt and pepper. Let cool.

Measure the burgundy and write this measurement on a sticky note. Pour onto lined dehydrator trays and dry for

1 tablespoon plus 1 teaspoon olive oil

2 tablespoons butter or vegan butter substitute

1 pound cremini mushrooms, diced

1 pound portobello mushrooms, diced

½ cup carrot, finely diced

½ cup yellow onion, finely diced

2 cloves garlic, minced

1 cup red wine (use something full bodied, preferably a Burgundy)

2 cups vegetable stock

2 tablespoons tomato paste

1 cup frozen pearl onions

1½ tablespoons potato flour

½ teaspoon dried thyme

Freshly ground black pepper to taste

Kosher salt to taste

7 to 10 hours. Place the dried stew and the sticky note in a ziplock freezer bag.

At Camp

Add enough boiling water to the Mushroom Burgundy to equal the measurement on your sticky note. Be sure to account for and add your dried ingredients to the rehydration container prior to adding the water. You can always add more water if you need to. Once the meal has rehydrated, reheat if necessary and serve over broad noodles or with potatoes or French bread.

Tip

The day you plan to have the stew for dinner, start rehydrating it at lunchtime by mixing the dried ingredients with cool water in a leakproof container. The stew will be fully rehydrated at dinnertime.

Red Peppers and Artichokes with Saffron

Dehydration Time: 7–10 hours
Makes 4–6 servings

This sauce is fairly versatile and can be used over pasta, couscous, quinoa, pitas, or rice. My husband loves it with penne, while I prefer to have it with rice that has been cooked with a little vegetable stock and saffron.

AT HOME

Heat 1 tablespoon of olive oil in a skillet over medium heat. Add the onion and cook until it starts to become translucent. Add the garlic, paprika, crushed red chilies, and saffron. Sauté for a few minutes, then add the peppers, artichoke hearts, and vinegar. Season the sauce with salt and pepper. Let cool.

Measure the sauce and write this measurement on a sticky note. Pour onto lined dehydrator trays and dry for 7 to 10 hours. Place the dried sauce and the sticky note in a ziplock freezer bag. Pack your pasta or rice. Add 3 tablespoons of olive oil to the other oil you will take on your trip.

AT CAMP

Add enough boiling water to the sauce to equal the measurement on your sticky note. Be sure to account for and add your dried ingredients to the rehydration container prior to adding the water. You can always add more water if you need to. Once the sauce has rehydrated, add 3 tablespoons of olive oil and reheat.

Tip

The day you plan to have the sauce for dinner, start rehydrating it at lunchtime by mixing the dried sauce with cool water in a leakproof container. The sauce will be fully rehydrated at dinnertime.

1 tablespoon plus 3 tablespoons olive oil

⅓ cup onion, chopped

2 cloves garlic, minced

½ teaspoon Spanish paprika

¼–½ teaspoon crushed red chilies

A pinch of Spanish saffron

1½ cups roasted red peppers, chopped (about 2 whole peppers)

1 cup canned artichoke hearts, drained and chopped

3 tablespoons red wine or white wine vinegar

A pinch of kosher salt

Fresh cracked black pepper to taste

Rosemary and Garlic Sweet Potatoes

3 cups sweet potatoes, peeled and cubed

¼ cup olive oil

3 cloves garlic, peeled

2 teaspoons fresh rosemary, stems removed

¼ teaspoon kosher salt

⅛ cup Parmesan cheese, finely grated (optional)

Dehydration Time: 8–10 hours
Makes 3–4 servings

This is a filling I typically make for ravioli, but it is great on its own. Sometimes I cook broken lasagna noodles at camp and stir them into the potatoes, creating a sort of deconstructed ravioli. If I am feeling really adventurous, I'll carry in fresh wonton wrappers and make little ravioli, which I serve tossed in a little olive oil and Parmesan cheese or nutritional yeast.

At Home

Preheat oven to 425°F. Toss the sweet potatoes with the olive oil and the whole cloves of garlic, rosemary, and salt in a shallow baking pan large enough to place the potatoes in a single layer. Bake for 25 to 30 minutes until the sweet potatoes are fully cooked. Stir halfway through cooking. If using the Parmesan cheese, add it during the last 10 minutes of cooking. Let cool.

Transfer the potato mixture to a food processor and pulse until smooth and well combined.

Spread the sweet potato mixture on lined dehydrator trays and dry for 8 to 10 hours. When it is dry, it will be leathery.

Break the dried mixture into small pieces by hand and run it through a blender or coffee grinder until it has broken up into small flakes. Package the sweet potatoes in a ziplock freezer bag. Store the sweet potatoes in the freezer until your trip.

At Camp

Add equal amounts of potato flakes and boiling water in a pot and let reconstitute for 10 to 15 minutes or until fully rehydrated. Add a little olive oil, if desired, and stir.

Tips

This dish can also be made into a soup by adding a half cup of vegetable stock for each serving.

Leftover potatoes are also wonderful fried for breakfast.

Sweet Potato and Black Urad Dal Burritos

Dehydration Time: 5–10 hours
Makes 4–6 servings

Mexico meets South India in this unique take on a bean bur-
rito. Whole black urad dal, *also known as black gram or black*
matpe beans, *is a South Indian ingredient similar to lentils.*
The skins impart an earthier flavor than the black beans typi-
cally found in traditional Mexican fare, and the insides are
white. Whole black urad dal *needs to be soaked before cooking.*
If you can't find these beans, use turtle or black beans.

AT HOME

Soak the whole black *urad dal* in cold water for 1½ to 2 hours.
Drain and transfer to a pot with 3 cups of water. Bring to a boil
and simmer for 45 minutes to an hour or until the *urad dal* is
tender. Drain and set aside. While the *urad dal* cooks, place
the sweet potatoes in a medium saucepan and cover with
water. Add ½ teaspoon salt, bring to a boil, and let simmer for
about 10 minutes or until fork-tender. Drain the sweet potatoes and let them cool. Heat the oil in a frying pan and sauté
the onions until they start to soften. Add the garlic, jalapeño,
cumin seeds, ground cumin, and coriander and sauté for an
additional 2 minutes, stirring so that the garlic doesn't burn.
Add the fresh cilantro to the onion mixture and set aside to
cool. Place the sweet potatoes, *urad dal,* and lime juice, with
salt and pepper to taste, in a food processor and pulse until
the mixture is smooth. If the mixture is too thick and binds in
the food processor, add a tablespoon or two of water.

Dehydrate the sweet potato mixture and onion mixture,
separately, on lined dehydrator trays for 8 to 10 hours or until
completely dried. When the sweet potato mixture is dry, it
may be leathery.

Measure the amount of salsa you will dry and write this
measurement on a sticky note. Dry the salsa on a lined dehydrator tray for 5 to 10 hours.

⅔ cup dry whole black *urad dal* (2½ cups cooked)

3 cups sweet potatoes, peeled and cubed

½ teaspoon salt

1 teaspoon vegetable oil

1 cup onion, diced

2 cloves garlic, minced

1 jalapeño pepper, minced

2 teaspoons whole cumin seeds

1 teaspoon ground cumin

2 teaspoons ground coriander

½ cup fresh cilantro, coarsely chopped

Juice of 2 limes

Kosher salt to taste

Freshly ground black pepper to taste

Salsa verde or your favorite salsa

4–6 soft tortillas

¼ cup roasted pepitas (optional)

Break the dried sweet potato mixture into small pieces by hand and run it through a blender or coffee grinder until it has broken up into very small pieces and place in a medium-size ziplock freezer bag. Add the onion mixture to the same bag. Package the salsa in a separate freezer bag with your sticky note and put that bag in the sweet potato bag. Store the meal in the freezer until your trip. Before your trip, package the tortillas in a large ziplock freezer bag with a piece of parchment paper between each one. Wrap the roasted pepitas, if using, them, in plastic wrap and place the bundle in the bag with the sweet potato mixture.

At Camp

Remove the salsa bag and the pepitas, if using, from the bag containing the sweet potato mixture. Add enough boiling water to the salsa to equal the measurement on your sticky note. Be sure to account for and add your dried ingredients to the rehydration container prior to adding the water. Add ¾ part boiling water to 1 part sweet potato mixture. Let reconstitute for 15 to 20 minutes, adding more hot water as needed. When the mixture has rehydrated, dollop a portion of the mixture onto a tortilla, top with salsa and pepitas, if using, and roll up and enjoy.

Tips

Always check *urad dal* carefully for foreign matter before cooking.

Warming the tortillas for 10 to 15 seconds in a frying pan will make them more pliable and prevent them from cracking when you are rolling them.

You could also bake these in a backpacking oven. Assemble the burritos but leave out the salsa. Then place the burritos seam side down in your pan, top with salsa, and bake for 15 to 20 minutes or until hot.

Red Quinoa and Curried Lentil Stew

Dehydration Time: 6–10 hours
Makes 4–6 servings

This spicy stew is definitely a fusion of cultures with red quinoa, a food of the Incas, and yellow lentils, also known as moong dal, *from India. If you cannot find red quinoa, by all means use white, although it does have a slightly stronger flavor than the red variety. Red lentils can be used in place of yellow lentils; however, you might have to adjust the cooking time by a few minutes.*

At Home

Place the quinoa in a fine sieve and rinse for at least 3 minutes to remove the bitter coating. Drain and set aside. Check over, rinse, and drain the lentils and set aside with the quinoa. Put the oil in a large pot over medium heat. Sauté the onion, carrots, celery, and celery leaves until the onions are translucent and the carrots are tender, about 10 minutes. Stir in the garlic, ginger, and curry powder. Add the stock and bring to a boil. Then add the tomatoes, quinoa, lentils, and sambal oelek. Reduce to a simmer and cook for 15 minutes or until the lentils are tender but not mushy. Add the chickpeas and let simmer for an additional 5 minutes. Season with salt and pepper to taste and stir in the cilantro. Then add the yogurt if you are using it and stir until incorporated. The stew will thicken as it stands.

Measure the stew and write this measurement on a sticky note. Spread the stew on lined dehydrator trays and dry for 6 to 10 hours. Put the stew and the sticky note in a ziplock freezer bag.

At Camp

Add enough boiling water to the dried stew to equal the measurement on your sticky note. Be sure to account for and add your dried ingredients to the rehydration container prior to

⅓ cup red quinoa, uncooked

¾ cup yellow or red lentils

2 teaspoons vegetable oil

½ cup onion, diced

½ cup carrot, diced

½ cup celery, diced

2 tablespoons celery leaves (optional)

3 cloves garlic, minced

1 tablespoon fresh ginger, grated

1 tablespoon curry powder

3⅓ cups vegetable stock

1 28-ounce can diced tomatoes

1 teaspoon–1 tablespoon sambal oelek to taste

1 19-ounce can chickpeas, rinsed and drained

Salt to taste

Pepper to taste

2 tablespoons fresh cilantro

⅓ cup plain yogurt or soy yogurt (optional)

adding the water. You can always add more water if you need to. Once the stew has rehydrated, you might have to reheat it. If the stew is too thick for your taste, add a little more water.

Tips

Always check lentils carefully for foreign matter before cooking. If you do not want to use canned chickpeas, use an equivalent amount of dried beans that have been soaked and cooked.

Greek Lentils

Dehydration Time: 5–8 hours
Makes 3–4 servings

A dear friend and paddling companion, Roula Loukas, made us this simple but memorable dish on our final night of a 9-day wilderness paddling trip near the world's largest old-growth red pine forest. Later that evening we enjoyed cedar tea around the campfire as we chatted about the pictographs, left by the Ojibwa people hundreds of years before us, across the lake from our campsite. This is my interpretation of Roula's lentil meal, but it has been dehydrated to reduce weight and cooking time.

1½ cups dried green lentils

2¼ cups water plus ¼–½ cup

2 bay leaves

1¼ cup onion, diced

4 cloves garlic

2 tablespoons tomato paste

Kosher salt and black pepper to taste

2 tablespoons olive oil

At Home

Look over the lentils and remove any debris. Place the lentils in a large pot and cover with 2¼ cups of water and simmer until tender or about 30 minutes. Do not add salt at this time, as it can cause the lentils to toughen. Drain and return the cooked lentils to the pot. Add the bay leaves, onions, garlic, and tomato paste. Heat through and then add enough water to just loosen the mixture; about ¼ to ½ cup. Let simmer for 10 minutes. Remove the bay leaves and season with salt and pepper.

Measure the lentils and write this measurement on a sticky note. Pour onto lined dehydrator trays and dry for 5 to 8 hours. Place the dried lentil mixture and the sticky note in a ziplock freezer bag. Pack the olive oil with any other olive oil that you will take with you on your trip.

At Camp

Add enough boiling water to the lentils to equal the measurement on your sticky note. Be sure to account for and add your dried ingredients to the rehydration container prior to adding the water. You can always add more water if you need to. Once the lentil dish has rehydrated, stir in 2 tablespoons olive oil and reheat if necessary.

Lentils with Apples and Wild Rice

1 cup dry red lentils

Enough vegetable stock to cook the lentils

1 cup water, plus glass of cold water

¼ cup wild rice, well rinsed

1 teaspoon vegetable oil

⅓ cup onion, chopped

1 clove garlic, minced

1 cup Fuji or Royal Gala apple, chopped

2 tablespoons fresh lemon juice

½ teaspoon lemon zest

½–¾ teaspoon smoked paprika to taste

½ teaspoon cumin

Salt and pepper to taste

Dehydration Time: 8–12 hours
Makes 2–3 servings

Wild rice, a grass native to North America, has double the protein of brown rice and, just like brown rice, has a lengthy cooking time. This recipe requires that you cook the rice at home and dehydrate it, which will save you valuable time and fuel at camp. Wild rice has a nutty, slightly smoky flavor that is enhanced by the addition of smoked paprika and offset by the sweetness of the apples. This also makes a good stuffing for squash baked in a campfire.

At Home

Cook the lentils, according to the package directions, using vegetable stock instead of water. Set aside. Bring 1 cup water to a boil. Add the wild rice and cook on low for 40 to 50 minutes. Remove the rice from the heat as soon as you see some of the grains start to pop open. Add a glass of cold water to the pot to stop the cooking. Drain. Heat the oil in a large frying pan over medium heat. Sauté the onion until it starts to turn slightly golden. Add the garlic and cook for 1 minute. Then add the chopped apples, lemon juice, lemon zest, smoked paprika, and cumin. Cook until the apples are tender but still hold their shape. Stir in the cooked lentils and wild rice. Season with salt and pepper to taste.

Measure the mixture and write this measurement on a sticky note. Spread evenly on lined dehydrator trays and dry for 8 to 12 hours until the rice and lentils are completely dry and the apples leathery. Place the dried meal in a medium ziplock freezer bag with your sticky note.

At Camp

Add enough boiling water to the dried mixture to equal the measurement on your sticky note. Be sure to account for and add your dried ingredients to the rehydration container prior to adding the water. You can always add more water if you need to. Once the dish has rehydrated, you might have to reheat it.

Tips

Always check lentils carefully for foreign matter before cooking. You can use leftover wild rice from dinner at home for this. You'll need ½ cup of cooked rice. You can also cook extra wild rice and dehydrate it for other meals.

Late Harvest Soup with Saffron

Dehydration Time: 5–8 hours
Makes 4–6 servings

⅔ cup celery, diced

⅔ cup carrots, diced

⅔ cup onions, diced

1 cup sweet potatoes, diced

1½ cups Yukon gold
potatoes, diced

1 cup squash, such as acorn
or butternut, diced

1 cup leeks, chopped

½ teaspoon saffron

⅓ cup fresh parsley

1 cup Royal Gala apples,
chopped

1 tablespoon fresh sage
leaves, chopped

⅓ cup roasted, salted
cashews, coarsely chopped
(optional)

Soups are always an integral part of our backcountry menu, as well as something we enjoy at home. I find that soup tastes better the second day because flavors have had the opportunity to infuse, so I often let the soup hang out in the fridge overnight and dry it the second day. Saffron adds a beautiful hue to the broth of this soup and an interesting flavor. I like to serve this with Greek-style pitas that we drizzle with a little olive oil and toast over the flame of our backpacking stove.

At Home

Put the celery, carrots, and onion in a large pot and just cover with water. Let simmer for 20 minutes, and then add the sweet potatoes and potatoes. Add enough water just to cover the potatoes and let simmer an additional 15 minutes. Next add the squash, leeks, saffron, and parsley. If the soup is too thick at this point, add a bit more water. Continue simmering until the squash is tender. Remove from heat and stir in apples and sage leaves. Let cool.

Measure the soup and write this measurement on a sticky note. Pour onto lined dehydrator trays and dry for 5 to 8 hours. Place the dried soup mixture and the sticky note in a ziplock freezer bag. Wrap the cashews in a piece of plastic wrap and add that to the bag.

At Camp

Add enough boiling water to the soup to equal the measurement on your sticky note. Be sure to account for and add your dried ingredients to the rehydration container prior to adding the water. You can always add more water if you need to. Once the soup has rehydrated, you might have to reheat it. Sprinkle with cashews if desired.

Chickpea Soup with Olive Oil Drizzle

Dehydration Time: 5–10 hours
Makes 4 servings

This simple but flavorful soup rehydrates very quickly at camp and can be used as a dinner or lunch. A generous drizzle of olive oil adds to the flavor of the soup. Serve it with your favorite pita, flatbread, or bagel crisps, and if you have leftover trail sprouts, put a good pinch of those on top of the soup. Sometimes I like to pack a little smoked hot paprika to sprinkle on top.

1 teaspoon plus 2–3 tablespoons olive oil

1 medium onion, chopped

1 clove garlic, chopped

1 bay leaf

1 teaspoon dried thyme

½ cup vegetable stock plus extra to cover the chickpeas

3 ½ cups canned chickpeas, rinsed and drained

¼–¾ teaspoon Spanish paprika to taste

Salt and pepper to taste

AT HOME

Place a pot over medium heat and add 1 teaspoon olive oil and sauté the onions until they start to soften. Add the garlic, bay leaf, and dried thyme and sauté for an additional minute. Add ½ cup vegetable stock to the pot and let simmer for 15 minutes so that the flavors of the herbs infuse the stock. Add the chickpeas and pour in enough stock just to cover. Simmer for 20 minutes and then discard the bay leaf. Use an immersion blender to purée the soup or very carefully pour into a standard blender, being cautious not to burn yourself. Blend until smooth. Return to the pot. Add the Spanish paprika to suit your taste. It is better to add a bit at a time and taste between additions than to add too much.

Measure the soup and write this measurement on a sticky note. Dehydrate on lined trays for 5 to 10 hours. Once it is dry, grind it to a powder in a spice or coffee grinder or a blender. Place the dried soup in a medium-size ziplock freezer bag with your sticky note. Add the 2 to 3 tablespoons olive oil to the other oil you will take on your trip.

AT CAMP

Add enough boiling water to the dried soup to equal the measurement on your sticky note. Be sure to account for and add your dried ingredients to the rehydration container prior to adding the water. With this particular soup, it is best to add a little less water than what your measurement stated and add more as needed to reach the desired consistency. Once the soup has rehydrated, you might have to reheat it. Pour into bowls and drizzle each serving with up to 1 tablespoon olive oil.

Black Bean, Corn, and Sweet Potato Soup

Dehydration Time: 6–10 hours
Makes 5–6 servings

We jokingly call some of my soups Kitchen Soup because they're made with whatever I can find in the kitchen. This is one of those recipes that started out as a way to use up the sweet potatoes in my pantry.

At Home

Toast the cumin seeds in a dry nonstick frying pan until they become fragrant, about 3 minutes. Set aside. Heat the olive oil in a large pot. Add the onion and sauté until soft and translucent. Add the sweet potatoes and cook until the mixture starts to brown slightly. Then add the garlic, cumin seed, cumin, chili powder, salt, and pepper. Stir in the lime juice, tomatoes, and enough vegetable stock to cover the mixture. Bring to a boil and then simmer for 10 minutes or until the potatoes are tender. Add the coriander, cilantro, corn, and black beans and more vegetable stock if necessary. Heat through. Add the sour cream if you are using it. Let cool.

Measure the soup and write this measurement on a sticky note. Spread the soup on lined dehydrator trays and dry for 6 to 10 hours. Put the soup and the sticky note in a ziplock bag.

At Camp

Add enough boiling water to the dried soup to equal the measurement on your sticky note. Be sure to account for and add your dried ingredients to the rehydration container prior to adding the water. You can always add more water if needed. This soup will take a little longer to rehydrate than most because of the corn. Once rehydrated, you might have to reheat it.

Tip

To rehydrate this soup faster, make it according to the directions but omit the corn. Add ½ cup of freeze-dried corn to the soup once dehydrated and follow the "At Camp" instructions.

1 teaspoon cumin seeds, toasted

1 tablespoon extra virgin olive oil

1 red or white onion, minced

1¼ cups sweet potatoes, diced

2 cloves garlic, minced

1 teaspoon cumin

1 teaspoon ancho chili powder (optional)

½ teaspoon kosher or coarse salt

½ teaspoon black pepper

1 tablespoon lime juice

1 28-ounce can diced tomatoes

2–3 cups vegetable stock

1 teaspoon coriander

1 teaspoon cilantro

1 cup frozen corn

2 14-ounce cans black beans, rinsed and drained

2 tablespoons sour cream (optional)

Mediterranean Vegetable and Balsamic Soup

1 teaspoon vegetable oil

1 cup leeks, chopped

1 cup celery, diced

4 cups vegetable stock

1 cup artichoke hearts

3 cloves garlic, minced

1 large carrot, grated

1 cup shredded russet potato

½ cup sweet red pepper, chopped

1 cup cremini mushrooms, quartered

1 cup eggplant, diced

1 cup Roma or plum tomatoes, seeds removed and diced

4 cups Swiss chard

½ cup water

3–4 tablespoons balsamic vinegar

Salt and pepper to taste

Dehydration Time: 5–8 hours
Makes 4–6 servings

The first time I ate this soup was in a wilderness campsite at Potters Lake in the backcountry of Ontario, Canada's Algonquin Provincial Park. As our family was enjoying our dinner, we heard a splash out in the middle of the lake. To our surprise it was a big bull moose going for a swim. Sadly, we didn't get a decent photo, but the soup was good. Bannock bread or toasted pitas are a nice accompaniment.

At Home

Heat the vegetable oil in a large pot over medium heat. Add the leeks and celery and cook until the celery softens. Add the vegetable stock and remaining vegetables, water, and balsamic vinegar and simmer for about 15 minutes or until the vegetables are tender. Season the soup with salt and pepper to taste. Let cool.

Measure the soup and write this measurement on a sticky note. Pour onto lined dehydrator trays and dry for 5 to 8 hours. Place the dried soup mixture and the sticky note in a ziplock freezer bag.

At Camp

Add enough boiling water to the soup to equal the measurement on your sticky note. Be sure to account for and add your dried ingredients to the rehydration container prior to adding the water. You can always add more water if you need to. Once the soup has rehydrated, you might have to reheat it.

Nacho Pizza

Dehydration Time: 5–10 hours
Makes 2 servings

We love to have homemade pizza in the backcountry, especially after being in the woods for a week. This twist on pizza was inspired by a friend who makes a similar pizza for her dinners at home.

AT HOME

Prepare the Basic Yeast Dough mix per the instructions on page 222 or the Gluten-free Pizza Dough from page 223 and put it in a small ziplock freezer bag. Put the dough mix and its instructions along with any herbs you might want to use in the crust into a large ziplock freezer bag.

Dry the onion and green pepper together on a dehydrator tray. Dry them for 5 to 10 hours, depending on the size of the pieces. Dry the jalapeño slices on a separate tray. Also dry ½ cup of your favorite tomato salsa. Place the pepper and onion mixture, jalapeño slices, and salsa in separate ziplock freezer bags and place the bags in with the dough mix. Wrap the cornmeal, if you are using it, in a piece of plastic wrap and put that in the bag with the others. Wrap the cheese. Add the oil to what you are taking.

AT CAMP

Using an equal amount of boiling water and dried ingredients, add water to the bag containing the pepper and onion mixture, being very careful not to burn yourself. Add boiling water to the jalapeño slices as well. Add boiling water to the salsa bag, using a little less water than dried salsa. Prepare the dough according to the recipe directions and rub a little olive oil on it before letting it rise. If the weather is cold, you can place the ziplock bag inside your jacket to aid in rising.

For wheat pizza dough

Once the dough has risen, press the dough out into the pan. Slice or grate the cheese. Drain any excess water from the

1 recipe Basic Yeast Dough (page 222) or 1 recipe Gluten-free Pizza Dough (page 223)

⅛ cup onion, diced

⅓ cup green or red sweet peppers, diced

8–10 sliced jarred jalapeños to taste

½ cup tomato salsa

1–2 teaspoons cornmeal (only necessary if making gluten-free dough)

¼–½ pound Monterey Jack, cheddar, or vegan cheese that melts well

2–3 tablespoons olive oil

pepper and onion mixture. Spread the salsa over the crust and then layer with the cheese and pepper and onion mixture. Drain any excess water from the jalapeño slices and place them on the pizza. Bake the pizza in the oven for 10 to 12 minutes, allowing a few minutes for the oven to preheat with the pizza in it before you start timing. Once the cheese is melted and the crust is golden, remove it from the heat and let it cool a few minutes before eating it.

For gluten-free pizza dough

Once the dough has risen, sprinkle your pan with a little cornmeal and press the dough out into the pan. Bake the pizza, without toppings, in the oven for 10 minutes, allowing a few minutes for the oven to preheat with the pizza in it before you start timing. Meanwhile, slice or grate the cheese. Drain any excess water from the pepper and onion mixture. Remove the pan from the oven and spread the salsa over the crust and then layer with the cheese and pepper and onion mixture. Drain any excess water from the jalapeño slices and place them on the pizza. Put the pizza back in the oven for 10 minutes, allowing a few minutes for the oven to preheat again with the pizza in it before you start timing. Once the cheese is melted and the crust is golden, remove it from the heat and let it cool a few minutes before eating it.

Mediterranean Pizza

Dehydration Time: 5–15 hours
Makes 2 servings

This pizza reflects the flavors of Italy and has kicked-up flavor with the addition of basil and roasted garlic in the dough. My husband asks for this one on every longer trip. Of course, you can use this basic recipe and add your own toppings as you see fit.

AT HOME

Prepare the Basic Yeast Dough mix per the instructions on page 222 or the Gluten-free Pizza Dough from page 223 and put it in a small ziplock freezer bag. Add ½ teaspoon of basil and ¼ teaspoon roasted garlic powder to the dough. Put the dough mix and its instructions into a large ziplock freezer bag.

Dry the roasted peppers, olives, mushrooms, and artichoke hearts separately on dehydrator trays. Dry them for 5 to 15 hours, depending on the size of the pieces. Also dry ¼ to ½ cup of your favorite pizza or marinara sauce. Place the vegetables and sauce in separate ziplock freezer bags and place the bags in with the dough mix. Wrap the cornmeal, if you are using it, in a piece of plastic wrap and put that in the bag with the others. Wrap the cheese. Add the oil to what you are taking.

AT CAMP

Using an equal amount of boiling water and dried ingredients, add water to the bag containing the vegetables, being very careful not to burn yourself. Add boiling water to the sauce bag, using a little less water than dried sauce. Prepare the dough according to the recipe directions and rub a little olive oil on it before letting it rise. If the weather is cold, you can place the ziplock bag inside your jacket to aid in rising.

For wheat pizza dough

Once the dough has risen, press the dough out into the pan. Slice or grate the cheese. Drain any excess water from the

1 recipe Basic Yeast Dough (page 222) or 1 recipe Gluten-free Pizza Dough (page 223)

½ teaspoon dried basil

¼ teaspoon roasted garlic powder (page 7)

⅛ cup roasted red peppers, chopped (page 7)

3 or 4 large black olives, pitted and chopped (optional)

⅛ cup baby portobello (also known as cremini) mushrooms, sliced

¼ cup canned or jarred artichoke hearts, packed in water, drained and chopped

¼–½ cup pizza or marinara sauce

1–2 teaspoons cornmeal (only necessary if making gluten-free dough)

¼–½ pound block mozzarella or vegan mozzarella-style cheese that melts well

2–3 tablespoons olive oil

vegetables. Spread the sauce over the crust and then layer with the cheese and the vegetable mixture. Bake the pizza in the oven for 10 to 12 minutes, allowing a few minutes for the oven to preheat with the pizza in it before you start timing. Once the cheese is melted and the crust is golden, remove it from the heat and let it cool a few minutes before eating it.

For gluten-free pizza dough

Once the dough has risen, sprinkle your pan with a little corn-meal and press the dough out into the pan. Bake the pizza, without toppings, in the oven for 10 minutes, allowing a few minutes for the oven to preheat with the pizza in it before you start timing. Meanwhile, slice or grate the cheese. Drain any excess water from the vegetables. Remove the pan from the oven and spread the sauce over the crust and then layer with the cheese and the vegetable mixture. Put the pizza back in the oven for 10 minutes, allowing a few minutes for the oven to preheat again with the pizza in it before you start timing. Once the cheese is melted and the crust is golden, remove it from the heat and let it cool a few minutes before eating it.

Israeli Couscous with Eggplant, Walnuts, and Feta

**Dehydration Time: 6–10 hours
Makes 4–5 servings**

Israeli couscous is also known as pearl couscous and is similar to orzo or other small pasta. It is also a great addition to soups because of the small size. If you aren't an ovo-lacto vegetarian, you can use capers in place of the Feta cheese.

AT HOME

Toss the diced eggplant and garlic cloves in 2 tablespoons of olive oil. Arrange in a single layer in a casserole dish and roast at 400°F for 15 minutes. Then stir in 1 tablespoon of balsamic vinegar and return to the oven for an additional 15 minutes. Remove the eggplant and garlic from the oven and mash with a fork. Toast the walnuts in a dry frying pan for a few minutes. Let cool and package in plastic wrap. Measure the eggplant mixture and write this measurement on a sticky note. Dry the eggplant on lined dehydrator trays for 6 to 10 hours. Also dry the Feta or capers on a lined dehydrator tray. Place the couscous in a ziplock freezer bag. Be sure to include a note with the cooking instructions for the couscous. Put the dried eggplant mixture and the dried Feta cheese or capers in separate bags and place those, as well as the walnut bundle, in with the couscous. Wrap the mint or basil and chives in plastic wrap and add that to the bag. Add the remaining 2 tablespoons of olive oil to the other oil you will take on your trip.

AT CAMP

Add enough boiling water to the dried eggplant to equal the measurement on your sticky note. Be sure to account for and add your dried ingredients to the rehydration container prior to adding the water. You can always add more water if you

1 cup eggplant, diced

4 whole garlic cloves

4 tablespoons olive oil, divided

1 tablespoon balsamic vinegar

1 tablespoon walnuts

2 tablespoons Feta cheese or capers

1 cup Israeli couscous or orzo (uncooked measurement)

¼ teaspoon dried mint or basil

½ teaspoon dried chives

Black pepper to taste

need to. Add boiling water to the Feta cheese or caper bag using a little less water than you have dried ingredients. Be careful not to burn yourself. While the eggplant is rehydrating, cook the couscous according to the package directions you included. Drain the couscous, and then add the rehydrated eggplant mixture and return to the burner to heat through. Stir in the walnuts, mint or basil, chives, and 1–2 tablespoons olive oil. Top with the Feta or capers. Season with black pepper to taste.

Couscous Pilaf

Dehydration Time: 6–10 hours
Makes 3–4 servings

This simple dish is a trail favorite that comes together quickly at camp. The addition of olive oil boosts the calories.

At Home

Heat the vegetable oil in a frying pan over medium heat. Add the red onions and sauté until they start to soften. Add the remaining vegetables except the green onions and cook until tender. Add the green onions, stir, and remove from the heat. Spread the vegetable mixture on lined dehydrator trays and dry for 6 to 10 hours. Place the dehydrated vegetables in a ziplock freezer bag with the dried apricots and then put the bag into a larger freezer bag along with the couscous. Be sure to include a note with the cooking instructions for the couscous.

Wrap the spices in a piece of plastic wrap. Do the same for the sliced almonds. Put these bundles in the larger bag with the couscous. Add 2 tablespoons of olive oil to the other olive oil that you are taking.

At Camp

Cover the vegetables with boiling water and set in a cozy until they are reconstituted. Once they have rehydrated, drain any excess water into a pot. Set aside. Add enough water to the excess water from the vegetables to cook the couscous, referring to the package directions you included, and bring it to a boil. Add the couscous and, when it has cooked, add the vegetables, spices, olive oil, and sliced almonds. Stir over low temperature until heated through. Season with salt and pepper to taste.

Tip

To enhance the flavor of this dish, simply toast the couscous in a dry frying pan, stirring frequently, for about 2 minutes. Let it cool completely and package as indicated in the "At Home" instructions.

1 teaspoon vegetable oil

⅛ cup red onion, minced

1 large carrot, grated

½ cup zucchini, diced

½ cup sweet pepper, chopped

½ cup button mushrooms, sliced

½ cup green onions, sliced

¼ cup dried apricots, diced

1 cup instant couscous

¼ teaspoon caraway seeds

¼ teaspoon smoked paprika

½ teaspoon cumin

¼ cup sliced almonds

1–2 tablespoons olive oil

Kosher salt and black pepper to taste

Couscous with Chickpeas, Pomegranate, and Pistachios

1 cup canned chickpeas, rinsed and drained

¼ cup pomegranate seeds

1 teaspoon dried lemon zest

1 cup couscous

1 teaspoon dried cilantro

¼ teaspoon cinnamon

2 tablespoons unsalted pistachios, chopped

2 tablespoons olive oil

Salt and pepper to taste

Dehydration Time: 6–15 hours
Makes 3–4 servings

When I was a child, I had a pen pal from a place called Agadir in Morocco, and he was the first person who told me about couscous. Although I haven't made my way there yet, when I think of Morocco, I think of spices in open-air markets and brilliant colors such as the red of a pomegranate. This recipe is inspired by that.

AT HOME

Place the chickpeas on a dehydrator tray and dry for 6 to 10 hours. Dry the pomegranate seeds on a lined dehydrator tray. Don't be alarmed if these take 15 or more hours to completely dry, as they are full of juice. Package the dried chickpeas, dried pomegranate, and dried lemon zest together in a ziplock freezer bag. Put the couscous in another bag. Be sure to include a note with the cooking instructions for the couscous. Wrap the spices in a piece of plastic wrap. Do the same for the pistachios. Put the spice and nut bundles and the bag of chickpea mixture in with the couscous. Pack the olive oil with the other oil you will take on your trip.

AT CAMP

Cover the chickpeas and pomegranate seeds with boiling water and set in a cozy until they are reconstituted. Once they have rehydrated, drain any excess water into a pot. Set aside. Add enough water to the excess water from the chickpeas to cook the couscous, referring to the package directions you included, and bring it to a boil. Add the couscous and, when it has cooked, add the chickpeas, pomegranate seeds, spices, pistachios, and olive oil. Stir over low temperature until heated through. Season with salt and pepper to taste.

Tips

Dried cherries can be used in place of the pomegranate seeds, but they won't impart the same texture or flavor.

If you can't have nuts, you can substitute pepitas or toasted sunflower seeds.

To make this gluten free, use rice or quinoa instead of couscous. This will require a longer cooking time however.

Thai-inspired Couscous

Dehydration time: 6–8 hours
Makes 3–4 servings

1 teaspoon vegetable oil

1 onion, chopped

2 cups mixed vegetables, such
as carrots, broccoli, celery,
green beans, and eggplant,
cut into small pieces

4 teaspoons Thai red curry
paste

½ cup vegetable stock

3 tablespoons coconut cream
powder

½ cup salted peanuts,
chopped

1¾ cups instant couscous

*Thailand meets Morocco in this dish. We first enjoyed this
for dinner on a private wilderness beach that took a few days
of travel to get to. We ate the meal while watching the sunset
and listening to the call of the loons.*

At Home

Heat the oil in a large nonstick frying pan and cook the onion
until it starts to take on a golden color. If carrots are in your
vegetable mix, add them to the onion and cook for 3 minutes.
Add the remaining vegetables and cook for another 3 minutes,
then stir in the Thai curry paste and stock. Cover the pan and
simmer for 10 minutes or until the vegetables are tender-crisp.

Measure the amount you will dry and write the measurement on a sticky note. Place the vegetable mixture on lined
dehydrator trays and dry for 6 to 8 hours. Place the dried mix
in a medium-size ziplock freezer bag with the sticky note.
Put that bag in a larger ziplock freezer bag. Wrap the coconut
powder and peanuts, separately, in a piece of plastic wrap and
add the bundles to the larger freezer bag. Add the couscous to
the larger bag. Be sure to bring a note with cooking instructions for the couscous.

At Camp

Remove the peanut and coconut powder bundles. Set aside.
Add enough boiling water to the vegetable mixture to equal the
measurement on your sticky note. Be sure to account for and
add your dried ingredients to the rehydration container prior
to adding the water. You can always add more water if you need
to. When the vegetables are rehydrated, boil enough water for
the couscous plus ½ cup. Cook the couscous according to the
package directions you brought. Add the coconut powder to the
additional ½ cup of water, mixing thoroughly. Stir the vegetable
mixture and the coconut milk together and serve with the couscous. Sprinkle chopped nuts on top before serving.

Vegetable and Cashew Stir-fry

Dehydration Time: 6–8 hours
Makes 3–4 servings

I modified this quick weekday supper for use on the trail because my son loved it so much. If you like to spice things up a little, add a few chili pepper flakes. Serve over rice, rice noodles, soba noodles, or angel-hair pasta.

AT HOME

Heat the oil in a nonstick skillet over high heat. Add the garlic, gingerroot, carrots, peppers, broccoli, and mushrooms. Cook for 3 to 4 minutes until tender-crisp. Add the green onions and sauté for another minute. Let the mixture cool.

Measure the amount you will dry and write the measurement on a sticky note. Place the vegetable mixture on lined dehydrator trays and dry for 6 to 8 hours. Place the dried mix in a medium-size ziplock freezer bag with the sticky note. Put that bag in a larger ziplock freezer bag. Pour the agave nectar or honey and soy sauce into a leakproof container and put that in the large bag as well. Wrap the cashew nuts and crushed red chilies, if using, in a piece of plastic wrap and add the bundle to the larger freezer bag. Pack the rice or noodles in the larger bag along with cooking instructions.

AT CAMP

Remove the agave or honey and soy sauce bottle, cashew bundle, and noodles. Set aside. Add enough boiling water to the vegetable mixture to equal the measurement on your sticky note. Be sure to account for and add your dried ingredients to the rehydration container prior to adding the water. You can always add more water if you need to. Cook your rice or noodles according to the package directions. Drain and then add the agave or honey and soy sauce mixture, as well as the vegetables, to the rice or noodles. Stir to combine. Sprinkle with the cashew nuts and crushed red chilies, if using, before serving.

1 teaspoon vegetable oil

2 cloves of garlic, minced

1½ tablespoons fresh ginger-root, grated

3 carrots, diced

½ cup sweet red pepper, diced

½ cup sweet yellow pepper, diced

1 cup small broccoli florets

½ cup white mushrooms, thinly sliced

⅔ cup green onions, thinly sliced

1 tablespoon agave nectar or honey

1½ tablespoons soy sauce

⅔ cup salted cashew nuts

½ teaspoon crushed red chilies

3–4 servings of rice or noodles

Chapter 9

Desserts and Baked Goods

There is something about desserts and other baked goods that seems to complete a menu. Maybe it is just a creature comfort that reminds us of home. Or perhaps it is being able to celebrate a special occasion in the wilds with something decadent. Whether it is a light after-dinner treat or a main course, such as pizza, baked goods on a backpacking or paddling trip are treats we enjoy, treats that can lift spirits at the end of a rugged day. Of course, there are some important considerations that one must take into account when it comes to this part of the menu.

- Type of travel (backpacking, hiking, canoeing, kayaking, or portaging)
- Time of year and weather
- Length of trip
- Fuel consumption
- Baking methods
- Equipment
- No-bake options
- Weight and bulk
- Fit with menu (you don't want a heavy dessert after a hearty meal)
- Altitude, which can effect baking times
- Size of group

Recipe Modification

You may be pleasantly surprised at how simple it can be to convert a favorite recipe to suit a backcountry trip. Although some recipes are more easily adapted, with a little thought and some of the following tips, you'll be a regular backwoods baker. Be sure to try your creations at home first; you really don't want to end up with a dessert or meal that doesn't work out at camp. There is nothing more disappointing in the camp kitchen than waiting for that perfect baked delight to be ready, only to find that it is a disaster.

Substitute fresh eggs for one of the alternatives I mentioned on page 32. Powdered milk, powdered almond milk, or powdered soy milk can be used to replace fresh milk. Oil, vegetable shortening, ghee or butter, and margarine can be safely carried for baking. If you do choose a vegan butter substitute or margarine, make sure that it is a variety suitable for baking, as many spreads have too high of a water content.

Packaged single-layer cake mixes, muffin mixes, and cookie mixes can be easily modified. For cake you can bring a little icing sugar and butter to make frosting. Cake and muffin batters can be enhanced with the addition of dried fruit, chocolate pieces, or nuts.

Commercial pizza dough mix, cornbread mix, and biscuit mix can be used easily enough on the trail; however, I prefer to make my own so that I have control over the ingredients. The Basic Biscuits and Gluten-free Biscuits recipes in this chapter are good examples. You can use the recipe as basic dough and add anything you like. For savory biscuits add herbs, hot peppers, olives, or the like. To make sweet biscuits just add a teaspoon of sugar or maple sugar to the dry ingredients and then mix in a small handful of your favorite dried fruit. I like to use a little maple sugar with dried apples and a pinch of cinnamon. Using water instead of milk powder will make biscuits lighter.

Baking Methods

I'm a big fan of the Outback Oven; in fact you might say that it is one of my favorite bits of kitchen kit. It works very well with my pot set and white-gas stove, so I don't need to count on a fire, which is important during the summer season when fire risk is high. It's also multipurpose. The convection dome, a tentlike apparatus made from some space-age-looking fabric, can be used over a pot to keep it warm while foods rehydrate, and I've used it to reduce cooking times.

Another baking contraption that I quite like is called the Backpacker Oven—a two-level oven that also works with a stove that has a remote fuel bottle. It's a little bulkier than the Outback Oven but produces the same great results.

If you plan to have a campfire, then a reflector oven works very well. You can purchase one from Sproul's of Maine at **campfirecookware.com** or, if you are a bit handy, look on the resources page at **aforkinthetrail.com** for links to free instructions if you'd like to make your own.

I find Dutch ovens are a little too weighty and bulky for my taste, but they really do give great results and they are wonderful for car camping or base camping. The BakePacker is lightweight but tends to steam the food and you don't get that yummy golden crust that you get with the Outback Oven or your oven at home. Fry-baking has its place, but it doesn't work with some recipes.

If you are using cookware that isn't nonstick or you merely want to make cleanup easier, I suggest using bakers' parchment paper. It also makes it much easier to remove your baking from the pan. Another of my favorite finds is the silicone muffin cup. They come in several styles, and some even have little feet. The feet, in my opinion, are unnecessary unless you plan to use a steam-baking method, so I use ones that simply look like the paper muffin cup liners. They are less bulky and weigh very little. The silicone is rated for 450°F–470°F depending on the brand. What I like is that they are very lightweight and reusable.

You can make a simple aluminum foil pouch for baking things in the fire. Baked apples are a good example. Core the apple and fill the hole with cinnamon, raisins, and sugar. Then wrap it in foil and put it in the hot coals of your campfire.

Ziplock bags are handy for mixing ingredients, especially when you have dough that needs kneading. Not to mention, if it is cold out, you can keep the dough warm during the rising by placing the bag close to the fire (but not so close that you will melt the bag) or inside your jacket.

Baked and Fried Desserts

Fried desserts are often higher in fat, and you'll need to watch them carefully so that you don't scorch your food. Frying is sometimes faster than baking and can be an effective way to make cookies, dessert tortillas, crepes, and biscuit-based desserts. Fry-baking isn't the best choice for some cakes or for pies. To fry-bake you will need a deep-sided, nonstick frying pan with a lid. If you don't have a lid, a piece of foil works great.

Baking, even though it requires a bit of extra time, equipment, and fuel, adds versatility to the camp menu—an essential luxury that will make your trips even more memorable.

Uncooked Desserts

Uncooked desserts can be a great addition to a menu. Of course, the first thing that comes to mind is a bar of my favorite dark chocolate or a piece of fruit that I've carefully packed in. There are many other ideas for uncooked desserts. A simple vegetarian and gelatin-free pudding can be made in a wide-mouth Nalgene and served with gingersnaps. It won't be as thick as you would make at home, but the flavor and texture will be there. You can make desserts such as bars, fudge, or truffles at home and bring them with you. Leftover breakfast pancakes can be sprinkled with a little lemon juice and icing sugar or spread with apple butter or jam.

Gluten-free Flour

Please read the earlier section on flour substitutions starting on page 34. When I use all-purpose flour in a gluten-free version of a recipe, it is almost always Bob's Red Mill Gluten Free All Purpose Baking Flour, as I've found it gives the best results. If you decide to experiment with a different flour combination, be sure to test the recipe at home first. You don't want to be stuck with something inedible on your trip.

Baking Time

Please note that all baking times are approximate and that many variables can affect how long it will take for a recipe to bake. These include altitude, weather, heat source, cooking equipment, and size. Check items at the earliest suggested time to avoid overbaking or burning your food. Oh, and don't forget the riser if you are using an Outback Oven. Without it you will go from bake to burn in mere seconds. How do I know this? I learned the hard way.

Cherry, Hazelnut, Wild Rice Fry Cookies

Makes 12 cookies (3 per package)

Yes, you read that right: wild rice in cookies. I used wild rice powder to add a little more nuttiness to these cookies. You could also use acorn flour, if you can find it. I didn't have any so I used wild rice powder instead. The idea was inspired by a lady named Carly Joynt. I met her at the Wolf Den Hostel and Nature Retreat in Oxtongue Lake, Ontario, Canada, where we stayed for a weekend of snowshoeing. Carly harvests, dries, and processes her own acorn flour, and even though you can buy it online, she enjoys the process. She made us some wonderful chocolate chip cookies and taught me something new about a very old food source, the acorn.

At Home

Toast the whole wild rice in a dry frying pan over medium heat until it starts to get fragrant. Remove from the pan and let cool. Grind the rice in a coffee or spice grinder until it is a fine powder. Combine the wild rice powder, flour, brown sugar, baking soda, salt, and xanthan gum (if using). Add the cherries, white chocolate chips, and hazelnuts. Stir well. Divide into 4 equal parts and place each part in a ziplock bag. Package the oil with the other vegetable oil you are taking on your trip.

At Camp

Combine 1 package of the mix with 1 tablespoon of oil and 1 tablespoon of water. Put an additional teaspoon of oil in a frying pan and heat on a medium-low flame. Divide the batter into thirds and drop the balls of dough into the frying pan. Gently press each cookie down with a spatula.

Cook for about 3 minutes until the bottom browns. Flip and cook the other side. Cool for a few minutes before eating because the chocolate and nuts will be very hot.

Follow these same steps for each of the other three bags of cookies when you're ready to eat them.

¼ cup wild rice powder

¾ cup all-purpose flour or Bob's Red Mill Gluten Free All Purpose Baking Flour

¼ cup dark brown sugar

½ teaspoon baking soda

½ teaspoon salt

¼ teaspoon xanthan gum (omit if using regular all-purpose flour)

¼ cup dried cherries, chopped

¼ cup white chocolate chips

¼ cup chopped or slivered hazelnuts

1 tablespoon vegetable oil, per package, plus 1 teaspoon

1 tablespoon water, per package

¼ cup almond meal

¾ cup all-purpose flour or
      Bob's Red Mill Gluten Free
      All Purpose Baking Flour

¼ cup dark brown sugar

½ teaspoon baking soda

½ teaspoon salt

¼ teaspoon xanthan gum
      (omit if using regular
      all-purpose flour)

¼ cup dried blueberries

⅛ cup chopped candied
      ginger

¼ cup slivered almonds

1 tablespoon vegetable oil,
      per package,
      plus 1 teaspoon

1 tablespoon water,
      per package

Double Ginger, Almond, Blueberry Fry Cookies

Makes 12 cookies (3 per package)

To say that candied ginger is one of my favorite treats might be an understatement, as you've probably guessed from my earlier mentions of it. I've loved the sweet bite since I was a young child and my mother let me taste it for the first time. I'm addicted. It goes nicely with almonds and blueberries, so I've added it to this recipe. If you like, you can add a few tablespoons of chocolate or carob chips to the recipe too.

At Home

Combine the almond meal, flour, brown sugar, baking soda, salt, and xanthan gum (if using). Add the blueberries, candied ginger, and slivered almonds. Stir well. Divide into 4 equal parts and place each part in a ziplock bag. Package the oil with the other vegetable oil you are taking on your trip.

At Camp

Combine 1 package of the mix with 1 tablespoon of oil and 1 tablespoon of water. Put an additional teaspoon of oil in a frying pan and heat on a medium-low flame. Divide the batter into thirds and drop the balls of dough into the frying pan. Gently press each cookie down with a spatula.

Cook for about 3 minutes until the bottom browns. Flip and cook the other side. Cool for a few minutes before eating because the blueberries and nuts will be very hot.

Follow these same steps for each of the other three bags of cookies when you're ready to eat them.

Tip

If you don't have any almond meal/almond flour on hand and you are not in need of a gluten-free cookie, you can use a full cup of all-purpose flour instead of ¾ cup. You could also substitute the almond meal with unsweetened cocoa powder to make a chocolate variation.

Chocolate Chai Fry Cookies

Makes 12 cookies (3 per package)

This idea was originally for hot chocolate but somehow ended up becoming a cookie. Sometimes I just don't know where inspiration is going to take me. This spicy cookie is delicious with a cup of orange pekoe tea as you watch the sun go down on the horizon. I think the leftover cookies would make a great trail snack; however, my companions devour them so quickly that I never get the chance to test that out.

AT HOME

Combine the flour, cocoa powder, brown sugar, baking soda, salt, and xanthan gum (if using). Add the chocolate chips, raisins, walnuts, and spices. Stir well. Divide into 4 equal parts and place each part in a ziplock bag. Package the oil with the other vegetable oil you are taking on your trip.

AT CAMP

Combine 1 package of the mix with 1 tablespoon of oil and 1 tablespoon of water. Put an additional teaspoon of oil in a frying pan and heat on a medium-low flame. Divide the batter into thirds and drop the balls of dough into the frying pan. Gently press each cookie down with a spatula.

Cook for about 3 minutes until the bottom browns. Flip and cook the other side. Cool for a few minutes before eating because the chocolate and nuts will be very hot.

Follow these same steps for each of the other three bags of cookies when you're ready to eat them.

¾ cup all-purpose flour or Bob's Red Mill Gluten Free All Purpose Baking Flour

¼ cup unsweetened cocoa powder

¼ cup dark brown sugar

½ teaspoon baking soda

½ teaspoon salt

¼ teaspoon xanthan gum (omit if using regular all-purpose flour)

¼ cup mini chocolate chips or carob chips

¼ cup dark raisins or sultanas

¼ cup chopped walnuts

⅛ teaspoon ground ginger

⅛ teaspoon cardamom

⅛ teaspoon cinnamon

⅛ scant teaspoon cloves

⅛ teaspoon black pepper

1 tablespoon vegetable oil, per package, plus 1 teaspoon

1 tablespoon water, per package

Portuguese Fig Fudge

Makes 24 pieces

½ pound dried Turkish figs

1½ cups almond meal

4 tablespoons unsweetened cocoa or carob powder

1 teaspoon cinnamon

Fresh zest of 1 lemon

½ cup water less 2 tablespoons

1 cup fine granulated sugar

You will see fig and almond dishes on many a menu in the Algarve region of Portugal because of the abundance of both products there. This is one of those recipes that should be made at home and packaged for your trip. I recommend wrapping it in plastic wrap or waxed paper, as it can be a little gooey. While we like to have it as an after-dinner sweet, it also makes a great snack while hiking.

At Home

Line an 8-inch square pan with parchment paper and set aside. Purée the figs in a food processor or chop them very fine by hand. Mix the almond meal, cocoa powder, cinnamon, and lemon zest together. Mix the almond meal mixture in with the figs. Set aside.

Place the water and sugar in a heavy saucepan over medium-high heat. Stir until the sugar dissolves. Once the mixture starts to boil, let it bubble for 3 minutes without stirring. Remove the pot from the heat and stir in the fig and almond meal mixture. It will be thick. Return it to medium-low heat and cook it slowly until it has a slight gloss and pulls away from the sides of the pot in a large ball. This will take 3 to 5 minutes.

Put the mixture into the lined pan and pat it down with a wooden spoon. Let cool completely and cut into small squares with a sharp knife. Wipe the knife clean with a hot, wet cloth between cuts. Roll each piece in granulated sugar or almond meal to keep the fudge from sticking. Wrap each piece in plastic wrap or waxed paper and place in a large ziplock freezer bag.

Cherry Almond Truffles

Makes 12 truffles

These aren't your traditional chocolate truffles; in fact, the only chocolate flavor comes from the carob or cocoa that they are rolled in. These will only keep for about 5 days so it is best to make them right before your trip.

AT HOME

Toast the whole wild rice in a dry frying pan over medium heat until it starts to get fragrant. Remove from the pan and let cool. Grind the rice in a coffee or spice grinder until it is a fine powder. Combine the wild rice powder, almond meal, dates, cherries, and marzipan together in a food processor and pulse until well combined. Shape into 12 balls and roll each truffle in carob or cocoa powder. Wrap, individually, in plastic wrap and package in a ziplock bag.

⅛ cup wild rice powder

¼ cup almond meal

⅛ cup Medjool or honey dates, without pits

⅛ cup dried cherries

⅛ cup marzipan

⅛ cup carob or unsweetened cocoa powder

Mayan Black Bean Brownies

⅙ cup almond meal

⅙ cup black bean flour (see page 35)

¼ cup unsweetened cocoa or carob powder

½ cup brown sugar

½ teaspoon baking powder

¼ teaspoon salt

⅛ cup cocoa nibs, mini chocolate chips, or carob chips

⅛ teaspoon cinnamon

⅛ teaspoon cayenne pepper

Egg replacer equivalent to 1 egg

⅛ cup water plus enough for the egg replacer

⅓ cup almond butter

Parchment paper

Makes 4 servings

I'll never forget the day that I first served these to my son, Tobias. I was waiting for the grimace because they were made with beans. Instead I got a remark about his father being in the woods and his query as to whether he could devour his dad's portion too. I figured that was a pass for this recipe. If you like the combination of salt and sweet, you could sprinkle a little coarse salt on the top right before baking.

At Home

Mix the almond meal, black bean flour, cocoa powder, brown sugar, baking powder, salt, cocoa nibs, cinnamon, and cayenne pepper together and place in a ziplock freezer bag. Put the egg replacer powder in a snack-size ziplock bag with a note stating how much water to add for 1 egg. Put this bag in the bag with the dry ingredients. Add the almond butter to the other almond butter that you are taking on your trip or package it in a leakproof container and add it to the bag with the dry ingredients.

At Camp

Add the water to the egg replacer as indicated on your note and set aside. Melt the almond butter in a pan over low heat. Remove from the heat and add the butter, ⅛ cup of water, and the egg replacement mixture to the freezer bag containing the dry ingredients and mix well. Pour the batter into a pot or pan lined with parchment paper and bake for 25 to 30 minutes or until a toothpick or knife inserted in the center comes out clean. Let cool and serve. Wrap any leftovers in plastic wrap for the next day.

Tropical Blondies

Makes 4 servings

This tropical version of my white bean brownies uses some of the Grilled Cinnamon Pineapple from page 136, but if you don't have pineapple, you can use raisins.

AT HOME

Mix the almond meal, white bean flour, all-purpose flour, brown sugar, baking powder, salt, pineapple, and shredded coconut together and place in a ziplock freezer bag. Put the egg replacer powder in a snack-size ziplock bag with a note stating how much water to add for 1 egg. Put this bag in the bag with the dry ingredients. Add the almond butter to the other almond butter that you are taking on your trip or package it in a leakproof container and add it to the bag with the dry ingredients. Mix the extracts together in a small leakproof bottle and place in the bag with the dry ingredients.

AT CAMP

Add the water to the egg replacer as indicated on your note and set aside. Melt the almond butter in a pan over low heat. Remove from the heat and add the butter, ⅛ cup of water, the egg replacement mixture, and the extracts to the freezer bag containing the dry ingredients and mix well. Pour the batter into a pot or pan lined with parchment paper and bake for 25 to 30 minutes or until a toothpick or knife inserted in the center comes out clean. Let cool and serve. Wrap any leftovers in plastic wrap for the next day.

⅙ cup almond meal

⅙ cup white bean flour (see pages 35–36)

¼ cup all-purpose flour or Bob's Red Mill Gluten Free All Purpose Baking Flour

½ cup brown sugar

½ teaspoon baking powder

¼ teaspoon salt

⅛ cup Grilled Cinnamon Pineapple, dried pineapple, or raisins, chopped

⅛ cup shredded coconut

Egg replacer equivalent to 1 egg

⅛ cup water plus enough for the egg replacer

⅓ cup almond butter

½ teaspoon rum extract

½ teaspoon pure vanilla extract

Parchment paper

Apple Cinnamon Upside-down Cake

Makes 3–4 servings

½ cup all-purpose flour

¼ cup maple sugar

¾ teaspoon baking powder

1 teaspoon instant apple cider powder

½ teaspoon cinnamon

½ teaspoon salt

Egg replacer equivalent to 1 egg

⅛ cup vegetable oil

¼ cup water, plus enough to rehydrate apple slices and for the egg replacer

Parchment paper

Topping

¼ cup maple sugar

½ teaspoon cinnamon

⅔ cup dried apple slices

¼ cup pecan halves (optional)

This apple cake has a hint of maple with the use of maple sugar. It makes a nice dessert, and leftovers can be saved for breakfast or to munch on the next day while you hike. This never happens with us though.

At Home

Combine the flour, sugar, baking powder, instant apple cider powder, cinnamon, and salt. Pour the mixture into a ziplock bag. Put the egg replacer powder in a snack-size ziplock bag with a note stating how much water to add for 1 egg. Put this bag in the bag with the dry ingredients. Add the oil to the oil you are already taking on your trip. Mix the maple sugar and cinnamon for the topping, wrap it in plastic wrap, and put that in the bag with the flour mixture. Pack the apple slices and pecans.

At Camp

Rehydrate the apple slices in a little boiling water. Let sit until rehydrated, drain, and set aside. In a small pot or large ziplock freezer bag, add water to the egg replacer powder as indicated on your note and set aside. Add ⅛ cup vegetable oil and ¼ cup water to the egg mixture. Add the liquid mix to the dry ingredients and stir just enough to moisten.

Line the bottom and sides of a pot or pan with parchment paper. Place the apple slices in a single layer, with the pecans if you are using them, on the parchment paper and sprinkle with the cinnamon–maple sugar mixture. Gently spread the batter on top of the apple slices. Bake for 25 to 35 minutes or until a toothpick or knife inserted in the center comes out clean. Let cool slightly.

Tip

If you don't have maple sugar, use the same amount of white sugar for the batter and brown sugar for the topping.

Lemon Rosemary Cupcakes

Makes 6 cupcakes

This seems an odd combination for a dessert, but there is a fresh burst of summery flavor to these cupcakes and the rosemary works well with the lemon. This recipe was inspired by my friend in Louisiana, Karla Coreil. She often has an abundance of rosemary in her garden; when we were talking about uses for the herb, it sparked an idea. Why not use it in dessert?

At Home

Combine the flour, sugar, baking powder, and salt. Pour the mixture in a ziplock bag. Put the egg replacer powder in a snack-size ziplock bag with a note stating how much water to add for 1 egg. Put this bag in the bag with the dry ingredients. Wrap the rosemary in plastic wrap and put it in the bag with the flour mixture. Pack a lemon and add the oil to what you are taking on your trip. Put the icing sugar in a ziplock bag.

At Camp

In a small pot or large ziplock freezer bag, add water to the egg replacer powder as indicated on your note and set aside. Add ⅛ cup vegetable oil to the egg mixture. Juice the lemon using a fork and add ¼ cup lemon juice to the oil and egg mixture. Reserve 1 tablespoon of lemon juice.

Slice the lemon peel into thin layers, being careful to avoid the pith. Sliver 1 teaspoon of the lemon rind and mix it and the rosemary with the dry ingredients. Add the liquid mix and stir just enough to moisten.

Put the batter into silicone muffin cups placed in your baking pan or pour directly into a parchment paper–lined baking pan. Bake for 25 to 35 minutes or until a toothpick or knife inserted in the center comes out clean. Set aside.

Make a glaze by stirring the tablespoon of reserved lemon juice into ¼ cup icing sugar. Spread it over the warm cupcakes or cake.

½ cup all-purpose flour

¼ cup white sugar

¾ teaspoon baking powder

½ teaspoon salt

Egg replacer equivalent to 1 egg, plus water as necessary

¼ teaspoon dried rosemary, finely chopped, or ½ teaspoon fresh rosemary (it will keep for a few days in cooler weather)

1 fresh lemon

⅛ cup vegetable oil

Parchment paper

Icing

1 tablespoon lemon juice (from lemon above)

¼ cup icing sugar

¼ cup all-purpose flour or Bob's Red Mill All Purpose Baking Flour

¾ cup rolled oats

⅛ teaspoon cardamom

⅛ teaspoon cinnamon

⅛ teaspoon ginger

¼ cup brown sugar

A pinch of salt

1 tablespoon white or maple sugar

1½ teaspoons loose green tea with jasmine

1 star anise

1½–2 cups dried figs, dried apricots, raisins, dried cranberries, dried apples, and dried pears, chopped and mixed

1 tablespoon dried pomegranate, (optional)

½ teaspoon dried orange zest, (optional)

2 tablespoons butter or vegan butter substitute suitable for baking

Parchment paper

Winter Fruit Crumble

Makes 2–3 servings

This recipe started out as one of those panic moments. It was Christmastime, and we had last-minute guests come to visit and invited them to stay for dinner. I wanted to make a dessert and there was no time to run to the market, so I looked to see what was in the pantry. I had loads of dried fruit leftover from granola-making. I had the sudden idea to make a fruit crumble, and while my guests were raving about the dessert, it dawned on me that this would be a nice treat on the trail.

At Home

Mix the flour, rolled oats, cardamom, cinnamon, and ginger together and place in a ziplock bag. Put the brown sugar and salt in another smaller ziplock bag. Place 1 tablespoon white or maple sugar in a piece of plastic wrap and put it inside the brown sugar bag. Wrap the tea and star anise in a piece of cheesecloth and tie with kitchen string or use a tea filter, then wrap in plastic wrap. Put the dried fruit, including the pomegranate and orange zest if using, in another bag and add the bundle of tea. Then place all the small bags of ingredients inside the bag containing the flour. Pack the butter or vegan butter substitute with any other butter you are taking on your trip.

At Camp

Place the tea bag bundle in a pot with the dried fruit and cover with boiling water. Let sit until the fruit is rehydrated and then remove the tea bag, drain, and set aside. Line the bottom and sides of a pot or pan with parchment paper. Place the rehydrated fruit in the bottom of the pot and sprinkle it with 1 tablespoon white or maple sugar.

Add 2 tablespoons butter or vegan butter substitute to the ziplock bag containing the brown sugar mixture and knead until the sugar mixture and butter are creamed. Shake the bag of flour, oats, and spices to ensure it is well combined and then blend in the butter mixture. Sprinkle over the fruit mixture. Bake for 30 to 40 minutes until the top is golden. Allow to cool slightly and serve.

Monkey Bread

Makes 3–4 servings

No one really quite knows the origin of this recipe's name, but it certainly is delicious. In the USA this bread is typically served for breakfast. We usually make it after dinner and then save half of it for a quick breakfast the next morning.

AT HOME

Place a ziplock freezer bag of yeast dough mix and its instructions into a large ziplock freezer bag. Mix the brown sugar and cinnamon together. Package the sugar mixture in a small ziplock bag and the nuts in plastic wrap and add them to the ziplock bag containing the yeast dough mix. Add the butter to what you will take on your trip.

AT CAMP

Prepare the yeast dough and let rise according to the recipe directions. If the weather is cold, you can place the ziplock bag inside your jacket to aid in rising. Once the dough has risen, break off pieces and roll them into 1-inch balls.

Melt the butter or vegan butter substitute over medium-low heat. Dip each ball in melted butter and then in the cinnamon-sugar mixture. Place the pieces together to form a ring in a parchment paper–lined pot or pan, sprinkling with nuts between each layer.

Bake in an Outback Oven or reflector oven for 10 to 12 minutes after the oven is preheated. Once the bread is cooked through and golden, remove from the heat and let cool for a few minutes before heating so that the nuts don't burn your mouth. Pull apart and enjoy.

1 recipe Basic Yeast Dough (page 222)

¼ cup brown sugar

1 teaspoon cinnamon

⅛ cup pistachio nuts, finely chopped

¼ cup butter or vegan butter substitute suitable for baking

Parchment paper

Chocolate Hazelnut Spirals

1 recipe Basic Yeast Dough
   (page 222)

⅓ cup Nutella or other hazelnut spread

⅛ cup hazelnuts, finely
   chopped

Icing

¼ cup icing sugar

1 tablespoon Frangelico or
   Kahlúa liqueur

Makes 3–4 servings

Decadent might be an understatement when it comes to these super-hazelnutty spirals. Not only is there hazelnut spread in the rolls but they are also laced with finely chopped hazelnuts and glazed with a Frangelico icing.

AT HOME

Place a ziplock freezer bag of yeast dough mix and its instructions into a large ziplock freezer bag. Package the hazelnut spread in a leakproof container and the nuts in plastic wrap and add them to the ziplock bag containing the yeast dough mix. Place the icing sugar in a small ziplock bag and add that to the yeast dough bag. Put the liqueur in a leakproof bottle.

AT CAMP

Prepare the yeast dough and let rise according to the recipe directions. If the weather is cold, you can place the ziplock bag inside your jacket to aid in rising. Once the dough has risen, press it out into a rectangular shape.

Spread the dough evenly with hazelnut spread, keeping the spread 1 inch away from the edges. Sprinkle with the chopped hazelnuts and roll it up, starting on one of the long sides. Moisten the long edge with a bit of water and press to seal the roll. Cut into 6 pieces.

Place the rolls in an Outback Oven or reflector oven for 10 to 12 minutes after the oven is preheated. Once the bread is cooked through and golden, remove from the heat and let cool for a few minutes before heating so that the nuts don't burn your mouth.

Make a glaze by stirring 1 tablespoon of Frangelico or Kahlúa into ¼ cup icing sugar. Spread it over the warm hazelnut rolls.

Tips

An easy way to roll out the dough is to put it in a large ziplock freezer bag and use your water bottle as a rolling pin. Then all you have to do is cut off one side of the bag and add the filling.

If you are making this for the kids, use a tablespoon of reconstituted powdered almond milk or other powdered milk to make the icing.

Brandied Fruit Compote with Sweet Biscuits

1 recipe Basic Biscuits (page 220) or Gluten-free Biscuits (page 221) or leftover pound/loaf cake

2 teaspoons plus 1 table-spoon fine granulated sugar, maple sugar, or organic cane sugar

⅛ cup dried cherries

¼ cup dried peaches, coarsely chopped

⅛ cup dried blueberries

½ teaspoon dried orange zest

½ cup brandy or cognac

Makes 6 servings

This rich compote adds a bit of glam to dessert. It was another one of these recipes that came about while scrounging through my pack to see what I could make nearing the end of a trip. I just happened to be carrying a small flask of brandy and some extra dried fruit, and we had leftover biscuits from breakfast.

At Home

Combine the ingredients for your choice of biscuit recipe with 2 teaspoons sugar and place in a ziplock freezer bag with the "At Camp" instructions from the biscuit recipe. Put the dried fruit and orange zest in a ziplock freezer bag and place that in the larger bag with the biscuit mix. Place 1 tablespoon sugar in a piece of plastic wrap and put that in the bag with the fruit. Put the brandy or cognac in a leakproof bottle.

At Camp

Ensure that you are at least 6 feet away from anything flammable—do not make this recipe under a tarp or near your tent. Mix the fruit, 1 tablespoon sugar, and all but 2 table-spoons brandy in a frying pan and carefully heat the mixture. Let the fruit simmer in the hot brandy until it rehydrates and the mixture thickens. Remove from the heat and set aside. Follow the "At Camp" instructions for the biscuits. Bake as indicated in the instructions for the biscuit recipe. Add the remaining brandy to the fruit while it is off the burner. Put the pan of fruit back on the heat and carefully tilt the pan so that the alcohol catches fire. Alternatively turn off the stove and light the pan with a match—either way be very careful. When the flames go out, spoon the warm compote on top of the biscuits.

Tips

If you want to make this for children, use a bag of fruit tea such as peach or cranberry and ½ cup of water. Steep the fruit and tea in boiling water for 5 minutes.

Masa Dumplings for Chili or Soup

Makes 16 little dumplings

¾ cup masa harina

½ teaspoon salt

¼ teaspoon dried cilantro

2 teaspoons vegetable oil

These little dumplings work well in the Four Pepper Chili or the Black Bean, Corn, and Sweet Potato Soup from the Dinners chapter. Add a pinch of cayenne for a bit of heat.

At Home

Mix the masa harina, salt, and cilantro together and place in a ziplock bag. Add the vegetable oil to any other vegetable oil you are taking with you.

At Camp

Bring your chili or soup to a boil, ensuring that there is some liquid in the pot, as the dumplings will absorb some of the liquid. Add 2 teaspoons vegetable oil and enough water to the bag of dry ingredients to make soft dough. Cut a corner off the bag so that the opening is about ¾-inch across. Squeeze out dumplings, approximately the size of a large marble, into the boiling chili or soup. Reduce the heat, cover, and cook the dumplings for 10 minutes or until cooked through.

Flatbread

Makes 4–6 servings

2½ cups all-purpose flour plus ¼ cup extra all-purpose flour for kneading

1 envelope rapid-rise yeast (about 2 teaspoons)

1 teaspoon sugar

1 teaspoon salt

¼ cup vegetable oil

1 cup water

One of the things I'd miss on long trips is fresh bread. Pitas would only last for so many days before they would get stale or go bad on a 10-day trip. This recipe is adapted from one that my dear friend and canoeist Shelley Lauzon made for us on a quiet little lake after several days of paddling together. This bread is delicious when sprinkled with a little spice blend called za'atar.

At Home

Place the flour except for the additional ¼ cup in a large ziplock freezer bag with the unopened envelope of yeast. Wrap the ¼ cup extra flour and sugar separately in plastic wrap and the salt in a medium ziplock bag that has been labeled. Place the flour, sugar, and salt packages in the bag with the large amount of flour. Pack the oil with the other oil you will take with you on your trip.

At Camp

Put ½ cup warm water in your cup and mix in 1 teaspoon of sugar. Sprinkle the rapid-rise yeast into the water, and let it sit for 5 minutes. Meanwhile add ½ cup warm water to the freezer bag containing the salt. Remove the extra flour bundle from the large bag of flour and set aside. When the yeast is activated, pour the mixture, along with the salt water, into the large bag with the flour. Knead the bag for 8 to 10 minutes, adding more flour if needed. Divide the dough into 6 pieces and flatten each piece into a ¼-inch-thick circle. Heat a little of the oil in a frying pan over medium heat and fry each flatbread, flipping once, until golden brown on both sides.

Tip

If you prefer to use whole-wheat flour, you can replace half of the all-purpose flour with all-purpose whole-wheat flour.

Quinoa Chickpea Spiced Fry Bread

Makes 4 servings

This spicy and crispy flatbread combines quinoa and chickpea flour, which makes it a little higher in protein than other fry bread. These are best served right after cooking and make a nice accompaniment to a soup or lentil dishes.

At Home

Combine the flours, salt, cumin, and black pepper and place the mixture in a ziplock freezer bag. Pack the oil with the other vegetable oil you are taking on your trip.

At Camp

Add 1 to 1¼ cups water to the flour mixture to make a loose batter. Heat a ⅛-inch layer of oil in a frying pan over medium-high heat. Drop the batter by heaping tablespoonfuls into the pan, flattening and smoothing with the back of a spoon. Fry the bread until the top edges start to appear dry and the bottom is golden and crispy. Flip and cook on the other side. Serve immediately, while still warm.

½ cup chickpea flour

½ cup quinoa flour

1 tablespoon potato flour (not potato starch)

¾ teaspoon kosher salt

½ teaspoon cumin

½ teaspoon black pepper

¼ cup vegetable oil, for frying

1–1¼ cup water

Focaccia with Caramelized Balsamic Onions and Rosemary

1 recipe Basic Yeast Dough (page 222)

½ cup onion, thinly sliced

2 tablespoons balsamic vinegar

¼ teaspoon dried rosemary, crumbled

¼ cup fresh goat cheese or herbed goat cheese

2 teaspoons olive oil

Kosher salt and pepper to taste

Parchment paper

Dehydration Time: 8–10 hours
Makes 2–4 servings

This is delicious on its own, as a side for soup, or as the base for a sandwich. You can also use the caramelized onion and rosemary mixture as a topping for the gluten-free pizza crust. If you are vegan, omit the cheese or use a vegan alternative.

AT HOME

Place a ziplock freezer bag of the yeast dough mix and its "At Camp" instructions into a large ziplock freezer bag. Sauté the onion slices in a frying pan over medium heat until they start to turn golden brown. Add the balsamic vinegar and cook until the vinegar reduces. Dehydrate on lined dehydrator trays for 8 to 10 hours. Let cool and place in a ziplock freezer bag with the rosemary. Put the bag of onions and rosemary into the large ziplock with the bag of yeast dough mix. When you are ready to leave for your trip, wrap the goat cheese in a piece of plastic wrap and place that in a separate freezer bag and store in an insulated cooler bag or cozy. Package the olive oil with the other olive oil you will take on your trip.

AT CAMP

Add a little less boiling water than you have dried ingredients to the onion mixture and set it aside to rehydrate. Once it has rehydrated, drain off any excess liquid. Prepare the dough and let rise according to the recipe directions. If the weather is cold, you can place the ziplock bag inside your jacket to help the dough rise.

Once the dough has risen, press it into a pot or pan lined with parchment paper. Top with the rehydrated onion and rosemary mixture. Then crumble the goat cheese on top, if you are using it. Drizzle with 1 to 2 teaspoons olive oil and season with salt and pepper.

Place in an Outback Oven or reflector oven and bake for 10 to 12 minutes after the oven has preheated. Once the bread has cooked through and is golden, remove the focaccia from the heat. Let it cool for a few minutes before eating so that the onions do not burn your mouth.

Tip

You can also add 1 tablespoon of your favorite dried mushrooms to the onions when you are rehydrating them and omit the cheese to create a different flavor combination.

Basic Biscuits

Makes 6 biscuits

1 cup all-purpose flour

2 teaspoons baking powder

½ teaspoon salt

1 tablespoon butter, vegan
    butter substitute suitable
    for baking, or shortening

½ cup water

Parchment paper

This biscuit recipe is from my first book, A Fork in the Trail, *and is a great all-purpose biscuit that can be made sweet or savory. It is easy to make on the trail, so I felt it warranted inclusion in this book as well.*

AT HOME

Sift the dry ingredients once and place them in a ziplock bag. Package the butter (or shortening) separately and put it in the ziplock bag with the dry ingredients.

AT CAMP

Mix the butter (or shortening) with the flour mixture using your fingertips until the mixture looks like small beans.

Mix in ½ cup of water until you have a very soft dough. Do not knead. Shape into 6 biscuits.

Place in a pan lined with parchment paper for baking. Bake for 20 minutes. If you are preparing these in a frying pan, cook until they are golden on the bottom, then flip them and cook them until they're done.

Tip

Do not use margarine or oil because it will make the biscuits tough and they will not cook properly.

Gluten-free Biscuits

Makes 6 biscuits

My first attempt at gluten-free baking was with biscuits. Back then, I didn't understand how not having gluten in flour could affect a recipe and I created biscuits that could have been used for hockey pucks; hockey is, after all, a Canadian pastime. Then I discovered that with the use of tapioca flour and xanthan gum, I could make a light, fluffy biscuit that is gluten free.

AT HOME

Sift the dry ingredients together and place them in a ziplock bag. Package the butter (or shortening) separately and put it in the ziplock bag with the dry ingredients.

AT CAMP

Mix the butter (or shortening) with the flour mixture using your fingertips until the mixture looks like small beans.

Mix in ¼ cup of water until you have a very soft dough (add more water if needed). Do not knead. Shape into 6 biscuits.

Place in a pan lined with parchment paper for baking. Bake for 20 to 25 minutes.

⅓ cup white rice flour

⅓ cup tapioca flour

¼ cup brown rice flour

1½ teaspoons xanthan gum

1 tablespoon soy milk powder

2 teaspoons baking powder

¼ teaspoon baking soda

½ teaspoon salt

2 tablespoons butter, vegan butter substitute suitable for baking, or shortening

¼ cup water

Parchment paper

Basic Yeast Dough

Makes 2–3 servings

This all-purpose dough recipe is from A Fork in the Trail. *It can be used for buns, pizza, desserts, and focaccia.*

1 heaping teaspoon
(½ envelope) rapid-rise
yeast

1 cup all-purpose flour

½ teaspoon salt

½ teaspoon sugar

2 teaspoons vegetable or
olive oil

½ cup warm water

AT HOME

If the yeast you buy does not come packaged in an envelope, put it in a small ziplock freezer bag. Mix the flour and salt together and place it in a ziplock freezer bag. Put the yeast envelope or package into the bag with the flour. Add the sugar and the oil to what you are taking on your trip.

AT CAMP

Put ½ cup warm water in your cup and mix in ½ teaspoon of sugar. Sprinkle the rapid-rise yeast into the water and let it sit for 1 or 2 minutes. Pour the yeast mixture into the dry ingredients and add 2 teaspoons of vegetable or olive oil. (Use olive oil to make pizza or herb bread and vegetable oil to make sweet bread like Monkey Bread.)

Knead for 5 minutes or until the ingredients are well combined and the dough is elastic. Let rise for 5 minutes, then shape it into 6 buns, a loaf, or a pizza crust. Bake for 10 to 15 minutes or until golden.

Gluten-free Pizza Dough

Makes 1 pizza crust

This pizza dough is full of flavor but must be twice-baked for best results. Don't be alarmed; it doesn't use a lot of fuel, and pizza in the backcountry is definitely a treat.

At Home

Mix the herbs, white rice flour, brown rice flour, potato starch, and tapioca starch together and place in a large ziplock freezer bag. Mix the salt and xanthan gum together and bundle in a piece of plastic wrap. Wrap the cornmeal in a piece of plastic wrap and put that, and the xanthan gum bundle, in the freezer bag with the flour and herb mixture. If the yeast you buy does not come packaged in an envelope, put it in a small ziplock freezer bag. Put the yeast envelope or bag into the bag with the flour. Pour the apple cider vinegar into a small leakproof bottle and place that in the bag of flour. Add the sugar and the oil to what you are taking on your trip.

At Camp

Put ½ cup warm water in your cup and mix in 1 teaspoon of sugar. Sprinkle the rapid-rise yeast into the water and let it sit for 1 or 2 minutes. While you are waiting for the yeast, add 2 tablespoons of olive oil to 1 teaspoon of apple cider vinegar and add the salt and xanthan gum mixture. Add it to the yeast mixture once the yeast has sat for a few minutes. Add the liquid ingredients to the flour and herb mixture and knead for 2 to 3 minutes. Line a pan with parchment paper and lightly oil the top of the paper. Lightly sprinkle cornmeal on top of the oil. With wet hands press the dough out onto the lined pan. Bake the pizza crust for 10 minutes and then remove the pan from the heat. Flip it over and add your sauce and toppings and bake for 10 to 15 minutes or until all the toppings are heated through.

¼ teaspoon dried oregano

¼ teaspoon dried basil

⅜ cup white rice flour

⅜ cup brown rice flour

¼ cup potato starch

⅛ cup tapioca starch

½ teaspoon salt

½ teaspoon xanthan gum

1 tablespoon cornmeal

1 heaping teaspoon (½ envelope) rapid-rise yeast

1 teaspoon apple cider vinegar

1 teaspoon sugar

2 tablespoons olive oil

½ cup warm water

Parchment paper

Chapter 10

BEVERAGES

As backpackers and paddlers, we should be aware of the importance of staying hydrated, yet so many times I've traveled in the wilderness with people who ignore their thirst cues and start to suffer from the signs of dehydration. These include headache, nausea, irritability, muscle cramps, fatigue, and eventually a loss of coordination. I always keep electrolyte replacement crystals in my first-aid kit, and while I've never had to use them for myself, I have had to break them out for others. I have a dear friend who I've paddled and portaged with on many a trip and I find that I have to remind her to drink. Hydration is important in the winter too, especially if you are sweating due to warm clothing. Dehydration is serious and can cause death, so it isn't something to be taken lightly.

Drinking plain water, for some, can get mundane, and while it's necessary, there are ways to jazz it up. I travel in the Canadian Shield, and sometimes the water is brackish or mineral laden and the color of weak tea, and it doesn't taste as beautiful as water from a fresh spring. Adding a flavoring makes it more palatable and can be very helpful if you are traveling with younger children who might be put off by the taste of such water.

On shorter trips where a cooler or cooler bag is feasible, you can freeze a few Tetra packs of juice or almond milk and use them to chill the foods in your cooler. The juice is often still cool once the food from the cooler bag has been consumed and can be a nice treat. Cold drinks are definitely one of the things I miss on those hot summer trips because I usually only take a cooler if we are camping in a campground with our Jeep. We also enjoy a variety of hot drinks on our trips. Because we are often out for 10 to 14 nights at a time, we generally get into some cool and rainy conditions. In fact, my husband's record for rain is so bad that family tease about booking their vacations when we won't be camping in the backcountry. Where you put Bryan in a situation with a tent, there will be rain—lots of it. One trip in particular always comes to mind. We were in the wilds for 7 days, 6 of which brought snow, rain, hail, sleet, and more rain. One of the things that got us through and kept morale up, especially with that damp cold that chills you to the bone, was the variety of hot drinks I had brought.

The following are some ideas for cold and hot drinks to keep you well hydrated on your trips:

- Tang, served hot or cold or with soy or almond milk instead of water
- Hot chocolate (look for vegan and organic varieties or make your own)
- Cocoa
- Lemonade, served hot or cold
- Herbal and fruit teas
- Coffee
- Chicory

- *Mate* (also known as *chimarrão* or *cimarrón*)
- Crystal Light or other drink crystals
- Apple cider (this can be purchased as a powder and consumed hot or cold)
- Jolly Rancher (Drop one hard candy in your drinking bottle—kids really like this one)
- Powdered Gatorade

I always try to choose organic and fair trade coffees, hot chocolates, and cocoas. For tea, I look for products that are part of The Ethical Tea Partnership.

If you will be making hot drinks, there are a few things to keep in mind. The first is how you will brew loose tea or ground coffee. Of course, you could use a tea bag, as they are convenient, but if you are like me and prefer the higher quality of loose tea, then you have a few options. Some people use percolators specifically designed for camping and others use a kettle. There are a variety of presses designed for camping—some of which are big enough for a family and others that are designed for a single cup. These presses also work terrifically for loose tea. Most backcountry travelers I know opt for the simple camp pot and boiling water merely poured into a cup over the tea leaves or other ingredients. This is my preferred method too, as I like to use gear that has multiple uses. For some recipes or larger group settings, it is preferable to brew your beverage right in the pot. Also, be aware that some herbal teas and green tea are brewed in water that has gone off the boil, whereas black or orange pekoe varieties need boiling water for the perfect brew.

If you plan to make a camp pot of coffee or tea, it is a great idea to put the ingredients into a cone-style filter. Roll down the top and staple it a few times. Alternatively you can use what I use, the t-Sac. This product is an unbleached tea or coffee filter that is basically just a tea bag that you fill yourself. They come in a variety of sizes ranging from a single serving to pot size. Cheesecloth spice bags are also great for this. They have a little drawstring, and you can rinse and reuse them. If you can't find these, you can put your loose tea on a small square of cheesecloth, bundle it up, and tie the top closed with kitchen string. You can also use a metal tea strainer, and these come in several different designs.

Instant coffees come in all qualities, and some are flavored. I found Kava brand to be one of the better ones, and Starbucks Via is very good too, albeit a little pricey. Instant espresso is delicious, especially when mixed with a little hot chocolate. You can also add these powdered alternatives to baked goods.

Hot chocolate, lattes, or cocoas make a nice dessert replacement in the backcountry. The extra calories will help you stay warm in the colder weather, and the warmth of the drink helps take the chill off. If you are of age, a liqueur such as Grand Marnier, Kahlúa, Frangelico, or Irish cream can certainly add a bit of a twist. Care must be taken when consuming alcohol in a wilderness setting, as it can give you a false sense of being toasty warm. Consume in moderation and remember that effects are often more powerful at higher altitudes.

Water Treatment

Just because a water source looks safe and the water is crystal clear doesn't mean that it is free of cysts, bacteria, or protozoa. It is important to take the proper measures to ensure you don't end up contracting giardia, cryptosporidium, or other parasites. Having an intestinal issue when you are in the backcountry is no picnic. There are several methods for treating water, and some are more effective than others. Boiling your water for 1–3 minutes works well, but you have to allow it to cool and then aerate it by transferring it quickly and repeatedly from one container to another in order to keep it from tasting flat. Water filters, although my preferred method, will not remove viruses; however, this is not an issue in North America. Filters are faster than chemical treatments but can be weighty depending on the model. Filters also remove some of the other harmless particulate floating in the water. Another benefit to filtering is that you can get water faster on the fly, whereas you might have to wait upwards of 30 minutes for chemicals to take effect. Chlorine dioxide treatments, such as Aquamira and Pristine, work by combining two chemicals together and adding them to the water. A chemical reaction is created and that kills everything in the water. It's basically a smaller-scale version of what happens at many local water treatment facilities. The water may have little floating particles in it because it didn't go through a filter. A way to avoid some of this is to strain the water through a clean bandana when pouring it into your water container before you treat it. Or you can simply let the particles settle to the bottom while you wait for the chemicals to do their work. Chemicals can be more expensive, and they have an expiration date. I avoid iodine because it leaves an awful taste and isn't fully effective with cryptosporidium parasites. Do not use iodine if you are pregnant. Another method is the SteriPen. SteriPen uses ultraviolet light to kill 99.9% of bacteria; this is the smaller-scale version of another method used by municipalities and homeowners to treat water. You can purchase it with or without a pre-filter. It treats the water quickly, and the only downfall is that it is battery operated.

Almond Milk Powder

Dehydration Time: 15–18 hours
Makes 2 servings

2 cups almond milk, sweetened or unsweetened

⅞ cup water

The writing of this book came with a quest to find instant almond milk powder. Of course, you can make almond milk with ground almonds, but it takes about 24 hours and then you have to deal with the pulp. My husband, Bryan, was off to Ohio and I asked him to look in some of the American grocery stores to see if such a product existed south of our border. I already knew that it was going to be a fruitless search because the Internet hadn't turned up anything either. When he came up empty handed, he said to me, "You have food dehydrators; why don't you just make your own?" So I did—right after I gave my forehead a smack for not seeing the obvious.

AT HOME

Pour 2 cups of almond milk on a solid dehydrator tray. Dehydrate at 135°F for 15 to 18 hours or until the milk is completely dry and brittle. Remove it from the trays and grind into a fine powder using a coffee grinder or spice grinder. Put the powder in a ziplock freezer bag.

AT CAMP

Squish the bag of powder with your fingertips to break up any lumps. To make 1 cup of almond milk, add ⅛ cup or 2 tablespoons to your cup and add enough water to bring the mixture up to 1 cup or about ⅞ cup water. Stir and let hydrate for a few minutes. Stir again before drinking.

Tips

It is very important to use a solid tray with a lip designed for fruit leather. If you don't have one, you can use plastic wrap or good-quality parchment paper. If you are using parchment paper, you need to make a lip on it so that the almond milk won't flow off the sheet.

Please note that almond milk is dried until brittle and can be a little fussy to get off the tray. I usually put my trays in the freezer for 20 minutes or so and then it comes off easier. It will come off in tiny little pieces. I use a plastic scraper to get some of the pieces up. Sometimes, if I remember, I use plastic wrap over the solid tray to make removal easier.

I prefer to use sweetened almond milk if we are going to be drinking it straight and unsweetened for use in place of milk in hot chocolate and baking. The sweetened milk will be slightly sticky.

While this recipe is for 1 tray or 2 servings of almond milk, I recommend drying several trays at a time. Besides drying the unsweetened vanilla almond milk, I often dry sweetened chocolate almond milk and sweetened vanilla almond milk, so we have variety.

Green Tea Chai Vanilla Latte

½ cup nonfat powdered milk or almond milk powder (see page 228)

1 tablespoon loose chai tea

1 tablespoon loose gunpowder (green) tea

1½ teaspoons pure vanilla extract

Sweetener such as agave, raw cane sugar, or honey to taste

2½ cups water

Makes 2 servings

Sometimes, when we plan a trip with friends, we meet at a local coffee pub. I always have a chai latte. There is something comforting about sipping the combination of spices and vanilla while sitting with friends as we pore over maps and discuss trip menus. You could use two tea bags here, but I prefer the flavors of loose tea.

AT HOME

Put the powdered milk in a ziplock freezer bag. Measure the loose chai tea and loose gunpowder green tea separately into cheesecloth bags or tea filters and then place them in a ziplock freezer bag. Put this bag inside the bag with the powdered milk. Put the vanilla extract in a small leakproof bottle and put that in the bag with the milk powder or add it to any other vanilla that you will take on your trip. Pack the sweetener with the other sweetener that you will take on your trip.

AT CAMP

Put 2½ cups of water in a pot with the chai tea bag and the powdered milk. Bring to a simmer over medium-low heat, stirring often so that the milk does not stick. Simmer for 3 minutes, add the gunpowder green tea bag, and reduce the heat to low. Let steep for another 3 minutes and add the vanilla extract.

Remove the tea bags and divide the tea between two camp cups. Sweeten to taste.

Tips

You could swap out the vanilla extract and sweeten with vanilla sugar but you will have a less intense vanilla flavor.

If you happen to be base camping or car camping and have a cooler with ice, this makes a delicious iced drink too.

Bay Leaf–infused Apple Tea

Makes 2 servings

1 bay leaf

1 single serving package
    instant apple cider mix

¼ teaspoon cinnamon

1 orange pekoe tea bag

Enough water for 2 cups tea

This sweet tea came about on a wilderness camping trip. It was a cold, wet day and we wanted something hot to drink. My husband, Bryan, isn't much of a cider fan, but we were down to one tea bag and one packet of cider and we were out of sugar. He likes his tea sweet. So I improvised and it's now on the list of favorites.

AT HOME

Place all the ingredients in a ziplock bag.

AT CAMP

Boil enough water to make 2 cups of tea. Break the bay leaf in half and add it to the pot. As soon as the water boils, add the cider packet, cinnamon, and tea bag. Let steep to taste. Remove the tea bag and bay leaf pieces. Stir well and pour into cups.

Cranberry Ginger Green Tea

3 tablespoons dried cranberries, finely chopped

1 tablespoon gunpowder green tea

¼ teaspoon dried orange or lemon zest (optional)

¼ teaspoon ground ginger

Sweetener, such as sugar, agave nectar, or honey to taste

Enough water for 2 cups tea

Makes 2 servings

This tea is my go-to for when I feel under the weather or if the weather is just getting me down.

AT HOME

Use two cheesecloth bags or tea filters and put half of the ingredients, except for the sweetener, in each bag. Put the tea bags into a ziplock freezer bag. If you are using a reusable tea infuser, package each serving of tea in a snack-size ziplock bag. Pack the sweetener with the other sweetener that you will take on your trip.

AT CAMP

Bring enough water for 2 cups of tea just to the boiling point. Put a tea bag in each cup and pour the water over the bag. Let steep for 3 to 5 minutes or until the tea is the strength you desire. Sweeten to taste.

Tip

You can substitute dried peach pieces for the cranberries to change the flavor, or use a combination of chopped cranberries and peaches.

Cocoa-nutty Hot Chocolate

Makes 4 servings

This is one of those happy accidents that I often refer to. I was preparing hot chocolate for a trip at the eleventh hour. I realized that I didn't have any coffee creamer or enough milk powder for my recipe so I improvised and used some of the leftover coconut powder I had from another recipe.

At Home

Mix the dry ingredients together and place them in a ziplock freezer bag.

At Camp

Shake the bag of dry ingredients to ensure that they are well combined. Place 5 tablespoons of mix in a cup and carefully fill it with boiling water. Stir until the ingredients dissolve. Repeat for each desired serving.

Tip

A pinch each of cinnamon and crushed red chili pepper can be added to the mix if you like things a little spicy.

⅓ cup unsweetened cocoa powder

½ cup Nestlé Nido, soy milk powder, or other milk powder

½ cup coconut cream powder

¼ cup sugar

Enough water for 4 cups hot chocolate

Lemon Ginger Hot Chocolate

Makes 4 servings

1 cup (4 servings) hot cocoa mix

1 teaspoon ground ginger

1 teaspoon pure lemon extract

Enough water for 4 cups hot chocolate

This was inspired by one of my favorite chocolate treats— laced with candied lemon and ginger pieces. This is the hot chocolate version and is best made with a dark cocoa mix, if you can find it.

AT HOME

Mix the dry ingredients and lemon extract together and place them in a ziplock freezer bag.

AT CAMP

Shake the bag of dry ingredients to ensure that they are well combined. Place 4 tablespoons of mix in a cup and carefully fill it with boiling water. Stir until the ingredients dissolve. Repeat for each desired serving.

Peanut Butter Banana Hot Chocolate

Makes 4 servings

This recipe was created for my little monkey, Tobias. It's the perfect kid-friendly hot chocolate recipe and a good way to give the little ones some extra calories. It's also delicious with almond butter, and if you wanted to have an adult version, you could omit the extract and use some banana liqueur.

At Home

Mix the dry ingredients and banana extract together and place them in a ziplock freezer bag. Package the peanut butter in a leakproof container or add it to any other peanut butter you are taking.

At Camp

Shake the bag of dry ingredients to ensure that they are well combined. Place 4 tablespoons of mix and 1 teaspoon of peanut butter in a cup and carefully fill it with boiling water. Stir until the ingredients dissolve. Repeat for each desired serving.

⅔ cup hot cocoa mix

⅓ cup Nestlé Nido, soy milk powder, or other milk powder

1 teaspoon banana extract

4 teaspoons peanut butter

Enough water for 4 cups hot chocolate

Chocolate Anise Coffee

Makes 4 servings

4 tablespoons non-dairy
  powdered coffee creamer

4 teaspoons sugar

4 teaspoons instant coffee

8 teaspoons unsweetened
  cocoa powder

1 teaspoon anise extract
  (if using anise oil, use a
  scant ⅛ teaspoon)

32 ounces water

This nonalcoholic drink is made with anise extract or anise oil. Anise has a licorice-like flavor and is used in liqueurs such as Italian sambuca, Greek ouzo, and French Pernod. The extract will be less expensive and less concentrated than the oil, so if you are using the oil, do so sparingly or it may overpower the other flavors.

AT HOME
Mix the dry ingredients and anise extract together and place them in a ziplock freezer bag.

AT CAMP
Shake the bag of dry ingredients to ensure they are well combined. Place 4 tablespoons of mix in a cup and carefully fill it with 8 ounces of boiling water. Stir until the ingredients dissolve. Repeat for each desired serving.

Coconut Crème Coffee

Makes 4 servings

This recipe was inspired by a delicious coffee bean flavor from a local store that we call Serenity for short. The store started out as a stall at our local farmers' market. Store owners Jan and Lynda have a motto—"wish it, dream it, do it"—and that is how I feel about backpacking. This is my instant version of their great coffee flavor.

AT HOME

Mix the dry ingredients and rum extract together and place them in a ziplock freezer bag.

AT CAMP

Shake the bag of dry ingredients to ensure they are well combined. Place 3 tablespoons of mix in a cup and carefully fill it with 8 ounces of boiling water. Stir until the ingredients dissolve. Repeat for each desired serving.

½ cup coconut cream powder

3 teaspoons sugar

4 teaspoons instant coffee

1 teaspoon rum extract

32 ounces water

Orange Spice Mocha

Makes 4 servings

⅔ cup hot cocoa mix or vegan hot chocolate mix

⅓ cup Nestlé Nido, soy milk powder, or other milk powder

1 tablespoon instant coffee

Scant ⅛ teaspoon ground cloves

1 teaspoon orange extract (not orange oil)

32 ounces water

The aroma of this mocha reminds me of the clove-studded oranges I used to make for friends as Christmas gifts when I was a broke student at the University of Guelph. I would don a pair of gloves and pierce the skin with the whole cloves, often creating elaborate patterns. The scent was deliciously crave-able and comforting. Just remember that cloves are strong so use them very sparingly.

At Home

Mix the dry ingredients and orange extract together and place them in a ziplock freezer bag.

At Camp

Shake the bag of dry ingredients to ensure they are well combined. Place 4 tablespoons of mix in a cup and carefully fill it with 8 ounces of boiling water. Stir until the ingredients dissolve. Repeat for each desired serving.

Berry White Chocolate

Makes 4 servings

I know this anecdote has nothing to do with the outdoors, but it is kind of funny. As I was typing the title of this recipe, I started to smile. Why? Well, I couldn't get Barry White's voice out of my head and I ended up having to listen to "You Sexy Thing." Funny how a little bit of wording can trigger a totally unrelated thought. This might be one of those "had to be there" moments.

AT HOME

Grind the white chocolate in a coffee grinder or blender until the chocolate is in fine pieces. Grind the freeze-dried berries until you have a fine powder. Mix the chocolate and berries with the powdered milk and place the powder in a ziplock freezer bag.

AT CAMP

Shake the bag of dry ingredients to ensure they are well combined. Place 3 heaping tablespoons of mix into a cup and carefully fill it with 8 ounces of boiling water. Stir until the ingredients dissolve. Repeat for each desired serving.

Tip

Don't use chocolate chips for this recipe. They tend to clump because they are made to hold their shape, to an extent, when heated.

⅓ cup white chocolate

3 tablespoons plus 1 teaspoon freeze-dried blueberries or raspberries

½ cup Nestlé Nido or other whole milk powder

32 ounces water

Chai Hot Chocolate

Makes 4 servings

⅓ cup white chocolate or milk chocolate

⅛ teaspoon ground ginger

⅛ teaspoon cardamom

⅛ teaspoon cinnamon

1/16 teaspoon cloves

⅛ teaspoon black pepper

½ cup Nestlé Nido or other whole milk powder

32 ounces water

This decadent and spicy hot chocolate can be made with white or milk chocolate or a combination of the two. It makes a great dessert or a warming treat on a snowy hike.

At Home

Grind the white or milk chocolate in a coffee grinder or blender until the chocolate is in fine pieces. Mix the chocolate and spices with the powdered milk and place the powder in a ziplock freezer bag.

At Camp

Shake the bag of dry ingredients to ensure they are well combined. Place 3 heaping tablespoons of mix into a cup and carefully fill it with 8 ounces of boiling water. Stir until the ingredients dissolve. Repeat for each desired serving.

Tip

Don't use chocolate chips for this recipe. They tend to clump because they are made to hold their shape, to an extent, when heated.

Gingerbread Spice Coffee Creamer

Makes 4 servings

This spiced coffee creamer is delicious in coffee or espresso. It can also be used to sweeten oatmeal for breakfast.

AT HOME
Mix the dry ingredients together and place them in a ziplock freezer bag.

AT CAMP
Add the gingerbread creamer to your brewed cup of coffee to suit your tastes.

Tip
Use Gingerbread Spice Coffee Creamer in place of sugar with 1 tablespoon unsweetened cocoa powder, 1 cup water, and enough milk powder to make 1 cup milk to create Gingerbread Hot Chocolate.

⅛ cup firmly packed dark brown sugar

½ cup non-dairy powdered coffee creamer

½ teaspoon ground ginger

½ teaspoon cinnamon

Scant ⅛ teaspoon ground cloves

Raspberry Peach Breakfast Nectar

1 cup fresh raspberries

1 cup canned peaches packed in juice, drained

1¼ cups vanilla almond milk, unsweetened

1 tablespoon lime juice

¼ cup agave nectar or honey

**Dehydration Time: 7–12 hours
Makes 3–4 servings**

This is a cross between fruit smoothie and fruit nectar and was something I craved when I was pregnant with our little Kaia. It takes a while to rehydrate, so we usually break down camp while we wait. Sometimes I'll start the rehydration process the night before.

AT HOME

Blend the raspberries until they are puréed. Strain through a fine sieve to remove any seeds. Return the berries to the blender and add the peaches, vanilla almond milk, lime juice, and agave nectar or honey in a blender until smooth. Measure the amount that you will be dehydrating and write that measurement on a sticky note. Spread on lined dehydrator trays and dry for 7 to 12 hours or until you have a dry leather. Package the leather in a ziplock freezer bag with your note.

AT CAMP

Tear the leather into small pieces and place in a large wide-mouth water bottle. Add enough water to the leather pieces to equal the measurement on your sticky note. Let rehydrate for 30 minutes shaking well at 5- to 10-minute intervals. Serve warm or cool.

Chocolate Almond Blueberry Smoothie

Makes 2 servings

¼ cup freeze-dried blueberries

¼ cup chocolate almond milk powder (made from sweetened milk; see page 228)

2 cups water

While we generally have this with an energy bar for a speedy breakfast when we want to break camp quickly, it could be enjoyed at any time of day. Try it hot for an after-dinner treat.

AT HOME

Grind the freeze-dried blueberries in a blender or coffee grinder until you have a fine powder. Mix the dry ingredients together and place in a ziplock freezer bag. Alternatively, divide the mixture into 2 individual servings and package separately.

AT CAMP

If you didn't package each serving individually, then shake the package of dry ingredients to ensure they are well combined. Break apart any lumps. If you are making both servings together, put the powder in a wide-mouth water bottle and add 2 cups of water. If you packaged them separately, add 1 serving of powder to 1 cup of water. Stir or shake and let it sit for a few minutes for the flavors to infuse and to let the almond milk rehydrate.

Tip

You can substitute chocolate protein powder mixed with a little milk powder for the almond milk powder.

Vanilla Almond Tropical Spiced Smoothie

⅛ cup freeze-dried mangoes

⅛ cup freeze-dried bananas

¼ cup vanilla almond milk powder (made from sweetened milk; see page 228)

⅛ teaspoon cinnamon

2 cups water

Makes 2 servings

This tropical smoothie is great when served alongside a breakfast muffin or biscuit. It's also yummy as a hot drink in colder weather.

AT HOME

Grind the freeze-dried fruit in a blender or coffee grinder until you have a fine powder. Mix the dry ingredients together and place in a ziplock freezer bag. Alternatively, divide the mixture into 2 individual servings and package separately.

AT CAMP

If you didn't package each serving individually, then shake the package of dry ingredients to ensure they are well combined. Break apart any lumps. If you are making both servings together, put the powder in a wide-mouth water bottle and add 2 cups of water. If you packaged them separately, add 1 serving of powder to 1 cup of water. Stir or shake and let it sit for a few minutes for the flavors to infuse and to let the almond milk rehydrate.

Tip

You can substitute vanilla protein powder mixed with a little milk powder for the almond milk powder.

Pumpkin Nog

Makes 4 servings

This take on eggnog has the added nutrition from the use of pumpkin flour. It's like Thanksgiving in a cup. A shot of rum could be added to make this an adult treat.

At Home

Mix the dry ingredients and vanilla extract together and place them in a ziplock freezer bag. Pack the sweetener with the other sweetener that you will take on your trip.

At Camp

Shake the bag of dry ingredients to ensure that they are well combined. Place 4 tablespoons of mix in a cup and carefully fill it with 8 ounces of boiling water. Stir until the ingredients dissolve and let sit for 5 minutes or more so that the pumpkin flour can fully rehydrate. Sweeten to taste. Repeat for each desired serving.

½ cup Nestlé Nido, other whole milk powder, or ½ cup almond milk powder (see page 228)

8 teaspoons pumpkin flour (made from pumpkin meat)

⅛ teaspoon cinnamon

⅛ teaspoon ginger

⅛ teaspoon nutmeg

1 teaspoon pure vanilla extract

Sweetener such as agave, raw cane sugar, or honey to taste

32 ounces water

Blueberry Mango Lemonade

⅓ cup freeze-dried blueberries and mangoes, mixed

4 servings instant lemonade powder

32–40 ounces water

Makes 4 servings

There is nothing better than lemonade to mask some of the undesirable flavors that can be tasted in some water sources when in the backcountry.

AT HOME

Grind the freeze-dried fruit in a blender or coffee grinder until you have a fine powder. Put the lemonade powder in a measuring cup with the freeze-dried fruit powder. Mix. Divide the measurement by 4, and record the single serving amount on a piece of paper. Put the note and both powders in a ziplock freezer bag or package each serving individually.

AT CAMP

If you didn't package each serving individually, then shake the package of dry ingredients to ensure they are well combined. Measure 1 serving of powder into a cup or water bottle. Add 8 to 10 ounces of water, depending how strong you like your lemonade. Stir or shake and let it sit for a few minutes for the flavors to infuse.

Spiked Winter Latte

Makes 4 servings

This warming drink is perfect as an after-dinner treat on a cold or rainy day. It can be made with Amaretto or crème de cacao, but the hazelnut flavor of the Frangelico makes it a little more special.

AT HOME

Grind the white chocolate in a coffee grinder or blender until the chocolate is in fine pieces. Mix the powdered milk and espresso powder with the white chocolate and place the powder in a ziplock freezer bag. Pack the liqueur in a leakproof bottle and place it in the freezer bag with the powder.

AT CAMP

Shake the bag of dry ingredients to ensure they are well combined. Place 3 tablespoons of mix into a cup and carefully fill it with 8 ounces of boiling water. Stir until the ingredients dissolve, then add 1 ounce of Frangelico liqueur. Repeat for each desired serving.

Tips

Don't use chocolate chips for this recipe. They tend to clump because they are made to hold their shape, to an extent, when heated.

To make this nonalcoholic, you could substitute 1 teaspoon almond or other nut extract for the 4 ounces of liqueur.

⅓ cup white chocolate

½ cup Nestlé Nido or other whole milk powder

2 tablespoons instant espresso powder

4 ounces Frangelico or other hazelnut-flavored liqueur

32 ounces water

½ teaspoon dried lime zest

½ teaspoon dried lemon zest

¼ cup fine sugar or maple sugar

2–3 whole cloves

½ cinnamon stick

½ bay leaf

½ cardamom pod

1 star anise

Small pinch of nutmeg (about ¹⁄₁₆ of a teaspoon or 5 gratings of whole nutmeg)

1 heaping tablespoon dried pomegranate seeds or dried chopped cranberries (optional)

1 teaspoon vanilla extract

2 ounces cognac or brandy

1 fresh clementine or tangerine

25 ounces or one small bottle red wine such as Merlot, Rioja, or Shiraz

Mulled Wine

Makes 6–8 servings

Mulled wine is wonderful for a backcountry celebration when you have a larger group.

At Home

Put the dried zests and sugar together and place in a ziplock freezer bag. Mix the spices together with the dried pomegranate seeds or dried cranberries, if you are using them, and bundle in a piece of cheesecloth tied with kitchen string or place in a tea filter. Put the bundle in the bag with the sugar mixture. Pack the vanilla extract in a leakproof bottle or with any other vanilla that you will take on your trip. Put the cognac or brandy in a small leakproof bottle. Pack the clementine and decant the wine into a leakproof and unbreakable container right before you leave for your trip.

At Camp

Use your camp knife to cut a few strips of peel from the clementine, being careful not to get any of the white pith. Place the clementine peel in a pot with the sugar mixture. Squeeze the juice from the clementine into the pot and add enough red wine just to cover the mixture and heat on medium-low just until the sugar has dissolved. Add the spice bundle, 1 teaspoon vanilla extract, and cognac or brandy, then bring to a boil and let simmer for about 5 minutes. Turn off the heat, add the remaining wine, and let the mulled wine sit for 5 minutes so the flavor can develop. Remove the spice bundle, pour the wine into camp mugs, and serve.

Tip

See the instructions for drying pomegranates in the recipe on page 143.

Chapter 11

More Elaborate Dishes

This book, just like *A Fork in the Trail,* wouldn't be complete without a small section to cover fare for car-camping and base-camping trips. From time to time we will car camp with people in our circle who just aren't into the type of roughing it that comes with a wilderness trip. Sometimes we car camp because the long drive to the trailhead or canoe put-in prohibits setting off into the wilds on the same day. Front-country camping is something we did the summer our daughter, Kaia, was born because she was far too tiny for backpacking or canoeing. These foods are also suitable for backcountry trips that involve a base camp or cabin. In a few of the backcountry places we travel, you can stay at the old ranger cabins or a yurt. Some weekend backpacking trips also lend themselves well to this type of food—trips where a soft-sided cooler would be feasible. In a few recipes I have included alternate instructions for creating these for the first 2 or 3 days of a wilderness excursion. There are many differences between backcountry and front-country camping and one of them is the ability to bring a large, hard-sided cooler, giving you the most flexibility in your menu. You'll want to keep your vehicle organized on these trips, and here are a few tips that will help with that.

• Use a large Rubbermaid container with a lid for your kitchen equipment and dry goods.

• Store baked goods in a small cardboard box.

• Keep fruits and vegetables out of direct sunlight.

• Hard-sided plastic containers are great for storing food in a cooler.

- Bring a plastic sink and store your camp soap, dishcloth, and drying towels inside.

- Keep cutlery in a plastic container.

- Transfer peanut butter, jams, agave nectar, maple syrup, and condiments to small leakproof containers.

- Remove excess packaging from store-bought items. (Take individually wrapped granola bars out of the box, for example, and pack in a storage bag.)

- Freeze juice boxes and water bottles to keep the contents of the cooler cold.

- Larger blocks of ice take longer to melt than cubes. Use large, empty cardboard juice cartons to make larger blocks of ice in your freezer at home.

- Only open the cooler if you need to.

- Keep the cooler in the shade unless you are in bear country and must keep it in the car.

Pumpkin French Toast

Makes 2 servings

This yummy French toast usually graces our menu for camping on the Canadian Thanksgiving weekend, but it is delicious at any time of year. This is best made with bread that is 2–3 days old. Fresh bread produces a soggy end product, so if you don't have stale bread, put the slices in the oven at about 300°F for 10 minutes.

AT HOME

Toast the pecans just until fragrant in a dry nonstick frying pan. Let cool and wrap in plastic wrap. Mix the cornstarch, cinnamon, ginger, and salt together and wrap in plastic wrap. Combine the vanilla, pumpkin, and milk in a leakproof container and refrigerate until you are ready to pack your cooler. Wrap the bread slices in plastic wrap. Pack the bread and cornstarch mixture with the other dry goods you are taking. Add the vegetable oil to any other vegetable oil you are taking. Package the syrup in a leakproof bottle and put that, along with the container of milk and pumpkin, in your cooler before you leave.

AT CAMP

Combine the cornstarch mixture with the milk-and-pumpkin mixture. Place the bread slices in a single layer in the pan. Pour the pumpkin mixture over the bread and let sit for 10 minutes. Flip the slices and let sit for an additional 15 minutes. Preheat a frying pan over medium heat and add a little oil. Fry the toast, turning once, until both sides are a deep golden color. Transfer to a pot or plate and put in a cozy to keep the pieces warm. Repeat with each slice of bread. Top with syrup and toasted pecans.

Tip

This can easily be made gluten-free by using your favorite gluten-free product with a texture similar to French bread.

⅛ cup pecans

1 tablespoon cornstarch

1 teaspoon cinnamon

¾ teaspoon ground ginger

A pinch of salt

¼ teaspoon pure vanilla extract

½ cup canned, puréed pumpkin

¾ cup vanilla almond milk, sweetened

4 slices stale French bread, cut 1 inch thick

Vegetable oil for frying

Maple syrup or other breakfast syrup (see the Breakfasts chapter for ideas)

Poached Eggs with Lentils

Makes 2 servings

1 tablespoon plus 2 teaspoons olive oil

⅓ cup onion, minced

⅓ cup carrot, diced

⅓ cup celery, diced

⅛ teaspoon dried thyme

¾ cup canned green lentils, rinsed and drained

Salt and freshly ground black pepper to taste

A pinch of crushed red chili pepper flakes (optional)

2 fresh eggs

My brother Bruce was an avid outdoors guy and was wild about poached eggs on toast. I was looking for a healthier alternative to bread and decided that lentils would fit the bill. This makes a terrific breakfast or brunch. If you can find truffle oil, it is delicious in place of olive oil drizzled over the egg.

At Home

Preheat 1 tablespoon olive oil in a pan over medium heat. Sauté the onion, carrot, and celery until the vegetables are soft. Add the thyme and lentils. Heat the mixture through and then season with salt and pepper to taste. Let cool and place in a ziplock freezer bag. Refrigerate until you are ready to pack your cooler. Wrap the crushed red chilies in a piece of plastic wrap and pack with the other dry goods you are taking. Pack the eggs and the lentil mixture in a cooler when you are ready to leave. Add 2 teaspoons olive oil to the other oil you will take with you.

At Camp

Warm the lentil mixture in a frying pan, place in a cozy, and set aside.

Put a pot of water on to boil, crack 2 eggs into the pot, and let the water simmer to cook the eggs. The eggs will be cooked when the whites are firm and the yolks are thick and runny. If you prefer your yolks harder, leave the eggs in the water a little longer.

As the eggs come close to being ready to remove from the water, put half of the lentil mixture on each plate. Drizzle the lentils with 1 teaspoon olive oil, top with a poached egg, and sprinkle a pinch of crushed red chili flakes, if desired.

Tip

If you're on a trip where spoilage would be an issue, you could dehydrate the lentil mixture for 6 to 10 hours and use a powdered scrambled egg mix in place of the poached egg.

Eggless Salad Wrap

Makes 3–4 servings

This tofu-based salad looks and tastes suspiciously like real egg salad. Serve the eggless salad in a wrap or on your favorite bread.

At Home

Set the tofu in a colander to drain. Once the tofu has drained, crumble it and place it in a ziplock freezer bag. Mix the vinegar, mustard, turmeric, and agave nectar together and transfer to a leakproof container. Chop the shallots and celery and place them together in a ziplock freezer bag. Package the spices in a piece of plastic wrap. When you are ready to leave, pack all the ingredients, except the spices, in a cooler.

At Camp

Make sure the tofu is well drained. Pour the dressing over the crumbled tofu in the bag, mix in the shallots, celery, and spices, and let sit in the cooler for 45 minutes to 1 hour. Spoon the mixture onto a wrap, bread, or Boston lettuce leaves.

2½ cups firm tofu, drained and crumbled

1 tablespoon apple cider vinegar

2½ teaspoons prepared yellow mustard

½ teaspoon turmeric

1 teaspoon agave nectar

2 tablespoons shallots or red onion, finely minced

2 tablespoons celery, finely minced

⅛ teaspoon Spanish paprika

½ teaspoon finely ground black pepper

Kosher salt to taste

Sort-of Ceviche

Makes 3–4 servings

¼ cup red onion, minced

Pickled jalapeños, finely minced, to taste

1 14-ounce can hearts of palm

1 avocado

1 fresh lime

2–3 plum tomatoes

2 tablespoons fresh cilantro

Salt and pepper to taste

Ceviche is usually a Peruvian dish that involves fish and lime juice. This version is meat-free, using hearts of palm, tomato, and avocado in place of seafood. Serve with flatbread, crackers, or tortilla chips.

At Home

Package the red onion and jalapeños in a container and place it in the refrigerator until you are ready to pack the cooler for your trip. Pack the hearts of palm and other fruits and vegetables with the other food items you will take on your trip. Make sure that the avocado is well protected. Pack the fresh cilantro, without chopping it first, in your cooler.

At Camp

Put the red onion and jalapeños in a bowl or pot. Quarter the hearts of palm and chop into ½-inch pieces. Cut the avocado in half and remove the pit. Scoop out the flesh and chop into ½-inch pieces. Put the hearts of palm and avocado in the bowl and then cut the lime in half. Squeeze the lime juice over the mixture and toss to coat. Cut the tomatoes in half and remove the seeds. Chop and place in the bowl. Chop or tear the cilantro leaves, add them to the mixture, and stir to combine. Let sit for 10 minutes so that the flavors can combine.

Tip

If you plan to have this later on in a trip, buy an avocado that is not quite ripe and let it ripen on your trip. I like to use something called a Froot Guard. If you don't have one, simply wrap the avocado in paper towels and put it in a hard-sided container so that it doesn't get bruised.

Quinoa and Avocado Salad

Makes 2–4 servings

I love to have dinner salads when we camp. Quinoa is packed with protein, and the avocado provides a good source of potassium. While this recipe is best served fresh when car or base camping, I've included alternate instructions in case you'd like to dry it for the trail.

At Home

Place the quinoa in a fine sieve and rinse for at least 3 minutes to remove the bitter coating. Drain and place in a nonstick frying pan; toast the quinoa, stirring frequently. As soon as some of the seeds start to pop, remove the quinoa from the pan. Put the toasted quinoa and water into a pot. Bring the mixture to a boil; cover and simmer for 10 minutes. Remove from the heat and leave the lid on for an additional 10 minutes. Fluff with a fork as you would for rice and let cool. Once the quinoa has cooled, pack it in a ziplock freezer bag. Put the black beans and roasted red peppers in a ziplock freezer bag and place that bag inside the quinoa bag. Place the bag in the refrigerator until you are ready to leave. Pack the pepitas, limes, and avocado carefully with the other vegetables that you will be taking. Put the quinoa and beans in the cooler along with the green onions and cilantro. Pack the olive oil with the other oil you will take on your trip.

At Camp

Remove the package of pepitas from the ziplock bag. Slice the green onion and chop or tear the fresh cilantro and add to the quinoa with the beans, roasted red peppers, and pepitas. Cut the limes in half and squeeze out 3 tablespoons of lime juice. Add ¼ cup olive oil and the lime juice to the salad. Mix well. Cut the avocado in half and remove the pit. Score the avocado while it is still in the skin and then scoop out the flesh and gently mix it in with the salad. Season with salt and pepper to taste.

1 cup quinoa, rinsed and toasted

1¾ cups water

½ cup cooked or canned black beans, rinsed

½ cup roasted red pepper, chopped

¼ cup roasted pepitas (hulled pumpkin seeds)

3 tablespoons lime juice (about 2 limes)

1 fresh avocado

⅓ cup green onions, sliced

¼ cup fresh cilantro, chopped

Kosher salt to taste

Ground black pepper to taste

¼ cup olive oil

Alternate Instructions for Dehydrating

Dehydration Time: 7–12 hours

Because you will use a fresh avocado, make this recipe in the first few days of a trip.

At Home

Mix the cooked quinoa with the roasted red pepper, green onions, black beans, and cilantro. Measure the mixture and write this measurement on a sticky note. Dry on lined dehydrator trays for 7 to 12 hours or until no moisture remains. Put the sticky note and dried mix in a ziplock freezer bag. Wrap the pepitas in a small piece of plastic wrap and add that to the ziplock bag. Pack the salt and pepper with the other salt and pepper you will take on your trip. Do the same with the olive oil. Just before your trip, pack 2 limes and an avocado.

At Camp

Remove the package of pepitas from the ziplock bag. Add enough cold water to the ingredients in the ziplock to equal the measurement on your sticky note. Be sure to account for the volume of your dried ingredients prior to adding the water. You can always add more water if you need to. Let rehydrate for 20 minutes or until fully hydrated. If you are planning to eat this as a lunch, you can start rehydration at breakfast. Use a leakproof container such as a wide-mouth Nalgene. Once the quinoa mix is reconstituted, drain off any excess water. Add salt, pepper, and roasted pepitas to the quinoa mixture. Cut the limes in half and squeeze out 3 tablespoons of lime juice. Add ¼ cup olive oil and the lime juice to the salad. Mix well. Cut the avocado in half and remove the pit. Score the avocado while it is still in the skin and then scoop out the flesh and gently mix it in with the salad.

Tips

If you plan to have this later on in a trip, buy an avocado that is not quite ripe and let it ripen in your pack. I like to use something called a Froot Guard. If you don't have one, simply wrap the avocado in paper towels and put it in a hard-sided container so that it doesn't get bruised. If you do this, you must let the air and humidity out of the container every day. If you don't want to use a hard container, you can use a ziplock bag and place the avocado in a safe spot in your pack.

Balsamic, Mushroom, and Spinach Salad

Makes 3–4 servings

I've used button mushrooms in this recipe because they are the most common; however, you could use baby portobellos, enoki, or any other mushroom in this dish. This salad is also good served in a pita pocket or wrap.

At Home

Mix the olive oil and vinegar together and place in a leak-proof container. Put the mushrooms in a paper bag. Pack the vegetables, except for the baby spinach, with the other vegetables you are taking with you. Toast the walnuts in a dry nonstick frying pan for 1 or 2 minutes until they start to become fragrant. Cool, wrap in plastic wrap, and pack with the vegetables. Put the baby spinach in your cooler when you are ready to leave.

At Camp

Slice the mushrooms and add them to a pot or bowl. Chop the onion, mince the garlic, slice the green pepper, and cut the grape or cherry tomatoes in half. Add them to the bowl along with the spinach. Shake the dressing well to combine and pour just enough on the salad to lightly coat the spinach leaves. Sprinkle with toasted walnuts and season with salt and pepper to taste.

Tips

If you are using less expensive balsamic vinegar, you may have to add 1 teaspoon dark brown sugar, agave nectar, or brown rice syrup to balance out the flavor of the dressing.

Ovo-lacto vegetarians could choose to crumble a bit of Gorgonzola or other blue cheese on top of the salad before serving.

½ cup olive oil

¼ cup balsamic vinegar

2 cups white button mushrooms

1 small onion

1 clove garlic

½ cup sliced green pepper

½ cup grape or cherry tomatoes

¼ cup toasted walnuts (optional)

6 cups baby spinach or 4 cups baby spinach and 2 cups baby arugula

Kosher salt to taste

Freshly ground black pepper to taste

Fire-roasted Moroccan Sweet Potato Salad

Makes 4 servings

1 pound sweet potatoes (about 2 medium-large)

5 saffron threads

⅛ teaspoon cumin

½ teaspoon paprika

⅛ cup dried apricots, finely chopped, or pomegranate seeds

⅛ cup pistachios, chopped

1 teaspoon fresh gingerroot, grated

1 fresh lemon

4 tablespoons olive oil

2 tablespoons fresh cilantro

Salt and pepper to taste

½ teaspoon kosher salt

A large piece of aluminum foil

Tongs

My best friend, Samantha Rogers, loves potato salad, and she's often the one to bring the sweet potatoes to family dinners. This recipe was inspired by her love of potatoes and my love of the exotic spices of Morocco. I prefer to use home-dried pomegranate seeds, or gems as I call them, because they impart such a beautiful color to the dish.

AT HOME

Package the sweet potatoes with the other dry foods you will take on the trip. Mix the saffron, cumin, and paprika together and place in a small ziplock bag. Wrap the dried apricots or pomegranate seeds in plastic wrap and put the bundle in the spice bag. Do the same with the pistachios. Put the grated gingerroot in a ziplock bag and keep it in the refrigerator until you are ready to pack your cooler. Pack the lemon with your other fruits and vegetables and add the olive oil to the other olive oil you will take on your trip. Put the fresh cilantro, without chopping it first, in your cooler. Pack a piece of aluminum foil large enough to wrap the sweet potatoes when they are chopped. Pack a pair of tongs.

AT CAMP

Add a little boiling water to the dried apricot pieces or pomegranate seeds. Make sure you have a well-established campfire with hot coals. Peel and cut the sweet potatoes into cubes. Place the cubes on the piece of foil, drizzle with 1 tablespoon olive oil, and sprinkle with salt. Seal the foil into a package. Place the bundle in the hot coals and bake for 15 to 20 minutes or until the potatoes are tender. Turn the package of sweet potatoes frequently, with tongs, so that the mixture doesn't burn. Remove from the coals and let cool but not all the way—you still want them to be warm.

Mix the 3 tablespoons of olive oil with 2 tablespoons of fresh lemon juice, the spice mixture, and grated ginger. Chop the fresh cilantro and add it to the dressing. Pour the dressing over the warm potatoes and let sit for 30 minutes, stirring from time to time, for the flavors to infuse. Stir in the rehydrated fruit and garnish with chopped pistachios. Serve with your favorite flatbread.

Tip

See the instructions for drying pomegranates in the recipe on page 143.

Tofu Souvlaki

Makes 4 servings

12–14 ounces extra firm or firm tofu, pressed

1 tablespoon olive oil

Juice of 1 lemon

1½ tablespoons fresh oregano, chopped

5 cloves garlic, minced

½ teaspoon kosher salt

6 bamboo skewers

1 8-ounce container tzatziki (optional)

A little vegetable oil

This grilled tofu, marinated in simple Mediterranean ingredients, has a taste similar to souvlaki. This should be marinated the day before your trip and is suitable for the first night of backcountry camping or for up to the second night of campground camping.

At Home

Remove the block of tofu from the package. If you don't have a tofu press, take the tofu and place it in a shallow casserole dish. Set a heavy pot that is weighted with a few cans on top of the tofu and let it press for 30 to 40 minutes. Drain off the excess liquid and chop the tofu into 1-inch cubes. Combine the olive oil, lemon juice, oregano, garlic, tofu cubes, and salt together and place in a large ziplock freezer bag, compressing as much air out as possible, and put the bag in the refrigerator. Just before you leave, pack the bag of tofu and tzatziki, if using, in your cooler. Pack the bamboo skewers. Add the vegetable oil to the other oil you will take on your trip.

At Camp

Fill a bag or container with water and soak the bamboo skewers for an hour. Put the tofu on the skewers and grill on a rack, which has been lightly oiled, over hot campfire coals or on a barbeque, turning frequently to prevent burning, until the tofu starts to brown lightly. Serve with a salad, rice, or Greek pitas, and tzatziki, if desired.

Tips

If you are an ovo-lacto vegetarian, you may want to have a dollop of tzatziki, a cucumber yogurt dip that sometimes contains a bit of dill, with this souvlaki knock-off.

It is very important to oil the grill before cooking the tofu, as it has a tendency to stick.

Grilled Tofu Kebabs with Red Cargo Rice

Makes 4 servings

This tofu dish has Asian-inspired flavor enhanced by the grilling process. We like to serve it with red cargo rice that has a sprinkle of lime juice to balance the slightly sweet and nutty flavor of the rice. This should be marinated the day before your trip and is suitable for the first night of backcountry camping or for up to the second night of campground camping.

At Home

Remove the block of tofu from the package. If you don't have a tofu press, place the tofu in a shallow casserole dish. Set a heavy pot that is weighted with a few cans on top of the tofu and let it press for 30 to 40 minutes. Drain off the excess liquid and chop the tofu into 1-inch cubes. Combine the vinegar, soy sauce, ginger, agave nectar, garlic, cilantro, and tofu cubes together and place in a large ziplock freezer bag, compressing as much air out as possible, and put the bag in the refrigerator. Package the rice in a ziplock freezer bag along with a note containing the cooking instructions from the package. Just before you leave, pack the bag of tofu in your cooler along with a fresh lime and pack the bag of rice with your dry goods. Pack the bamboo skewers.

At Camp

Fill a bag or container with water and soak the bamboo skewers for an hour. Make the rice according to the directions. While the rice is cooking, put the tofu on the skewers and grill on a rack, which has been lightly oiled, over hot campfire coals or on a barbeque, turning frequently to prevent burning, until the tofu starts to brown lightly. Sprinkle the rice with fresh lime juice and top with the tofu before serving.

Tip

It is very important to oil the grill before cooking the tofu, as it has a tendency to stick.

12–14 ounces extra firm or firm tofu, pressed

2 tablespoons rice wine vinegar

6 tablespoons soy sauce

4 teaspoons fresh ginger, finely grated

2 teaspoons agave nectar

2 cloves garlic, minced

1 teaspoon dried cilantro or 1 tablespoon fresh cilantro

1 cup red cargo rice

1 fresh lime

Bamboo skewers

Spicy Black Bean Burgers with Guacamole

1 19-ounce can black beans, rinsed and drained

½ cup salsa verde or other medium-hot salsa

½ cup dry bread crumbs (use gluten-free bread crumbs if you have celiac disease)

2 teaspoons vegetable oil

Salt and pepper to taste

4 medium-size Kaiser rolls or hamburger buns

Waxed paper

Avocado Topping

Makes 2 servings

1 ripe avocado

¼ teaspoon cumin

⅛ teaspoon garlic salt

1 tablespoon fresh cilantro (or ½ teaspoon dried)

1 lime

Makes 4 burgers

Burgers are probably one of the quintessential foods for car camping, so I created this bean burger with that in mind. Sometimes I use a little red pepper dip on these in place of the avocado topping. You could even use leftover guacamole. I've included alternate instructions in case you'd like to dry this recipe for the trail.

At Home

After you have drained and rinsed the black beans, mash them with a fork. It should be fairly smooth but it is OK to have some small pieces. Stir in the salsa, put the mixture in a ziplock freezer bag, and refrigerate until you are ready to leave. Package the dry bread crumbs in a ziplock bag or container and place them with the other dry goods you will take. Pack the vegetable oil with the other oil that you will take and do the same for the salt and pepper. Pack the buns with the other dry goods before you leave. Take a piece of waxed paper. Pack the avocado and make sure that it is well protected from bruising. Pack the spices, except the cilantro, in a small ziplock bag and put that, and the lime, with your dry goods. Put the fresh cilantro, without chopping it first, in your cooler.

At Camp

Mix the bean-and-salsa mixture with the bread crumbs. The mixture should be firm. Wet your hands and form into four ½-inch-thick patties. Place on waxed paper. Preheat 1 to 2 teaspoons vegetable oil in a nonstick frying pan and fry the patties, turning once, for about 5 minutes per side. They will be done when the outside is crispy and heated through. Season to taste with the salt and pepper.

While you are waiting for the burgers to cook, mash the avocado and chop the cilantro, and stir in the spices. Squeeze the juice of half the lime over the mixture. Use enough lime juice to lightly coat the mixture but don't make it too wet.

Put each cooked patty on a bun bottom, and top with the avocado mixture and the top of the bun. If you are an ovo-lacto vegetarian, a little dollop of sour cream is nice on these too.

Alternate Instructions for Dehydrating
Dehydration Time: 5–10 hours

Because you will use a fresh avocado, make this recipe in the first few days of a trip. Take an extra ⅛ cup of bread crumbs in case your bean-and-salsa mixture is too wet when you rehydrate it.

AT HOME
After you have drained and rinsed the black beans, mash them with a fork. It should be fairly smooth but it is OK to have some small pieces. Stir in the salsa. Measure the mixture and write this measurement on a sticky note. Dry on lined dehydrator trays for 5 to 10 hours or until no moisture remains. Put the sticky note and dried mix in a ziplock freezer bag. Place the bread crumbs in a small ziplock freezer bag and put this in the bag with the dried bean-and-salsa mixture. Wrap the cumin, garlic salt, and ½ teaspoon dried cilantro in a piece of plastic wrap and put this in the bean-and-salsa bag. Pack the salt and pepper with the other salt and pepper you will take on your trip. Do the same with the olive oil. Just before your trip pack the buns, a lime, and an avocado.

AT CAMP
Rehydrate the bean-and-salsa mixture with enough boiling water to equal the measurement on your sticky note. Be sure to account for and add your dried ingredients to the rehydration container prior to adding the water. Let reconstitute for 15 minutes and add more water as needed. Mix the bean and salsa mixture with ½ cup bread crumbs. The mixture should be firm. Wet your hands and form into four ½-inch-thick patties. Place on waxed paper. Preheat 1 to 2 teaspoons vegetable oil in a nonstick frying pan and fry the patties, turning once, for about 5 minutes per side. They will be done when the

outside is crispy and heated through. Season to taste with the salt and pepper.

While you are waiting for the burgers to cook, mash the avocado and stir in the spices. Squeeze the juice of half the lime over the mixture. Use enough lime juice to lightly coat the mixture but don't make it too wet.

Put each cooked patty on a bun bottom, and top with the avocado mixture and the top of the bun.

Tips

You can substitute red kidney beans or fava beans for this.

If you plan to have this later on in a trip, buy an avocado that is not quite ripe and let it ripen in your pack. I like to use something called a Froot Guard. If you don't have one, simply wrap the avocado in paper towels and put it in a hard-sided container so that it doesn't get bruised. If you do this, you must let the air and humidity out of the container every day. If you don't want to use a hard container, you can use a ziplock bag and place the avocado in a safe spot in your pack.

Grilled Portobello Sandwiches

Makes 2 sandwiches

Portobello mushrooms have a meatiness to them that makes it seem as if you are biting into a regular burger. They also soak up a marinade beautifully, which gives them lots of flavor.

At Home

Mix the olive oil, vinegar, Dijon mustard, garlic, and vegan Worcestershire sauce (if using). Pour the marinade in a leak-proof container and store it in your refrigerator until you are ready to leave. Do the same for the mayonnaise. Put the grated cheese in a ziplock bag and refrigerate. Pack the mushrooms in a paper bag and take along a large ziplock freezer bag or container for marinating them. Pack the tomatoes. Pack the buns or bread with any other dry goods you are taking. Pack the vegetable oil with any other vegetable oil you are taking and bring a few paper towels. Pack a pair of tongs.

At Camp

Place the mushrooms in the freezer bag and add the marinade. Season with salt and pepper, and let sit for 10 minutes. Preheat the grill and pour a bit of vegetable oil on a paper towel. Using the tongs, very carefully oil the grill with the oil-moistened paper towel. Cook the mushrooms for 5 minutes per side until they start to take on color and are cooked through. Meanwhile, cut the buns and spread mayonnaise or vegan mayonnaise on the bottom cut side. If you are using rye bread, spread the mayo on one side of two pieces of bread. Place a mushroom on top of the mayonnaise-spread bun, followed by a tomato slice, and the grated cheese. Place the top of the roll or other piece of bread on top. Gently press the sandwich and return it to the grill. Toast for 1 to 2 minutes, then flip the sandwich and toast on the other side. Remove as soon as the bun or bread is golden and crisp and the cheese is melted.

Tip

Don't refrigerate the tomatoes; it adversely affects their flavor.

---

1 tablespoon olive oil

1 tablespoon balsamic vinegar

1½ teaspoons Dijon mustard

1 garlic clove, minced

¼ teaspoon vegan Worcestershire sauce (optional)

2 tablespoons mayonnaise or vegan mayonnaise substitute

½ cup shredded aged white Cheddar cheese or vegan cheese suitable for melting

2 large portobello mushrooms, stems removed

2 slices tomatoes

2 medium-sized Kaiser rolls or 4 slices rye bread

Salt and pepper to taste

2 tablespoons vegetable oil

Tongs

Zucchini Canoes

Makes 4 servings

⅓ cup panko crumbs, or crumbs from flaky crackers or gluten-free crackers

2 large zucchini

¾ cup mozzarella or vegan mozzarella suitable for melting

1 small tomato

1 tablespoon fresh basil or ¼ teaspoon dried basil

Salt and pepper to taste

Small pinch of crushed red chili pepper flakes (optional)

1–2 tablespoons olive oil

A large piece of aluminum foil

16 toothpicks

At home I call these Zucchini Boats, but it seemed fitting to rename them for our wilderness trips; after all we call it a canoe, not a boat. If we are going into the backcountry, the hike or portage to camp isn't too difficult, and we are in an area where a campfire would be permitted, I sometimes take these for the first night. If you are vegan, choose a vegan mozzarella substitute that melts well.

At Home

Package the crumbs in a small ziplock bag. Package the zucchini with the vegetables you will take on the trip. Place the grated cheese or cheese substitute in a ziplock bag and keep it in the refrigerator until you are ready to pack your cooler. Pack the tomato with your other fruits and vegetables you will take on your trip. Put the fresh basil, without chopping it first, in your cooler. Pack the crushed red chili pepper flakes, if you are using them, and put the olive oil in with any other olive oil you will take on your trip. Pack a piece of aluminum foil large enough to wrap each of 4 zucchini halves when they are cut in half lengthwise and pack the toothpicks.

At Camp

Cut the zucchinis in half, lengthwise, and drizzle with olive oil. Season the cut sides with salt and pepper. Grill them, cut side down, over the fire for 5 to 8 minutes or until tender. Let them cool enough so you can handle them. Scoop out the flesh and reserve it, being careful to leave the skins intact as you will be using the skins as a dish.

Chop the zucchini meat, the basil, and the tomato, and then mix with ½ cup of the cheese, crushed red chili pepper flakes if you are using them, and the cracker crumbs. Spoon the mixture back into the zucchini skins and sprinkle with the remaining cheese.

Place each zucchini half on a piece of foil big enough to wrap it completely. Put 4 toothpicks in each half to keep the foil up off the cheese. Wrap and seal the foil around the half, being careful not to tear the foil or disturb the topping. Place in the hot coals of your campfire or on your grill for about 10 minutes or until the cheese is melted. Remove from the heat and let cool enough so that the cheese doesn't burn your mouth. Serve with a side of your favorite pasta tossed in a little garlic and olive oil or with a side of garlic bread.

Veggie Quesadillas

Makes 6 quesadillas

¼ teaspoon cumin

1 cup mushrooms

2 green onions

¼ cup sweet green pepper

3 plum tomatoes

1 tablespoon vegetable oil

Salt and pepper to taste

1 cup Monterey Jack or sharp
    Cheddar cheese, grated

¼ cup cabbage, shredded

½ cup salsa

⅓ cup sour cream (optional)

6 10-inch tortillas

My twist on a traditional quesadilla is full of flavor and is a favorite with the kids. We like to switch the mushrooms for other vegetables depending on what is in season and serve them with a salad.

At Home

Wrap the cumin in a piece of plastic wrap and pack it with your dry foods. Put the mushrooms in a paper bag. Pack the remaining vegetables, except for the cabbage, with the other vegetables you are taking on your trip. Put the oil in with any other oil that you will be taking. Put the grated cheese and shredded cabbage in separate ziplock bags and package the salsa and sour cream, if you are using it, in leakproof containers. Refrigerate until you are ready to pack your cooler. Package the tortillas with any dry goods you are taking. Before you leave on your trip, put the cheese, cabbage, salsa, and sour cream in your cooler.

At Camp

Chop the mushrooms and slice the green onions. Then chop the pepper and tomatoes. Heat a little vegetable oil in a pot and add the cumin. Sauté the mushrooms and green peppers until tender. Remove from the heat and add the onions, cabbage, and tomatoes. Season with salt and pepper and set aside.

Heat a frying pan over medium-heat. Put a tiny bit of vegetable oil in the bottom of the pan and place a tortilla in the pan. Warm the tortilla for 10 seconds on each side. When you see little air pockets starting to form in the tortilla, spread one-sixth of the vegetable mixture on one half. Sprinkle the vegetables with one-sixth of the cheese. Fold the tortilla in half so that the bare side covers the filled side in a half moon shape. Use your spatula to press down on the tortilla for a few seconds until the cheese starts to melt. Turn the quesadilla over to toast the other side. The quesadillas are done when the cheese has melted and the outside is crispy and golden. Garnish with salsa and sour cream.

Grilled Pound Cake with Peaches, Honey, Lime, and Basil

Makes 4 servings

This came about as a way to use up some leftover pound cake. You can use any type of loaf cake, but a plain or vanilla-flavored cake works best with the lime and basil. When buying the cake, pay attention to the ingredients; some of these cakes contain eggs. You can make your own vegan version too.

AT HOME

Wrap the cake in plastic wrap and pack it with the other dry goods you are taking. Add the olive oil to the other olive oil you are taking. Do the same for the honey. Pack the peaches so they won't bruise and put them, and the fresh lime, in with the other fruit and vegetables you will take on your trip. Pour the Grand Marnier in a leakproof bottle. Put the fresh basil, without chopping it first, in your cooler. Pack the skewers.

AT CAMP

A half hour before dinner, soak the bamboo skewers in water. At the same time, chop the fresh basil; mix it with 1 tablespoon honey and the juice from the lime. Let sit until you are ready to make dessert so the flavors have a chance to infuse. Preheat the grill or make sure you have good campfire coals. Cut the peaches into 1-by-2-inch chunks and thread them on the skewers. Grill the fruit for about 10 minutes on a rack over hot coals or a barbeque grill that has been well oiled. Turn the skewers often so that the fruit doesn't burn. Remove the fruit from the fire and set aside. Grill the pound cake slices just until they are toasted and start to take on some golden brown color. Sprinkle each slice with a little bit of Grand Marnier and then top with one-fourth of the peaches. Drizzle each serving with one-fourth of the lime juice–basil syrup.

Tip

You can use a little bit of peach juice instead of Grand Marnier.

4 slices leftover stale pound or loaf cake

1 tablespoon olive oil

1 tablespoon honey

4 fresh peaches

1 fresh lime

1 ounce Grand Marnier liqueur

1 tablespoon fresh basil

4 bamboo skewers

Fresh Berries with Balsamic Reduction and Black Pepper

½ cup balsamic vinegar

2 tablespoons maple syrup, blueberry syrup, or agave nectar

3 cups mixed fresh berries (strawberries, blackberries, raspberries, and blueberries or any combination)

Freshly ground black pepper

Make 4 servings

This simple dish sounds much more difficult and fussy than it is. The very first time I made this fruit dish was for an Easter brunch I was hosting. It was lovely, but I prefer it as a light dessert. You can make the reduction days ahead of time and at camp all you need to do is prepare the fruit. I've used berries here, but you can use any combination of fruits that you like. Peaches are a delicious substitute.

AT HOME

Put the balsamic vinegar in a pot over medium heat and simmer until it has reduced and starts to thicken. Remove from the heat and stir in the syrup. Let it cool and package it in a leakproof container. Store the reduction in the refrigerator until you leave for your trip. Package the berries carefully, so that they don't get damaged, and put them in your cooler with the reduction. Pack the pepper.

AT CAMP

Take the balsamic reduction and fruit out of the cooler about 45 minutes before you plan to have dessert. After dinner, hull and quarter the strawberries and mix with the other berries. Divide into 4 servings and drizzle with the balsamic reduction and sprinkle with a very small amount of black pepper.

Bananas Foster

Makes 3 servings

This rich, warm, and decadent dessert is heavenly over leftover cake or mini-shortcakes, with leftover plain pancakes, wrapped in a warmed tortilla, or with leftover rice. We usually just eat it on its own.

3 large ripe bananas

¼ cup butter or
  vegan butter substitute
  suitable for baking

½ cup dark rum

½ cup plus 1 tablespoon dark
  brown sugar

¼ teaspoon cinnamon

¼ cup pecans (optional)

AT HOME

Carefully pack the bananas, to prevent bruising, with the other fruit and vegetables you will take on your trip. Put the butter or vegan butter substitute in a leakproof container and do the same for the rum. Package the brown sugar, cinnamon, and pecans separately in plastic wrap and put them in a ziplock bag.

AT CAMP

Melt 2 tablespoons of the butter or vegan butter substitute. Peel the bananas and cut them in half lengthwise. Cover the bananas with the melted butter, then sprinkle them with 1 tablespoon brown sugar. Grill the bananas on a rack over hot coals or a barbeque grill for 5 minutes, turning once during cooking. Remove from the heat and set aside.

Melt the rest of the butter or vegan butter substitute in a frying pan over medium heat. Add the remaining brown sugar and cinnamon. Stir until the sugar has dissolved and then add the pecans. Remove the pan from the burner and add ½ cup dark rum. Put the pan back on the heat and carefully tilt the pan so that the alcohol catches fire. Alternatively, turn off the stove and light the pan with a match—either way, be very careful. When the flames go out, spoon the warm banana mixture into three bowls or use it as a topping.

Glossary of Special Ingredients

agave nectar *(agave syrup)* A thick sweet syrup that is made from the blue agave or maguey agave plants. Agave nectar has a similar taste to honey without the bitterness.

almond butter A nut butter similar to peanut butter. It can be purchased as natural almond butter, which, like natural peanut butter, you'll have to stir or you can buy it mixed with other ingredients. The natural variety is preferable.

almond meal A finely ground meal made from almonds. Also referred to as almond flour or finely ground almonds.

almond milk A flavorful and non-dairy milk alternative made by soaking ground almonds in water for 24 hours or more. There are many good commercial varieties available, in different flavors. This milk comes sweetened or unsweetened.

ancho chili powder A sweet-hot powder made from grinding dried poblano chili peppers. The peppers are referred to as ancho chili peppers once dried and they have a dark-brown hue.

aniseed *(anise seed)* A seed used in cooking and baking that has a mild licorice flavor. Fennel seed is slightly sweeter tasting but can be used as a substitute.

anise flavoring *(anise extract)* A liquid extract with a flavor similar to that of licorice. Anise oil can be used as a substitute but only use one-quarter of the amount because it is highly concentrated.

artichoke hearts The flower of a plant from the thistle family. The heart of the artichoke is the best tasting part and can be purchased in cans or jars.

balsamic vinegar A fruity and dark vinegar made from unfermented white grape juice. It has a slightly sweet flavor. It lasts 3–6 months after being opened.

black mustard seed A pungent mustard seed used in Indian cooking.

black *urad dal (black urad dhal, black gram, or black matpe beans)* A black bean that is similar to lentils. It has a white interior and a stronger flavor than lentils. These beans also have an earthiness to them and need to be soaked before cooking.

brown rice farina This cereal is made from brown rice and is much like cream of wheat in texture. It is especially good for people who have food allergies.

brown rice syrup A vegan-friendly sweetener made from brown rice. It is slightly buttery in flavor and can be used as a topping or in baking.

candied ginger *(crystallized ginger)* Pieces of peeled gingerroot or stem ginger that have been simmered in a mixture of sugar and water. Candied ginger can be found in the baking section of most grocery stores.

capers The buds of a plant related to the cabbage and popular in Mediterranean cuisine as a garnish. They are usually sold pickled, which imparts a slightly sour and salty flavor.

caraway seeds Often used in German cooking and in the making of rye bread, it has a slightly sweet and nutty flavor with a bit of tang.

cardamom *(green cardamom, black cardamom, cardamom pods)* This strong spice is common in Indian cooking and for baking in Scandinavian countries such as Sweden. It has a bit of a peppery note and a slight hint of lemon. Green cardamom has a fresher flavor and black cardamom has a hint of smoke.

carob *(carob powder)* A member of the legume family and often used as a replacement for chocolate or cocoa. It is sweeter but less flavorful than chocolate and it is caffeine free.

celery leaves The leaves of the celery plant. They have a milder flavor than the stalks and are a great addition to salads and wraps.

chia seeds *(Salba)* These seeds of the *Salvia hispanica* plant are full of omega-3 fatty acid and other nutrients. They become gelatinous with the addition of liquid and make a great replacement for egg. They can be eaten raw or cooked and are sometimes ground into flour.

chile de arbol A very hot dried pepper with a heat similar to cayenne. Their flavor is slightly smoky.

chipotle peppers Smoked jalapeño peppers that have a medium heat level. They are well suited to sauces and meat dishes as they add a smoky flavor and a little heat.

chocolate protein powder Made from whey protein, it can be found at health food stores and places that specialize in nutritional supplements.

clarified butter *(drawn butter or ghee)* Butter that has been heated and from which the milk solids have been removed. This process gives the butter a higher smoke point and reduces its risk of spoilage if it's being stored without refrigeration.

cocoa nibs The interior of the cocoa bean that remains after the bean has been roasted and the husk has been removed. The bean is then broken into pieces or nibs.

coconut cream powder Made from dried coconut that has been ground fine, this powder can be purchased in stores that specialize in Indian or Thai cuisine. Also known as coconut powder.

couscous Usually made from durum semolina in Moroccan and Israeli varieties. Moroccan couscous is a small grain couscous and is not as large or round as the Israeli or pearl couscous. Couscous also comes in instant varieties, which are more suitable for this book.

cumin seeds Flavorful seeds often found in Indian and Mexican cuisine. They impart a strong flavor, so a little goes a long way.

Dijon mustard A hotter and more pungent product than the more common yellow mustard. It has humble beginnings in Dijon, France.

dried mushrooms These fungi come in many varieties and can be easily reconstituted. Reserve the rehydrating liquid to add extra flavor to your dish.

fennel bulb The bottom section of the fennel plant, which has a slight licorice flavor. It can be eaten raw or cooked. The stalks, fronds, and seeds of the plant are all edible.

fennel seed *See* **aniseed.**

five spice powder A spice blend popular in Chinese cooking. It usually consists of fennel, cloves, Szechuan peppercorns, star anise, and cinnamon. In some regions the mixture will vary, with ginger replacing the fennel.

flax meal A coarse powder made from ground flaxseed.

flaxseed Oily seeds that have a slightly nutty flavor. They can be used in a variety of ways, from being an egg replacer to being soaked as an ingredient for crackers. Flax is nutrient dense and a good source of omega-3 fatty acids.

edamame beans A Japanese soybean that is harvested while still green. They can be enjoyed raw or cooked and are very high in fiber.

garam masala An Indian spice blend most often containing cumin, nutmeg, cinnamon, black pepper, chili powder, mace, cardamom, fennel, fenugreek, and coriander, but this can vary by region.

ghee *See* **clarified butter.**

goji berries Dried red berries, also known as wolfberries, that have a slight tang similar to a cranberry. High in antioxidants and regarded, in some circles, as a superfood.

guacamole A condiment made primarily of avocado and cilantro. It often has a creamy texture and is commonly served with Mexican foods.

gunpowder green tea Leaves from green tea that have been individually rolled into little "bullets" and dried. Look for a shine to the pellets, as that is an indicator of freshness.

herbes de Provence A blend of herbs usually containing basil, bay leaf, lavender, marjoram, orange peel, rosemary, and thyme. Be sure to use edible lavender if you are making your own blend, as some forms of lavender are not edible.

instant espresso powder A fine powder made from freeze-dried espresso. It is used as a drink and in baking.

instant polenta *See* **polenta.**

instant wild rice A variety of natural wild rice that has been processed to shorten its cooking time.

Israeli couscous *See* **couscous.**

jalapeño A small, hot, green pepper often used in Mexican cooking. Much of the heat is in the seeds.

Jamaican jerk seasoning paste A hot paste made from allspice, habanero peppers, cloves, cinnamon, scallions, nutmeg, thyme, garlic, salt, and pepper. It is often used as a marinade.

jarred jalapeños *See* **pickled jalapeños.**

jicama A slightly nutty and sweet-flavored root vegetable with the texture of a water chestnut. Although it looks like a turnip and is often referred to as Mexican turnip or Mexican potato, jicama is actually a legume.

kale The slightly bitter relative of cabbage that is packed with nutrition. Kale is best if it is cooked and is a good ingredient for soups. It is also used with mashed potatoes to create the Celtic dish colcannon. It is a good source of calcium.

kosher salt Coarse and flaky in comparison to table salt, it is also noniodized. Because of its coarse texture, kosher salt adheres to food much better than table salt does.

lavender Lavender is a flower with a strong fragrance used to flavor syrups and as an ingredient in herbes de Provence. Care should be taken to make sure you are using an edible variety.

lemon zest The exterior yellow part of the lemon rind without the white pith. The zest contains lemon fragrance and flavor along with oils and adds another layer of flavor to salads and other foods.

lime zest Similar to lemon zest, it comes from the exterior green part of the lime rind, without the white pith. The zest contains lime fragrance and flavor along with oils and can be used in a variety of ways.

maple sugar Maple syrup that has been boiled down until granulation occurs. It has an intense maple flavor, is a nice addition to hot drinks, and can be reconstituted into syrup.

marzipan Formed by almonds and sugar ground together into a paste. It is usually found in the baking section of the grocery store.

masa harina A fine corn flour also known as masa flour. Sometimes it is called Maseca, which is actually a popular brand of corn flour.

moong dal *(moong dhal)* A small, yellow split lentil that cooks quickly and has a mild flavor.

mustard powder *(English mustard)* A hot mustard that should be used in smaller quantities than the prepared mustard commonplace in North America.

Nido A whole milk powder found in the Mexican section of many grocery stores. Its high milk-fat content, 2%, makes it ideal for increasing the fat content in hot drinks and cereals on winter trips.

Nutella A spread made from ground hazelnuts, cocoa, and milk.

nutritional yeast A deactivated yeast with a cheesy and slightly nutty flavor.

orange zest Similar to lemon zest, it comes from the exterior of the orange rind, without the white pith. The zest contains a strong orange scent and flavor along with oils and can be used in a variety of ways.

pepitas Hulled pumpkin seeds that make a nice addition to trail mix and salads.

pickled jalapeños Sliced jalapeño peppers that have been preserved in vinegar.

plum tomato *(Roma tomato or Italian tomato)* An oval-shaped tomato with a firmer texture and more concentrated flavor than regular tomatoes due to the reduced amount of juice and seeds.

pomegranate gems *(pomegranate seeds)* The fresh or dehydrated segments of the pomegranate fruit.

powdered egg Made from whole eggs, it can be used to replace the eggs in most recipes.

powdered egg replacer A vegan and allergy-free alternative to eggs for baking. Powdered egg replacer usually contains leavening agents and potato starch.

powdered scrambled egg mix A combination of whole egg powder, powdered milk, and powdered vegetable oil to which one just adds water. It is excellent for making scrambled eggs, omelets, and French toast.

pumpkin seed butter A spread similar to natural peanut butter made from hulled pumpkin seeds that have been ground.

quinoa The seed from the goosefoot plant, which is native to South America. It is an excellent and complete protein, containing essential amino acids and also magnesium, riboflavin, and iron. Quinoa should be rinsed before cooking to remove any bitterness caused by the natural coating of saponin. It has a fluffy consistency with a slight nuttiness and a bite similar to pasta. There are different colors of quinoa. The red variety is a little milder than the white.

Roma tomato *See* **plum tomato.**

rooibos An African shrub known as "red bush." The fermented leaves are sun-dried for tea.

rubbed sage Dried and crumbled sage leaves that are aromatic and a great accompaniment to poultry. It can also be used to make sage butter, which is delicious on ravioli or other pasta.

saffron threads The handpicked stamens from the saffron crocus or *Crocus sativus* L. Because saffron is handpicked, it is quite expensive compared to other spices and herbs. It imparts a gentle flavor and wonderful yellow color.

salsa verde A spicy green salsa often made from tomatillos.

sambal oelek A condiment made from spicy red chilies. It is unlike some other chili condiments in that it doesn't have the addition of garlic or other spices. It has a good heat and slight tartness.

smoked paprika A spice made from smoked, ground pimento peppers.

star anise A dried, star-shaped fruit that has a slightly stronger licorice flavor than anise.

stem ginger *See* **candied ginger.**

stone ground mustard *(Creole mustard)* Similar to whole-grain mustard except that the seeds are slightly crushed or ground, giving the mustard an interesting texture. It has a spicier flavor than prepared mustard.

sun-dried tomatoes Made from Roma tomatoes that have been dried in the sun, they have a concentrated flavor and can be bought dry or in jars with oil. The dry kind can be used in trail mix, salads, soups, pasta, and bannock. The kinds that are packed in oil aren't suitable for backcountry trips.

Swiss chard *(spinach beet)* A leafy vegetable with properties similar to spinach. It tastes a little like beets and is sturdier than spinach. Chard is great on its own or in soups.

tahini *(sesame paste)* Ground white sesame seeds with a texture similar to that of peanut butter. It's most often used to make hummus.

tamari sauce Very similar in taste to soy sauce, but it does not contain wheat. It has a lighter flavor than regular soy sauce.

teriyaki sauce A Japanese sauce typically made from mirin, soy, and sake. Mirin, a type of rice wine, gives teriyaki its sweetness.

Thai green chilies Small, very hot chilies that are also known as bird chilies.

Thai red curry paste An aromatic paste used in Thai dishes. It contains fresh red chilies, lemongrass, spices, and galangal, which is an ingredient similar to ginger.

turmeric A very yellow and pungent spice often found as an ingredient in Indian cooking and in prepared mustard.

tzatziki sauce A condiment used in Greek cuisine that contains cucumbers, dills, and sometimes garlic. It is usually made from yogurt but is sometimes made with sour cream.

vanilla protein powder *See* **chocolate protein powder.**

vanilla sugar Made by placing a vanilla bean in white granulated sugar so that the sugar absorbs the vanilla flavor. You can sometimes find vanilla sugar in the baking section or in specialty shops, but it is just as easy to make your own.

wasabi paste A Japanese condiment that comes from Japanese horseradish. If you can't find the paste, you can buy wasabi powder and follow the package directions to make the paste.

wasabi peas Peas that have been dried with a coating that contains wasabi. They are crunchy and hot—a great addition to a savory trail mix.

wasabi powder A spicy Japanese powder of horseradish, Japanese wasabi, and mustard, used to make wasabi paste.

white pepper Less pungent than black pepper with a milder heat, it is often used for aesthetic reasons.

xanthan gum A natural bacterium from the fermentation process. It is often used in baked goods.

za'atar A blend of sumac, thyme, sesame seeds, hyssop, and oregano, typically used with olive oil to spice flatbread and in Middle Eastern cuisine.

Glossary of Cooking Terms

beat Mix ingredients until they are smooth.

blanch Cook fruits or vegetables briefly in boiling water and then dunk them in ice water.

blend Mix ingredients together well by hand or in a blender.

combine Stir ingredients just until they come together.

chop Cut into small pieces.

dice Cut into ⅓-inch cubes.

grind Create very fine pieces or a powder using a blender, food processor, or spice grinder.

mince Chop into fine pieces.

mix Stir ingredients together until they are well combined.

purée Mash or blend food until it becomes a paste.

sauté Cook food quickly in a hot pan while constantly moving the ingredients.

simmer Cook a liquid on a stove at a temperature at which small bubbles just break the surface.

Measuring Tips and Suggestions

These tips will help you measure ingredients more precisely at home or at camp and help prevent cooking disasters.

- Always use level measurements unless indicated otherwise in a recipe.

- When dividing commercial ingredients such as muffin or cake mix, be sure to shake or mix the dry ingredients well before splitting the portions.

- Never measure spices or seasonings over your food—a mistake can easily ruin your meal.

- The measurements marked on some water bottles and other gear are inaccurate; verify the markings at home before your trip.

- Measure liquid ingredients at eye level.

- A large folding measuring spoon that doubles as a scoop is a great addition to a backcountry kitchen.

Measurement Conversions

Conversions Within the American System	
A pinch	⅛ teaspoon
3 teaspoons	1 tablespoon
1 tablespoon	1/16 cup
2 tablespoons + 2 teaspoons	⅙ cup
2 tablespoons	⅛ cup
4 tablespoons	¼ cup
5 tablespoons + 1 teaspoon	⅓ cup
6 tablespoons	⅜ cup
8 tablespoons	½ cup
10 tablespoons + 2 teaspoons	⅔ cup
12 tablespoons	¾ cup
16 tablespoons	1 cup
48 teaspoons	1 cup

Metric Conversions	
Mass	
½ ounce	15 grams
1 ounce	30 grams
3 ounces	85 grams
3¾ ounces	100 grams
4 ounces	115 grams
8 ounces	225 grams
16 ounces or 1 pound	340 grams

Metric Conversions	
Volume	
⅛ teaspoon	0.5 milliliter
¼ teaspoon	1 milliliter
½ teaspoon	2 milliliters
¾ teaspoon	3 milliliters
1 teaspoon	4 milliliters
1 tablespoon	15 milliliters
¼ cup	60 milliliters
⅓ cup	80 milliliters
½ cup	120 milliliters
⅔ cup	160 milliliters
¾ cup	180 milliliters
1 cup	225 milliliters
1 cups or 1 pint	450 milliliters
3 cups	675 milliliters
4 cups or 1 pint	1 liters
½ gallon	2 liters
1 gallon	4 liters

Metric Conversions	
Temperature	
250° Fahrenheit	130° Celsius
300° Fahrenheit	150° Celsius
350° Fahrenheit	180° Celsius
400° Fahrenheit	200° Celsius
450° Fahrenheit	230° Celsius

Index

About the Author

Laurie Ann March is an avid backpacker, hiker, and wilderness canoeist. So much so, that she has turned her passion into her day job as owner and editor of the popular e-zines **www.OutdoorAdventureCanada. com** and **www.WildernessCooking.com.**

photo credit: Bryan March

Laurie started her backcountry cooking adventures as a child camping with her big brother and mentor Bruce. As a preteen, she took a 4-H outdoor living course that taught her the basic foundations of roughing it, as well as how to preserve foods through dehydration. She hosts wilderness cooking workshops, where she teaches and supports students learning the special skills needed to prepare food for their wilderness excursions. Her first book, *A Fork in the Trail*, has been enjoyed by backpackers and paddlers around the globe.

Laurie is not just an author and outdoorswoman; she is also a mom, wife, artist, and photographer. Laurie lives in Brant County, Ontario, Canada, near the picturesque Grand River and the Great Lakes. Ontario's beautiful backcountry regions are perfect for Laurie to backpack, hike, snowshoe, and paddle with her husband, Bryan, and her children, Tobias and Kaia. Experiencing the wonder of nature through her children's eyes is one of her greatest rewards.

For more information about wilderness cooking and printable trail instructions, please visit **www.aforkinthetrail.com.** Laurie's blog, where she posts recipes and food finds, is found at **www.wildernesscooking.com.**